BENTLEY
SIX-CYLINDER MODELS
In Detail

BENTLEY
SIX-CYLINDER MODELS
In Detail

BY JAMES TAYLOR

Herridge & Sons

Acknowledgments
The author and the publisher are grateful to the Bentley Drivers' Club and their archivist Alan Bodfish for access to the club's archive. Thanks are also due to Tim Houlding, who gave freely of his time, provided a great many photographs from his collection and advised on a number of historical and technical points. Other photographs were kindly loaned by Bryan Goodman and the David Hodges Collection.
The co-operation of the owners who allowed their cars to be photographed for this book is gratefully acknowledged. They are: Bonham's (6½-Litre Vanden Plas tourer), David Low (Speed Six Gurney Nutting saloon), James Medcalf (Speed Six Vanden Plas tourer), Bentley Motors (8-Litre HJ Mulliner saloon), Jens Pilo (8-Litre HJ Mulliner limousine) and George Tanner (4-Litre Freestone & Webb drophead coupé)

Published in 2012 by
Herridge & Sons Ltd
Lower Forda, Shebbear,
Beaworthy, Devon EX21 5SY

© Copyright James Taylor 2012
Designed by Ray Leaning, MUSE Fine Art & Design

Special photography by Simon Clay

All rights reserved. No part of this publication may be reproduced in any form or by any means without the prior permission of the publisher.

ISBN 978-1-906133-42-9
Printed in Singapore

Contents

Introduction	6
Chapter 1: **Bentley, the Company**	8
Chapter 2: **The 6½-Litre**	15
Chapter 3: **The Speed Six**	38
Chapter 4: **Coachwork on the 6½-Litre Chassis**	58
Chapter 5: **The Six-Cylinder Cars in Competition**	84
Chapter 6: **The 8-Litre**	99
Chapter 7: **Coachwork on the 8-Litre Chassis**	116
Chapter 8: **The 4-Litre**	141
Chapter 9: **Coachwork on the 4-Litre Chassis**	158
Chapter 10: **Legend: The Afterlife of the Six-Cylinder Bentleys**	162

Introduction

This book is intended as a companion volume to *Bentley Four-Cyliner Models In Detail*. Publisher Charles Herridge and I are in absolute agreement that the four-cylinder and six-cylinder cars deserve separate coverage, and that there is nothing worse than trying to cram too much into a single book. So, to give the subject of the Vintage Bentley the room it deserves, we decided to cover it in two volumes.

As I have noted in the introduction to the four-cylinder book, nobody writes about vintage Bentleys without first reading Michael Hay's *Bentley: The Vintage Years 1919-1931* and *Bentley Factory Cars, 1919-1931*. Hay's research is detailed and meticulous – qualities which any lover of motoring history can only admire. *Bentley Speed Six* by the same author, this time writing as Clare Hay, is another magnificent work but sadly printed in such limited numbers that few will ever see it.

However, I also found several other books very helpful in preparing this one. My absolute favourite has to be Elizabeth Nagle's *The Other Bentley Boys*, which recorded the memories of some key members of the company which made the cars. Necessarily biased, it is nonetheless essential further reading for anybody who begins to sense the magic of the Bentley legend.

Also necessarily biased, but indispensable in their own way are the books written by WO Bentley himself, *WO, The autobiography of WO Bentley*, and *An Illustrated History of the Bentley Car*. Michael Frostick's *Bentley, Cricklewood to Crewe* contains many valuable insights, while Johnnie Green's *Bentley, Fifty Years of the Marque* and Brian Smith's *Vanden Plas* were enormously helpful to me in showing how so many of the cars looked when they were new. On that theme, Nick Walker's *Coachwork on Vintage Bentleys* was also enlightening. Nicholas Foulkes' *The Bentley Era* is an altogether less reverent but no less relevant look at Bentley's competition history and at the image that grew up around the marque in the 1920s.

Dozens of magazine articles, and in particular those written when the cars were new and published in *The Autocar* and *The Motor*, made their own contributions to this book. Enormously helpful was the immediate access to information on Robert McLellann's web site, www.vintagebentleys.org. Material held by the Bentley Drivers' Club in its archive provided more information, and I was fortunate indeed to make the acquaintance of Bentley enthusiast extraordinaire Tim Houlding, who gave me unrestricted access to a wealth of material as well as to his own considered thoughts on many matters pertaining to vintage Bentleys. Some photographs appear here unacknowledged because they have come from other collections, so my thanks go to their originators, together with an appeal for forbearance. As for the main colour photographs in this volume, I am once again indebted to Simon Clay.

Ultimately, what is between these covers is my responsibility. The interpretations of the facts are mine, and if I have omitted or misunderstood facts found elsewhere, the fault is mine. Most important, however, is that this book should provide an enjoyable overview of the six-cylinder Bentleys built at Cricklewood, in particular so that those who are merely curious rather than already hard-core enthusiasts should begin to understand something of the Bentley appeal and the Bentley legend.

James Taylor
Oxfordshire, April 2012

The winged B, a polished radiator surround, and a pair of huge headlamps. Such is the enduring image of a "WO" Bentley.

Chapter One

Bentley the Company

When Bentley Motors announced the 6½-litre at the Olympia Motor Show in October 1925 as its first six-cylinder model, the company had been building cars for just four years. In that time, it had also built up a formidable reputation as a maker of high-quality sporting machines for wealthy owners, and it had attracted considerable kudos through participation in motor racing, in particular through a win at the Le Mans 24-hour endurance race in June 1924.

It would be good to report that the company was also in robust financial health, but that would be very far from the truth. In fact, the glamorous Bentley Motors was existing on a hand-to-mouth basis. As several of its employees at the time have since made clear, it was sometimes touch-and-go whether there would be enough money in the kitty to pay the weekly wages bill at the Cricklewood works. As its Sales Manager, AF Hillstead, memorably put it, 1924 was a year "when the company could not buy a packet of cigarettes without increasing its overdraft".

Though 1924 may have been particularly rough, the fact was that Bentley Motors had always existed on a shoe-string. The details of the financial deals that kept it afloat are as tedious to us today as they undoubtedly were to WO Bentley, the company's founder, at the time. As an engineer, WO simply had no interest in the day-to-day transactions that are needed to run a successful business. He saw his job as guiding the development of the products, and he left it to others to keep the books. Those others, who included his older brother HM Bentley, did their best to shield him from what was happening, no doubt in the belief that the knowledge would only distract him from what he did best. It is Hillstead again who explains (in *Fifty Years with Motor Cars*), "I know something of the way HM battled in the early days to keep WO as free from financial problems as the circumstances permitted".

It was Michael Frostick, in his book *Bentley: from Cricklewood to Crewe*, who was brave enough to dig deeply into the financial records of Bentley Motors. What he found raised a number of questions, partly because records were incomplete and partly because some were apparently contradictory. While he concluded that there was no evidence of any deliberate wrongdoing, it does seem clear that a lot was never properly accounted for – in particular the company's racing activities. Perhaps naivety would be the best word to describe what was going on at Cricklewood. Had there been better financial control, Bentley's history might have been different, although realistically the difference might have been that it would have stopped making motor cars altogether in the early 1920s.

Right from the start, the company was under-funded. A complex series of transactions during 1919 saw it absorb certain assets from Bentley & Bentley, the car sales company formerly run by the two Bentley brothers. Money that WO had been paid by the British Government for his work on military aero engines during the Great War formed the start-up capital, and of course on top of that the company had signed up some shareholders. However, Frostick's analysis of the figures shows that the £200,000 nominal share capital recorded at the time Bentley car production started in 1921 was simply pie-in-the-sky. Most of that money existed only in the form of paper promises, and the actual figure in the bank was £18,575.

These were in any case not good times to be entering the motor manufacturing business. The immediate aftermath of the Great War brought a certain amount of euphoria and, inevitably, hope for a brighter future. Almost equally inevitably, economic recession followed the huge expenditure during the war and, although it was nowhere near as bad in Britain as in the defeated countries, the early 1920s were a period of belt-tightening for many people.

At the same time, the established larger car manufacturers were able to invest in the automation which facilitated mass production and to keep prices down. Smaller companies were unable to keep up, and many collapsed or were bought out. Against this background, Bentley's survival in the first half of the 1920s looks like something of a miracle but, of course, the company was selling to a wealthy clientele that was less affected by economic vicissitudes than less well-off sectors of the population.

Such money as did come in from the sale of the company's 3-litre chassis in the early 1920s was quickly used up. Quite apart from the need to buy-in the forgings and castings from which these chassis were made, money had to be spent on maintaining a central London showroom and head office, and not least on paying the workforce who assembled, maintained or sold the cars. Although Bentley Motors had already bought the land in Cricklewood on which their works stood, there was a constant need for new buildings as production and other activities expanded. One of WO's cherished dreams was to have his own machine-shop on site but, by the time it was up and running, the company was in terminal decline.

Even the assets that Bentley did own passed out of their hands in 1923. In June, the company mortgaged its assets, lock, stock and barrel, to the London Life Association Ltd for £40,000, in order to provide the liquidity to keep the business going. Even that was not enough, and Hillstead's account certainly adds colour to our understanding of the way things were. He remembers occasions when he had to do the rounds of the company's London agents, offering advanced delivery dates or substantial discounts in an attempt to gain a cheque which would pay that week's staff wages. There were occasions when HM Bentley dug into his own funds to pay that bill and keep the company going until the next influx of cash, and Hillstead remembered at least two occasions on which he had to perform a similar service himself.

Record sales during 1924 were not enough to turn the financial position around, and this situation could clearly not go on for ever. WO's understandable desire to meet customer requirements by offering a larger and more powerful chassis simply made matters worse, as from

W O in post-Bentley days. He remained a loyal supporter of "his" cars and a friend to their owners.

1924 resources were devoted to the design and development of the new six-cylinder 6½-litre model. The thinking undoubtedly followed the line that pain today would be followed by gain tomorrow, but the real question was whether tomorrow would ever dawn in quite the way WO and his supporters hoped.

Things came to a head towards the end of 1925. Bentley had spent a fair sum of money (though exactly how much is a subject for debate) on entering a team of cars for the 1925 Le Mans in June. The hope had been to repeat their success of 1924, which had been the best kind of publicity possible, but the 1925 event proved a disaster. One car ran out of petrol and the other caught fire. WO, by his own admission, took a lot of criticism from his fellow Directors on the Bentley Board, and even he must have been in despondent mood by the end of the year. He could see that Bentley racing would be vetoed unless the team achieved better results; without racing it would be much harder to gain publicity; and without favourable publicity it would be much harder to sell the cars. What Bentley Motors needed was major investment, and quickly.

With the company going downhill financially at an alarming rate, WO could see that it needed a financial backer. He determined to do something about it, and may have approached several people for that financial help, but the details are not recorded. Michael Hay's researches have shown that among those he approached was motor magnate William Morris, but without success. Such details are usually forgotten in the glamour and excitement of what happened next.

It was Hillstead who came up with the idea. He knew most of Bentley's customers personally, and the one who seemed to him most likely to respond favourably to the suggestion that he should invest in the company was Woolf Barnato. Joel Woolf Barnato was the son of a diamond merchant who had died and had left him a vast fortune. He had recently added to this after a successful court case against other relatives. Though he was still under 30 years old, and very definitely a rich playboy by nature, he was also quite shrewd and a talented sportsman. Among his favoured sports was

WO'S LATER CAREER

As the Receiver formally wound up the affairs of Bentley Motors in late 1931, it became clear that WO's position was in the balance. Bound by documents signed when Barnato had taken over at Bentley Motors in 1926, he had a lifetime's allegiance to the company and its successors. Rolls-Royce quickly signed him to a new three-year contract with the new company they had set up to look after the Bentley interests, Bentley Motors (1931) Ltd. That prevented him from doing any more work for Napier.

Napier did make some efforts to get him back, but without success. Their first attempt to present a case in court was bungled, and the Judge sent them away to re-present the case, this time properly.

Meanwhile, a new broom had arrived at Napier. The company's newly-appointed Chairman, Sir Harold Snagge, was not in favour of the plan to re-enter car production. At his very first Board meeting on 10 May 1932, he persuaded the Napier Board to agree "to go no further towards bringing WO Bentley into the business to design motor cars".

So WO served out his contract at Rolls-Royce, but his contribution there was not great. The company busied him with customer liaison duties and with test driving at the Brooklands track and across continental Europe. Not surprisingly, he was only too keen to accept an offer from Lagonda to join them in April 1935. Appointed Technical Director at the company's Feltham works and joined by many of his loyal colleagues from the Bentley racing days, he designed there what may well have been his masterpiece – the 4480cc Lagonda V12 engine announced in 1937 for the company's Rapide model.

During the 1939-1945 war, WO worked on armaments at Lagonda, but towards the end of hostilities he began work on a new twin overhead camshaft straight-six engine. This was released in 2.6-litre form in 1948, but Lagonda sold out soon afterwards to the David Brown Group, who had already bought car manufacturer Aston Martin. As a direct result, the Bentley-designed engine appeared in the new Aston Martin DB2 sports car. It proved a remarkably durable power unit – as had all of WO's earlier engines – and remained in production until 1959.

In the meantime, WO had moved on again, this time to Armstrong Siddeley. Here, he worked on the design of a new model with a 3-litre twin overhead camshaft engine based on his Lagonda unit, but the project was dropped and the 3.4-litre ohv Sapphire 346 emerged instead. WO died in 1971, at the age of 83.

motor racing, and he had already shown great promise as an amateur racing driver in his 3-litre Bentley at the Brooklands track. WO could see Hillstead's point. He made the first contact himself, and Hillstead was sent off to Barnato's mansion at Ardenrun, near Lingfield in Surrey, on the pretext of demonstrating to him the new 6½-litre car. The idea of owning a car manufacturer as well-known as Bentley immediately appealed to him, and he asked for time to think it over.

Many years later, WO admitted in his autobiography that some people – he avoided saying whether he was one of them – had thought at the time that Barnato only took the bait "because if he hadn't there would have been no more nice Bentleys for him to race". He added that such people thought "that this was a shame when several of us, to whom the firm was everything, were dedicating our lives to it". Misgivings like these aside, however, if Barnato had not taken the bait, Bentley Motors might well have folded or been taken over by the end of 1926. As it was, the company lived to fight another day.

Through his finance and investment company, Baromans Ltd, Barnato agreed to finance Bentley Motors, initially with a sum in excess of £100,000 and a further £75,000 to pay off existing creditors. So in February 1926, the company went into voluntary liquidation, and the liquidators were authorised to consent to the registration of a new company with the name of Bentley Motors Ltd. However, Barnato's reputation for shrewdness had been well earned, and he imposed some quite harsh terms on the deal. These were made known to existing Bentley shareholders in June, and Hillstead probably spoke for most others when he wrote in *Those Bentley Days*: "I had a shock. Our original one pound shares were to be devalued to one shilling [5p in today's decimal currency], which meant, so far as my holding was concerned, that I could regard the money as lost".

The new company's capital of £175,000 was made up of 250,000 ordinary shares at one shilling each, and 162,500 preference shares at £1 each. Preference shares brought a fixed return of 8% per annum, and would have priority if the company were to be wound up. Barnato owned 109,400 of those shares, plus 114,700 ordinary shares, overwhelmingly the lion's share and one which meant that he

Woolf Barnato, who for a long period effectively financed the Bentley company, and who also, according to WO himself, was their best racing driver.

controlled the company. He took the title of Chairman, making WO the Managing Director. Hubert Pike, John Kennedy Carruth and Ramsey Manners made up the rest of the Board. Pike oversaw the Service Division and had been on the Bentley Board since 1922; Carruth and Manners were newcomers appointed by Barnato, and seem to have had a joint role as Company Secretaries. Both Hillstead and WO's brother, HM Bentley, slipped quietly out of the picture.

Nothing much happened until May 1927, when Barnato tightened his grip on the Board a little further by appointing a Cuban banker friend, the Marquis de Casa Maury, as Joint Managing Director with WO. The founder's grip on his own company was gradually slipping, but apart from those initial misgivings about Barnato's motives for becoming involved in Bentley Motors (if they were indeed his), WO seems to have had nothing but respect for his company's new owner. This can only have been boosted by Barnato's ability as a racing driver: he entered the Le Mans 24-hour race in a Bentley team car three times, in 1928, 1929 and 1930, and won the event every time. He was, wrote WO, "The best driver we ever had and, I consider, the best British driver of his day. One who never made a mistake and always obeyed orders."

With his position in the company acknowledged but also weakened, WO began to see things slipping out of his grasp. In late 1928, he voiced his strong aversion to the plan to supercharge the 4½-litre engine for racing and to build a "homologation run" of 50 cars for sale to the public, but was over-ruled by Barnato and

The company's competition successes made a stark contrast with its financial difficulties. Here the Speed Six driven by Sammy Davis and Clive Dunfee is seen landing after a terrific jump off the Byfleet banking at about 126mph during the 1929 BRDC 500-mile race at Brooklands, where they finished second to a 4½-Litre Bentley driven by Clement and Barclay.

others on the Board. Around 18 months later, the Board decided that a new and cheaper car than the 8-litre was needed, and over-ruled WO when he objected that their plans for the 4-litre model would not produce a car that embodied the recognised Bentley characteristics.

Meanwhile, Barnato had injected more money into the business. In July 1927, he provided £35,000 as a debenture – a long-term loan with interest. In 1928, he added £40,000, and then in 1929 another £25,000. Given that business is supposed to be about making returns on investments rather than forever bankrolling business activities, his patience must have been starting to wear thin. But this was the period when Barnato was at his peak as a racing driver and, as long as he could continue to afford the Bentley indulgence, there was no real reason why he should stop.

More money came from the London Life Association over the summer of 1929, first a loan of £15,000 and then a loan of £10,000 to which some additional conditions were attached. The company was heavily in debt, and it was no surprise that outside events soon tipped the balance. October 1929 saw the Wall Street Crash, which precipitated losses around the world among those whose savings were tied up in the companies affected.

The timing was very bad for Bentley Motors. Their 4½-litre and its supercharged derivative were old models and were attracting few customers. The Speed Six was effectively out of production (although a further batch was sanctioned to tide the company over for a few months), and the only new model on the horizon was the 8-litre. The decision was taken to press on with the development and introduction of that car, more because that was the easiest option than because it was the most sensible one. Announced in October 1930 to a world where even the wealthy had stopped spending money on luxury items, it was precisely the wrong car at the wrong time. Sales got off to a very slow start.

Recognising that they had to do something radical, and quickly, the Bentley Board made hasty plans to expand sales into Europe, New Zealand and North America – although how far these plans actually went towards realisation is questionable. Barnato was said to have travelled to the USA to take them forward during October. Shortly afterwards, the Board also decided to use the 8-litre as the basis of a new and cheaper car with an engine half the size.

In the meantime, Barnato tightened his grip yet again on the Bentley management. The precise details are lacking, but WO himself and the Marquis de Casa Maury were eased out of their positions as Joint Managing Directors, and in their place John Carruth was appointed as sole Managing Director during December 1930. Robert Montgomerie replaced WK Forster as Company Secretary. Though WO remained a Director of Bentley Motors, he had thus been forcibly (though almost certainly in a very

British, gentlemanly way) removed from the head of his own company.

In January 1931, two new Directors were appointed to the Board, but Sir Walrond Sinclair (of the Goodrich Rubber company) and Dick Witchell (Bentley's long-standing Works Manager) had barely made their mark before another crisis engulfed the company. No more than half a dozen examples of the new 4-litre car, introduced in May 1931, had been built by that stage. This time, it was the London Life Association calling in their earlier £40,000 loan. Barnato decided that enough was enough: he was not going to bail Bentley out yet again. As Michael Frostick analyses the story, Barnato had been led by his advisers to believe that the Wall Street Crash had left him ruined, and probably believed quite honestly that he was in no position to meet Bentley's debts even if he had wanted to.

So the London Life Association obtained a court order, and a Receiver was appointed on 10 July 1931. This was Patrick Frere, and his financial counterpart on the Bentley side was John Carruth. WO found he got on well with Frere: "He was easy to work with, got on well with everyone, and created an atmosphere of confidence that we had not known for months, by such acts as retaining the design staff in the hope that the tide would turn," was the way he remembered it in his autobiography. Acting as a good Receiver should, Frere quite quickly found a potential buyer for Bentley Motors in the shape of the Napier company.

D Napier and Sons Ltd had their head office at Acton in London. By 1931, the company was best known for its Lion aero engine, but it had earlier been a builder of high-quality luxury cars too. Aero engine manufacture had absorbed most of its resources during the Great War, but the company had returned to car manufacture in 1919 – the same year that Bentley Motors was established – with a model called the 40/50. This was a 6.1-litre six-cylinder car, beautifully made and a serious rival for the Rolls-Royce 40/50 of the period. However, when sales proved to be very slow, Napier decided to withdraw from the car market to focus on aero engines, and the last Napier car had been built in 1924.

So Napier's interest in Bentley Motors signalled their intention to return to the high-quality car business – arguably an odd thing to be doing at a time when economic recession was severely limiting the number of potential customers. Nevertheless, they were serious about their intentions and their purchase of Bentley seemed to be a mere formality, so much so that WO went over to the Acton works on a number of occasions during the summer of 1931 to make contributions to the design of the new Napier car.

When the news of what was afoot reached Rolls-Royce, the company's Directors had little doubt about Napier's intentions. The new car was clearly going to be aimed at their traditional

Not all competiton outings turned out so well, however. In the 1929 Tourist Trophy Glen Kidston's Speed Six ended up like this after a skid, perilously close to a telegraph pole. Kidston remarked afterwards that he had "never seen a telegraph pole get out of the way so quickly".

market, and more competition in those tricky times was certainly not to be welcomed. They knew that WO was capable of designing a formidable competitor because he had already done so with the 8-litre. They knew, too, that Napier were capable of bringing a credible Rolls-Royce competitor to market; their earlier effort had demonstrated the fact very clearly. The developing situation presented a threat that they could not ignore.

By late September, negotiations between Bentley's Receiver and Napier had reached a satisfactory state. Napier were prepared to pay £103,675 for Bentley, and all that was needed was formal approval from the court. A hearing was duly arranged for November, and all was going according to plan until the Counsel for the British Central Equitable Trust Ltd (of whom nobody had ever heard) stood up and countered the Napier bid with a larger one. Napier asked for an adjournment, and returned to the court with a higher figure. As the unknown Trust was about to counter that bid with a yet higher one, the Judge pointed out that he was not an auctioneer, and adjourned the court until 4.30 that afternoon. At that time, he said, he would receive sealed bids from both parties. When the envelopes were opened, the Napier bid of £104,775 was completely trumped by the Trust's bid of £125,256. It was not until later that the British Central Equitable Trust turned out to have been a "front" for Rolls-Royce, who made public their acquisition of Bentley on 20 November.

If Bentley under Woolf Barnato had been tilting at the Rolls-Royce domination of the high-quality luxury car market, under Rolls-Royce itself its character changed completely. Rolls-Royce chose to draw on the marque's sporting reputation, and to build well-appointed sporting cars under the Bentley name. Inevitably, the 3 ½-litre and later 4¼-litre Bentleys of the 1930s shared many mechanical elements with contemporary Rolls-Royce chassis; Nick Walker has told their story admirably in his book, *Bentley 3½- and 4¼-litre In Detail*.

UNDERSTANDING THE 8-LITRE

Some commentators have suggested that Bentley Motors' decision to go ahead with the 8-litre chassis in 1930 was little more than business suicide. A year or so after the Wall Street Crash, surely it must have been clear at Cricklewood that an even more expensive chassis with an even more limited appeal than earlier types was the wrong move, particularly when there was no cheaper chassis to keep sales ticking over. As so often happens, however, the story is a little more complicated than it appears at first sight.

Firstly, there are indications that the plan was not to pin the company's entire future on the 8-litre. From the biography of Harry Weslake, it seems that Cricklewood had been looking at a new side-valve engine as early as 1927 or 1928; tests were made on a single cylinder of 600cc and that figure, multiplied by six for a six-cylinder engine, would have given a swept volume of around 3.6 litres. This certainly suggests that a smaller chassis formed part of Bentley's future plans. The intention may have been to lead with the 8-litre, and to follow with the smaller car afterwards. The big luxury model would bring Bentley Motors the prestige that would allow them to charge high prices for the smaller, cheaper chassis.

In the event, the economic slowdown hit Bentley both early and hard. Both the four-cylinder models and the 6½-litre became almost unsaleable before the 8-litre was ready, and the whole pack of cards collapsed before there was any chance of starting work in earnest on whatever new and smaller car may have been in the back of WO's mind. Money had already been spent on developing the 8-litre, and there was no turning back.

Other factors also come into play. For much of 1929, when the ideas behind the 8-litre were taking shape, long-standing Chief Designer FT Burgess was out of action as a result of illness. His down-to-earth approach might have been a steadying influence on WO, and it is not hard to imagine him pointing out to WO at the end of 1929 that going all-out for an expensive chassis such as the 8-litre was not the most sensible course of action at a time when even the rich were becoming nervous about spending money.

As it was, Burgess died at the end of November. Meanwhile, WO had probably been heavily influenced by Barnato, whom he undoubtedly respected very greatly. For all his wealth, education and ability, Barnato would have been seen as "nouveau riche" by many of the traditional upper-crust Rolls-Royce customers, who came from the "old money" sector of society. So the idea of outmanoeuvring them by producing a car to rival the Rolls-Royce with which they were so closely associated would have had immense appeal to him. It seems very likely that this was one of the reasons why Barnato put his weight behind the 8-litre.

Chapter Two

The 6½-Litre

Once the 3-litre model had begun to reach customers, the direction that Bentley Motors would take was dictated less by the ideas of WO himself than by customer demand. As the companion volume to this one makes clear, customers did not all choose the lightweight sporting bodywork for their Bentley chassis that WO had in mind; instead, many of them took advantage of the engine's lugging ability to have their 3-litre chassis fitted with heavy formal bodies which might knock as much as 10mph off the top speed of the complete car.

This in turn raised a problem of a new kind. While the chassis and engine were perfectly capable of coping with the extra weight of such bodywork, the chassis was not long enough to provide the space for rear-seat passengers that those who ordered formal bodywork typically wanted. So within a year of the first chassis deliveries, Bentley Motors was designing a new chassis with a longer wheelbase. From the autumn of 1922, they offered this as an alternative to the original chassis size.

It went down well. Although the balance of sales remained in favour of the short-chassis 3-litre during the 1923 model-year, it was clear that the long-wheelbase chassis was attracting the customers. So for the 1924 model-year, the long chassis became standard, with the short chassis as the optional alternative.

Nevertheless, the sporting pretensions of the Bentley marque remained to the fore, not least thanks to the numbers of enthusiastic amateurs who did their damnedest with 3-litres at the Brooklands circuit over weekends and Bank Holidays. At a time when interest in motor sport was growing in Britain – Henry Segrave had won the French Grand Prix in summer 1923 driving a Sunbeam – it made good business sense to capitalise on high performance. If customer demand was forcing the Bentley marque to shift towards heavier bodywork that acted against performance, then the only way forward was to fit a more powerful engine to regain that performance and ensure that the Bentley marque had an edge over its competitors.

Bentley Motors were of course not alone in finding that their large-engined chassis appealed to both the sporting fraternity and the carriage trade. Companies such as Sunbeam and Vauxhall experienced the same thing. But there were also companies catering for the carriage trade which took little or no interest in sporting matters, and among them was Rolls-Royce. Despite their small size and ever-precarious finances, by making a deliberate move into this area of the market Bentley Motors were taking on the really big guns. Hindsight is a wonderful thing, and perhaps it did not seem that way at the time, but it was probably not the most sensible business decision the company could have made.

One way or another, WO was in no doubt about what his company should do – or at least that was the way he remembered it many years later when writing *An Illustrated History of the Bentley Car*. As he explained it: "The noise-level, and the impulses of a 4-cylinder engine, were always unsuitable for the closed coachwork we were obliged by public demand to offer on our chassis. By 1924 we accepted the truth of this, and I knew that the only answer was six instead of four cylinders, with an increase in capacity to provide the greater power required to give adequate performance."

So Cricklewood set about the design and preparation of a new and more powerful engine. Although there is some uncertainty about its precise dimensions – WO thought in his Autobiography that it had a swept volume of 4¼ litres but in *An Illustrated History of the Bentley Car* decided that he was wrong and that it had been 4¾ litres – there is no doubt that it was a more or less logical and straightforward development of the 3-litre type. Darrell Berthon, incidentally, stuck to the original WO thesis in his Classic Car Profile on the 6½-litre and reported that the first prototype engine had a swept volume of 4224cc. This was achieved by using the same 80mm bore as the 3-litre engine with a slightly shorter stroke of 140mm; the 3-litre had a 149mm stroke. Using the 80mm bore of the 3-litre would have enabled the two engines to share pistons, and would have been a logical starting-point for the design.

The new engine had the same arrangement of four valves per cylinder as the 3-litre, and most of the other details seem to have been similar. However, the cross-flow combustion chambers had now in effect been turned round, so that the inlet manifold was on the left-hand side of the engine and the exhaust manifold on the right. The reason, it appears, was that the carburettors would have fouled the steering column if left in their earlier position on the right of the engine. This reversal of the gas-flow probably made no difference at all to the performance of the engine, but it seems to have gone somewhat against the grain with WO, because when designing the later 8-litre engine he returned to the earlier arrangement with carburettors on the right and exhaust on the left.

The camshaft drive was also redesigned for the six-cylinder engine. On the 3-litre, it was driven by a vertical shaft at the front of the engine, but on the new six-cylinder the drive

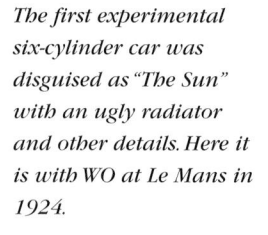

The first experimental six-cylinder car was disguised as "The Sun" with an ugly radiator and other details. Here it is with WO at Le Mans in 1924.

THE 6½-LITRE

> **THE PROTOTYPE ENGINE**
>
> As noted in the text, the prototype Bentley six-cylinder engine is thought to have had an 80mm bore and a 140mm stroke, giving a swept volume of 4224cc. WO thought, in *An Illustrated History of the Bentley Car*, that his earlier recollection had been wrong and that the bore may have been 83mm or 84mm. With an 83mm bore and a 140mm stroke, the swept volume would have been 4545cc; with an 84mm bore, it would have been 4655cc. Neither quite equates to the 4¾ litres of WO's later suggestion.

The first experimental 6½-litre engine, installed in EX 1. The car had been disguised as "The Sun", but by the time of this picture had been fitted with a Bentley radiator. The block follows the 3-litre pattern, with an internal water rail. Note also the rubber engine mounting.

was at the back of the engine – consistent with what was in effect turning the engine back to front to avoid that foul between steering column and carburettors. WO and his team also took the opportunity to redesign the drive itself to reduce noise, and the result was a most elegant design that used three coupling rods instead of shafts, chains, or gearwheels. The nose of the camshaft was now used to drive the water pump, as it would be on the production engines. As far as the output of the new "six" was concerned, Darrell Berthon's estimate of about 100bhp is probably reasonable. The 3-litre then gave about 70bhp, so this was a worthwhile increase in power.

The six-cylinder engine would first have been tested on the bench at Cricklewood but, once it had proved itself in such conditions, there would have been an understandable desire to see how it would perform on the road. As the new engine was intended for the carriage trade, it was put into a heavy car fitted with a rather ordinary (but therefore fairly typical) six-light saloon body with Weymann panelling by Freestone & Webb. The chassis may well have been a standard long-wheelbase 3-litre type, although no doubt some of its components would have been modified to cope with the extra stresses that the more powerful engine was likely to create – not to mention the extra weight. In *An Illustrated History of the Bentley Car*, WO claimed that the total weight of the car was more than two and a half tons.

The extra length of the engine of course demanded a longer bonnet than the 3-litre, and that would have given the game away to any onlookers who saw the car out on test. So the six-cylinder prototype, EX 1, was rather crudely disguised with a distinctly ugly radiator shell and with bonnet sides that were angled inwards at the bottom to match its shape. It carried the London registration number MF 7584 and Bentley Motors contrived to have it registered as "The Sun". Acknowledging that the disguise was created "for reasons of anonymity," WO nevertheless noted in *An Illustrated History of the Bentley Car* that it "drew more attention to ourselves than if we had proclaimed 'Six Cylinders' in large letters along the bonnet."

The car must have been complete and ready for testing in the early summer of 1924, and WO took it to France for a good long run on that country's clear and unrestricted Routes Nationales in the company of Hillstead, Bentley's Sales Manager. The plan was to take in the Le Mans event, at which John Duff and Frank Clement were to be racing a 3-litre Bentley. This was not entered as a "works" car, despite considerable support from Cricklewood, but rather under the name of Duff's Bentley dealership in London, Duff and Aldington. The Le Mans event was held over the weekend of 14-15 June, and from there WO and Hillstead motored on down to Lyons to catch the French Grand Prix on 3 August. Two months of trying out the car on French roads would be an excellent shake-down test.

At Le Mans, photographs survive to show that the engine compartment was covered in a tarpaulin to discourage the curious while the car was parked up at the circuit. Nevertheless, it would not have taken a genius to work out that an otherwise unidentifiable car driven to the circuit by two well-known individuals associated with Bentley Motors was likely to be a prototype of some sort. Indeed, WO remembered that the car had already attracted attention from the French customs when they had entered the country.

Le Mans that year was of course a triumph, with the Duff-Clement 3-litre coming home in first place. So, buoyed by this success, WO and Hillstead continued on their journey south. As WO remembered it in *An Illustrated History of the Bentley Car*, they were on "a long trial run to Tours" – which is just over 60 miles south of Le Mans and could well have been planned as their next overnight stop – when he "began to realise that we should not get enough 'steam' out of this engine, and that we should have to enlarge it." Perhaps the sight of John Duff hurtling round the Le Mans circuit had also made him think in terms of maximum performance, and made him find the six-cylinder prototype wanting in that department.

In the mean time, there were other things to worry about. The six-cylinder prototype was also being used to test the latest Dunlop "Balloon" tyres, which had only very recently been made available in sizes suitable for large cars like this one. They were wide tyres which ran at low pressures to give a softer ride than the beaded-edge tyres then in use on production Bentleys, but early examples were prone to blow-outs. Those on the Sun prototype did not last well, and all the spares had been used by the time WO and Hillstead reached Lyons.

There were no Bentleys running in the French Grand Prix. The test run in France merely gave WO a reason to indulge his interest in motorsport. However, the spectacle there no doubt also fuelled his thinking about maximum performance. Despite setting the fastest lap in his Sunbeam, British driver Henry Segrave finished only in fifth place behind two Alfas and two Delages. And with such disappointment in their minds, WO and Hillstead set off back north along the Routes Nationales.

It must have been a few days later when the decisive encounter with a prototype of the forthcoming Rolls-Royce Phantom took place. Rolls-Royce had their test centre at Chateauroux, some 245 miles north of Lyons and still 131 miles south of Le Mans, and it must have been somewhere around here – "somewhere in France" as WO put it – that a long trail of dust indicated to the occupants of the Bentley prototype that another car was approaching the Y junction on the road ahead. They reached the junction together, and there must have been a brief moment of recognition.

WO had heard rumours that a new and more powerful Rolls-Royce was being planned, and he realised what this other car must be. The Rolls-Royce driver may not have known that a new Bentley was on the cards, but he very probably recognised WO, who was driving at the time. There then ensued "a close and bitter trial of speed" along the empty Route Nationale for several miles. The impression that WO gives is that the two cars were fairly evenly matched, and indeed the Rolls-Royce had about the same 100bhp as the Bentley from its new and more lightly stressed 7.7-litre overhead-valve six-cylinder engine. The "race" ended when the Rolls-Royce driver's hat blew off and he stopped to retrieve it, but it had set WO thinking.

Rolls-Royce were already being criticised in some quarters for inadequate performance, and this new model was definitely going to remedy that deficiency. So if Bentley Motors were to offer the carriage trade a high performance model, they needed to ensure that it had more performance than the Rolls-Royce. These thoughts must have combined with the feeling WO already had that his prototype six-cylinder engine did not deliver enough performance – in particular, it seemed to be lacking in power low down. He would have to design a bigger one.

THE PHANTOM PROTOTYPE

Information published in Ian Rimmer's seminal book, *Rolls-Royce and Bentley Experimental Cars*, suggests that the Rolls-Royce prototype which WO and Hillstead encountered in France over the summer of 1924 was probably 93 NK, which carried a Park Ward cabriolet body. This car was then based at the Chateauroux test centre on a 20,000-mile trial, under the supervision of George Hancock.

The car was later rebodied and re-numbered as 11EX before being sold. The records available suggest that it no longer exists.

The production engine and transmission

Having neither the time nor the resources to design a completely new engine, and in any case being convinced of the merits of the existing 3-litre design, which had proved itself extremely reliable and durable, WO tackled the problem by increasing the bore of the six-cylinder engine. From the original 80mm (or 83mm or 84mm, depending on which dimension was the correct one), it went up to 100mm. The same bore centres were retained and, with the 140mm stroke of the original prototype six-cylinder engine, the swept volume went up to 6597cc. Strictly speaking, it was very nearly 6.6 litres, but WO decided that the name of 6½-litre would fit the bill very well, and so that was the name used for the production models.

The redesigned engine was probably running on the bench at Cricklewood long before the end of 1924, and the results were very promising indeed. Power was now 140bhp, which represented a massive 40% increase over the first, smaller-capacity, six-cylinder prototype. It was double the power obtained from the standard 3-litre production engine. WO and his team must have been delighted with the results. By the time production began, the new engine would be developing 147bhp at 3500rpm on a 4.4:1 compression ratio. It was clear that there would later be scope for further tuning to extract even more power and performance.

The new engine was almost certainly in a car by the start of 1925. EX1, "The Sun", was rebuilt with one of the new engines, and a second prototype, EX2, was constructed. This had the registration number MH 1030, which dates from summer 1924 and therefore suggests that the car may have been used for other purposes before becoming the second 6½-litre prototype.

It is impossible now to reconstruct the design and engineering processes which led to the production 6½-litre engine. However, research by Tim Houlding has shown that WO took out a patent for its remarkable three-throw camshaft drive as early as 1923. This must have been a good year or so before work started in earnest on the six-cylinder engine itself.

The overall design of the engine was an interesting one that bears examination. Today, we are familiar with six-cylinder engines having a crankshaft running in seven main bearings. The six-cylinder Bentley engine, however, had eight main bearings. The first seven were in their expected places; behind the seventh bearing

The second experimental car was known at Cricklewood as "The Box", and this picture makes clear why. The somewhat travel-stained car was pictured by WO himself somewhere in France while testing a steam-cooling system.

was a gearwheel for the new camshaft drive, and between that and the flywheel lay the eighth bearing, which ensured that this extra working section of the crankshaft did not cause an imbalance to the detriment of smooth operation. There was a damper on the nose of the crankshaft, as well.

As noted earlier, the nose of the camshaft was now being used to drive the water pump, and the camshaft itself was driven from the back of the engine. That drive gear on the crankshaft meshed with a fabric reduction gear twice its size, which thus rotated at half engine speed. The reduction gear in turn drove a miniature three-throw crankshaft, whose rotary motion was transmitted by three vertical connecting rods to a similar three-throw crank on the rear of the camshaft. The connecting rods were spring-loaded to cope with variations such as might arise from expansion in a hot engine, and the whole drive mechanism was protected within a large vertical tunnel-like casting. The camshaft itself also ran in eight bearings, the rearmost being of phosphor-bronze rather than white metal and serving the same function as the eighth bearing on the crankshaft.

The whole system was elegantly designed, and more than a little reminiscent of locomotive practice; WO had clearly not forgotten what he had learned as an apprentice with the Great Northern Railway. That three-throw camshaft drive is one of the details that so appeals to engineers today, and although there is little doubt that it could have been made both easier and cheaper to manufacture, it did prove reliable – and silent, which was an important element in Cricklewood's aims.

Like the four-cylinder engines, the cylinders and cylinder head of the six-cylinder engine were all part of the same casting. Each cylinder had two inlet and two exhaust valves, all operated by the same single camshaft running above them and acting through duralumin rockers. Each valve had concentric dual springs. Again like the four-cylinder engines, the six-cylinder had two spark plugs for each cylinder, one on each side of the block. These were fired by a magneto on each side of the engine, each driven by the same cross-shaft from a skew-gear on the back of the camshaft. The magnetos themselves were again manufactured by ML, but were GR6 types to suit the six-cylinder engine.

The six-cylinder engine had a cross-flow design like the 3-litre, too, but of course with the inlet manifold on the left-hand side and the exhaust on the right for reasons explained earlier. On the curvaceous inlet manifold was mounted a single Smith-Bentley five-jet carburettor similar to that used on the 3-litre engine of the time; on the six-cylinder engine, however, it was a type BVS 50 with a 50mm main jet instead of the 45mm size of the four-cylinder engine. This single carburettor was fed by an Autovac mounted on the bulkhead.

It scarcely needs to be said that this huge engine alone was enough to ensure that the 6½-litre Bentley would appeal to a limited market. It was rated by the RAC as a 37.2hp type, which meant that its road fund licence cost between six and seven times as much as that of the typical small family car – itself still something of a rarity in the middle of the 1920s. It also cost more than twice as much as the 15.9hp 3-litre. Nevertheless, Bentley Motors never doubted for a moment that their new model would attract a large enough slice of that limited market to make the model a fully viable product.

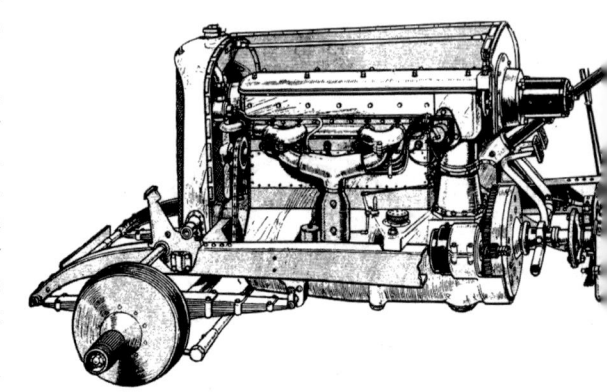

From the beginning, the new model had the latest design of single-plate clutch rather than the old cone type, and this had a completely new operating system with links and levers rather than the rollers used on the 3-litre chassis. There was also a new gearbox to suit the different power characteristics of the 6½-litre engine as well as the additional weight that the bodies were expected to have. Still mounted remotely from the engine and still operated by a change lever outboard of the driver, this was visually similar to the B-type then being fitted to 3-litre chassis but had a taller third-gear ratio and was known as the BS type. However, the close-ratio third was not compulsory, and it became possible early on to order a gearbox with a lower third gear ratio; this was known as the C-type box and was probably a recommended fit for cars destined to have heavier bodywork.

The engine's additional power also allowed taller final drive gearing to be fitted, with a 3.846:1 ratio being standard and a 4.166:1 available for especially heavy vehicles. The 3-litre in standard form, by contrast, had 4.23:1 gearing. The differential itself was much stronger than the 3-litre type, with additional support for the bearings and a double-row thrust race to take the thrust loads. The propshaft, meanwhile, had the same type of plunging joint as was found on the 3-litre.

The production chassis

The chassis frame had to be redesigned from the 3-litre type, partly to suit the extra length of the engine and partly to suit the anticipated extra weight of the bodywork. So the side members were made deeper than those on the 3-litre, with wider flanges. The six-cylinder chassis also had seven cross-members, four of them pressed steel and an additional tubular one taking the number to three from the 3-litre's two.

Again to counter the anticipated extra weight of the bodies, which would have tended to increase roll in cornering, the rear springs were outrigged rather than mounted directly under the frame as on the four-cylinder cars. The fuel tank, meanwhile, was increased in size to 19 gallons from the 11 gallons of the 3-litre, to ensure that the larger and thirstier engine did not compromise the car's range.

As for wheelbase sizes, there were three. The shortest was 11ft; although an inch and a half longer than the "long standard" 3-litre, this was rarely ordered. Next up came a 12ft wheelbase, which proved much more suitable for the large and heavy coachwork that 6½-litre customers usually wanted. Largest of all was a 12ft 6in size, prompted by the requirements of customers who wanted even more roomy bodywork.

Worth noting at this stage is that the longer wheelbase chassis demonstrated a certain instability in some conditions. More than one commentator has written of their tendency to "weave". Bentley Motors addressed this by moving the axle fixing point on the front road springs forwards not once but twice – in late 1927 or early 1928, and again early in 1929. In each case the wheelbase increased by an increment of 1¼in. This gave odd wheelbases for the longer chassis of 12ft 1¼in and 12ft 7¼in, and subsequently 12ft 2½in and 12ft 8½in. No doubt many older cars were modified at the works if customers complained of stability problems. Nevertheless, the chassis always seem to have been known to Cricklewood as "12ft" and "12ft 6in" types.

The 6½-litre also had a special multi-purpose bracket on top of the chassis at the front. This bore the Perrot shafts of the brakes and acted as a radiator trunnion, headlamp pillar and front wing stay mounting at the same time. The brake rods, which were in fact hollow tubes, ran inside it. Needless to say, brakes were fitted to all four wheels from the beginning of production, and were broadly similar to the 3-litre type with a balance-beam compensator system on the chassis.

As on the 3-litre, the new chassis came with Rudge Whitworth 21-inch wire-spoked wheels with centre locks, but the tyres were wider, with a 6.75-inch section. In view of the problems experienced on the prototype car's proving run in France with Dunlop "Balloon" tyres during 1924, Bentley held off on fitting them, and the 6½-litre chassis had beaded-edge tyres like its smaller-engined stable-mate. Nevertheless, as *The Autocar* confirmed when describing "A new six-cylinder Bentley" in its issue dated 19 June 1925, "the steering gear has been redesigned purposely to take low pressure tyres, the worm having more than the usual number of teeth engaged with the segment of the worm wheel ... so that the tooth load is very low."

As always, The Autocar *published a splendid cutaway drawing to show the important features of the new car. The general layout of the chassis was a continuation of earlier Bentley practice.*

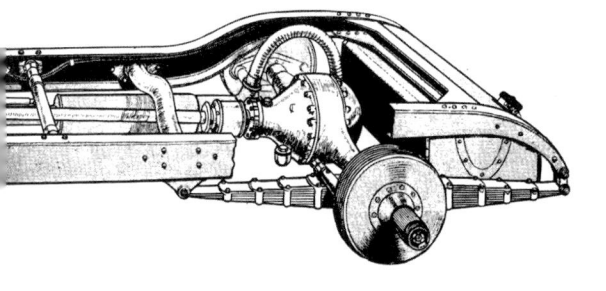

Chassis and bulkhead of TB 2538 are seen here during restoration. The car was a Standard Six delivered in October 1926 and originally had a Gurney Nutting limousine body.

Two views of the steering column and box on chassis TB 2538.

The Dewandre vacuum servo is seen here on chassis TB 2538 during restoration.

1925-26: announcement and the first 6½-litre chassis

Plans for the new six-cylinder Bentley were well in hand by the summer of 1925, and in mid-June the model was announced to the public by means of descriptive articles in the weekly motoring magazines. *The Autocar* dated 19 June carried four pages on "A new six-cylinder Bentley", while *The Motor* of 23 June (in practice both were published in the same week) revealed details of "A 6½-litre Bentley" in a three-page feature. Both magazines used photographs of EX1, still with its ordinary-looking Freestone & Webb saloon body but now of course wearing the production-style Bentley radiator. This tapered in gently towards the bottom, as it did on the Supersports version of the 3-litre introduced that March, and carried a blue enamel winged-B emblem at the top.

The announcement was premature to a degree or, at the very least, optimistic. The first the public got to see of the new 6½-litre was at the Olympia Motor Show in October 1925, when the Bentley stand displayed a specially prepared and polished long-wheelbase chassis and a complete car with a seven-seat Harrison saloon body incorporating a division. However, the first customers did not take delivery of their completed cars until March 1926, and then only four cars were delivered. So the 6½-litre Bentley did not really begin to make an impact until the spring and summer of 1926.

Michael Hay has speculated in *Bentley: The Vintage Years* that the polished chassis at Olympia in October 1925 was actually that of EX2, and it may well have been; however, that registration number was allocated around a year earlier, and it seems unlikely that the body would have been removed from the test car so that the chassis could be bulled-up for public viewing. Unlikely, but not impossible: funds were very tight at Cricklewood over the summer of 1925, and perhaps this was the only way to create a decent display for the Motor Show. As for the Harrison saloon, this was most probably the first production chassis, WB 2551, which was certainly bodied by Harrison and must have remained in the ownership of Bentley Motors until delivery to its first owner in July 1926.

Just 58 6½-litre chassis were delivered to their new owners during this first 1926 season. It was only a small number as compared to the 293 3-litre chassis delivered that year, but that was only to be expected because the 6½-litre was a more expensive car. More worrying for Bentley Motors was that the total chassis delivered in the 1926 season was only 351 – well short of the 392 chassis (all 3-litres) delivered during the 1925 season. The new 6½-litre was not replacing lost sales of the 3-litre.

1926-27: minor revisions

The 1927 season opened with the Olympia Show in October 1926, and this year there were no fewer than eight examples of the Bentley 6½-litre on display. Just one of those was on the Bentley Motors stand, where it was exhibited alongside a sectioned 6½-litre engine. The others were on coachbuilders' stands: William Arnold, J Blake & Co, Connaught, Offord and Vanden Plas were all showing limousine bodies, while Gurney Nutting and HJ Mulliner displayed four-light saloons. (The identification of the Offord limousine as a 6½-litre rather than a 3-litre is not conclusive.) On the Bentley stand, the 6½-litre carried a Sedanca de Ville body by Barker. Quite clearly, the carriage trade had taken to the new model in a big way.

Once the first customer cars were out on the roads, the usual feedback guided Cricklewood's next steps in development. Starting was evidently a problem on occasion, and by the end of 1926 chassis were being fitted as standard with a Ki-gass injector. This was essentially a hand-operated primer pump that squirted neat fuel into the cylinders to aid cold starting. By the end of the year, cars were also being fitted with ER6 magnetos in place of the original GR6 type. There had been a problem with clutch judder, too, and the original cork insert plate had been replaced by a spring-loaded pressure plate. No precise changeover points for these modifications are currently known.

The good news was that sales were picking up considerably. During the 1927 season there were 127 deliveries of 6½-litre models. That represented rather more than 10 cars every month, and compared very favourably with the 1926 season figure of just under five cars every month (58 cars had been delivered in 12 months).

The spiral bevel final drive is seen here from above on chassis TB 2530, dating from July 1926, and from below on LB 2348, delivered in May 1929.

Removed from Speed Six chassis NH 2750, this gearbox is visually typical of those fitted to the 6½-litre chassis.

This detail view of a 6½-litre chassis shows the gearbox and gearchange mechanism, and the location of the brake servo (just behind the cross-shaft for the gearchange) and the brake balance beam.

1927-28: more improvements

The 6½-litre was still big news at Olympia in October 1927, when no fewer than eight examples were on display. This compared with just two examples of the then-new 4½-litre model; the 3-litre remained in production, but there were no cars at that year's show.

All the big names still wanted to be associated with the car. There were limousines from Barker, Connaught, HJ Mulliner and Vanden Plas; Gurney Nutting and Weymann showed saloons; and in addition to a Barker "sports saloon limousine landaulette with division", the Bentley stand had a sedanca cabriolet by Hooper. This was something of a coup, as Hooper's were known as the Royal coachbuilders and were considered to be the *crème de la crème*. More than anything else, this car made clear that the 6½-litre Bentley was now considered a credible competitor for the Rolls-Royce Phantom.

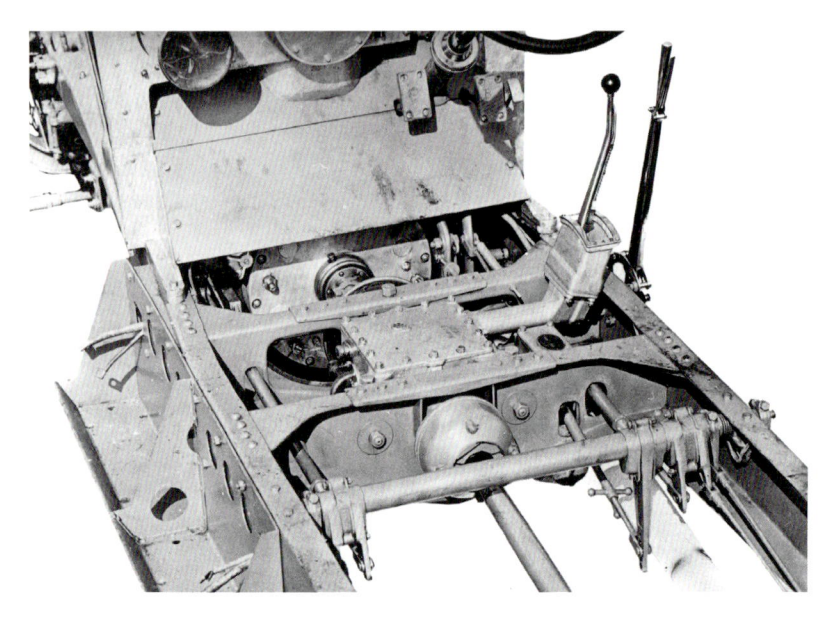

For the 1928 season, there were a few more changes to the chassis. The first example was on chassis KD2122, the Barker limousine-landaulette displayed on the Bentley stand at Olympia in October 1927. Wheelbases were increased by 1¼in as the front axle was mounted further forward on its springs. A louvred bonnet took over from the earlier type with three opening vents on each side, partly to aid cooling but probably more importantly helping to give an impression of power and performance. The chassis also gained an even more imposing frontal appearance thanks to a deeper radiator.

The deeper radiator came about because of a change from a camshaft-driven dynamo behind the engine to a crankshaft-driven dynamo at the front. The new dynamo was a five-brush Type 2 DAC5 made by Smith's, and was mounted between the front dumb-irons of the chassis, jutting out ahead of the radiator. Its casing was bolted to the front cross-member and the drive came from the nose of the crankshaft through a flexible coupling. To make space for this drive, the radiator matrix had to be redesigned, and ended up somewhat deeper than before although still tapering gently inwards towards the bottom. (In more recent times, countless small boys have misidentified the dynamo as a supercharger, almost always because the supercharger was mounted in the same place between the front dumb-irons when it was fitted to the 4½-litre chassis.)

The 1928-season cars also had better braking. As weight increased, so did the amount of effort the driver needed to stop the car, and Bentley responded by making a brake servo standard on the 6½-litre chassis. This was introduced at or very close to the start of the 1928 season. The servo was a vacuum type manufactured by Dewandre, and was mounted between the

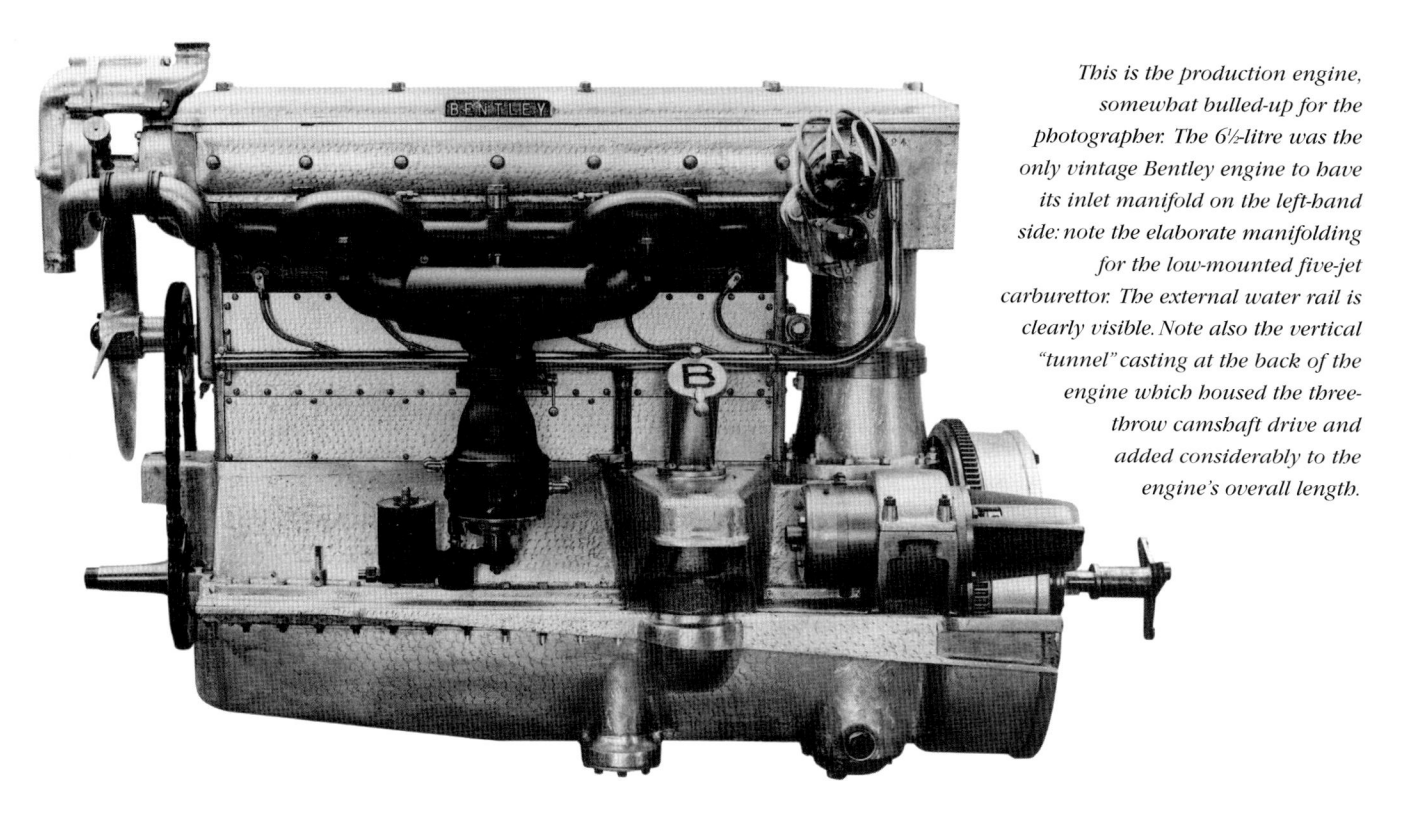

This is the production engine, somewhat bulled-up for the photographer. The 6½-litre was the only vintage Bentley engine to have its inlet manifold on the left-hand side: note the elaborate manifolding for the low-mounted five-jet carburettor. The external water rail is clearly visible. Note also the vertical "tunnel" casting at the back of the engine which housed the three-throw camshaft drive and added considerably to the engine's overall length.

chassis side-member and the gearbox on the right-hand side. It needed no special maintenance, brake adjustment being achieved by the compensator shaft in exactly the same way as on earlier chassis without a servo. However, the brake compensator shaft was also strengthened to suit the increased forces likely to be applied by the servo.

With the new brakes came a stronger front axle, with greater torsional rigidity, and both axle and brake compensator shaft were also fitted to the 4½-litre chassis at the same time, as they suited its new "self-servo" brakes. A great number of earlier 6½-litres were subsequently retro-fitted with the servo and the heavier axle beam at the Service Department from 1928 onwards. At the same time, Cricklewood often updated them to have the front-mounted dynamo and deeper radiator – a goodwill programme that must have cost the company a lot of money it could ill afford.

Less visibly, from engine MD2458 (installed in chassis PR2317) the rockers were drilled to provide an oil feed. This would not be the last modification in that area of the engine, however.

More changes followed as the season wore on, and towards the end of 1927 a Hardy-Spicer propshaft replaced the original plunging-joint type to reduce chassis maintenance, from chassis number BR2351. This was simply a running improvement, of course, and the new enclosed propshaft would also become standard on the 4½-litre a couple of months later. A further running improvement took care of a minor problem caused by the change to a front-mounted dynamo at the start of the 1928 season.

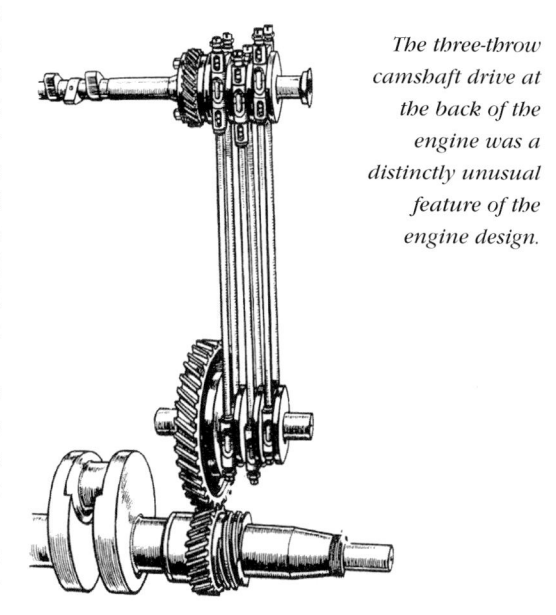

The three-throw camshaft drive at the back of the engine was a distinctly unusual feature of the engine design.

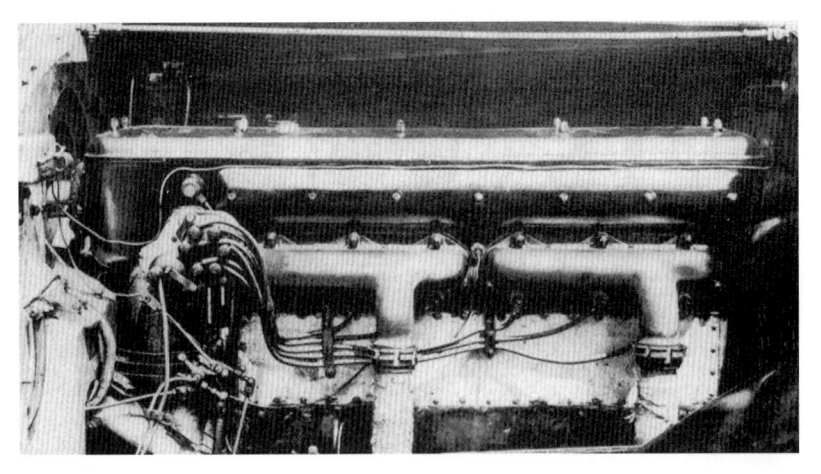

The exhaust side of the production six-cylinder engine. As this was the driving side, a system of rods and joints was needed to transfer the accelerator demands across to the carburettor on the far side of the engine.

The original dynamo drive had doubled as a damper but, with the dynamo no longer there, the camshaft had become prone to a certain amount of unwelcome movement. So its end was tapered and a torsional damper was fitted from chassis BR2366 at the start of 1928. From BR2367, the gear lever gate was redesigned.

This Bentley "works" photograph shows the front end of the engine. Note how the cylinder block is bolted to a separate crankcase, which in turn is bolted to the sump.

From chassis number WT2263, built right at the end of the 1928 season in the summer of that year, oil baffles were fitted to the rear axle to improve lubrication.

A long-term problem that had shown up was with excess heat finding its way into the body. That the exhaust ran under the driver's side probably exacerbated this (on other Bentleys, it ran on the left of the chassis and, of course, the passengers were less likely to detect the problem than the driver, who was always in the car). So from FA2504, delivered in July 1928, insulated floorboards were fitted.

All these changes undoubtedly improved the 6½-litre, but sales were slowing down during the 1928 season. Just 99 chassis were delivered, which compared poorly with the 128 delivered during the 1927 season. From the sales figures, it appears that the new and obviously less expensive 4½-litre might have been stealing sales from the bigger car: while 3-litre sales had dwindled to just 46, the new four-cylinder car had got off to a flying start with sales of 263 chassis. The overall picture was promising, however, with a total of 408 chassis sold in the 1928 season as against a miserable 268 for 1927.

1928-29: overshadowed by the Speed Six

The most important development for the six-cylinder chassis at the start of the 1929 season was of course the introduction of the Speed Six variant, which is discussed separately in Chapter 3. As a result, very little was done to the original 6½-litre, which became known as the Standard Six.

There seemed to be no significant lessening of interest among coachbuilders at the Olympia Show in October 1928, however. On the Bentley stand were a Barker saloon and a Hooper sports saloon, both with divisions. On their own stands, Thrupp & Maberly had a Cabriolet de Ville and Martin Walter a Weymann limousine, and there were saloons from Freestone & Webb and HJ Mulliner. But the most striking of all was on the Barker stand. It was a real show-stopper – a sports two-seater with "pontoon" type streamlined wings finished in blue, yellow and burnished aluminium. The body, which is discussed further in Chapter 4, would not have looked out of place on a Speed Six chassis and was perhaps intended as a demonstration of what

The bottom end of a 6½-litre engine, in fact the one from chassis number TB 2538. The engine bearers are an integral part of the crankcase casting, and the aperture behind the cylinder holes is for the three-throw camshaft drive.

Barker could do on the new high-performance chassis when they could get their hands on one. One way or another, it was very different from the grand and formal designs that the coachbuilders had built on earlier 6½-litre chassis.

The early 6½-litres had been fitted with a double-pole electrical system and single 12-volt battery, like the 3-litres in production when they were built. However, from chassis number FA2514, probably built right at the start of the 1929 season in autumn 1928, the 6½-litre changed to a single-pole fused system with twin 6-volt batteries. In this, it paralleled the 4½-litre, where the change was made at about the same time.

More changes followed as the 1929 season progressed. Lubrication of the top end of the engine was still giving problems, and at an undetermined date an oil bath was added to the base of the cam case. This lubricated the rocker rollers and prevented squeaks from the tappet ball-ends. A new Bosch fuse box was then fitted from chassis number LB2340, built towards the spring of 1929.

There were then several more changes in the spring and summer. Chassis strength was clearly giving some cause for concern, perhaps because of extra strains associated with the more powerful Speed Six model. So from chassis BA2597, strut gear was standardised to add rigidity to the frame, and shortly after that, from chassis KF2392, the frames were made from heavier-gauge steel, 3/16in (0.188in) thick instead of 5/32in (0.156in). In this latter case, the thicker metal was already in use for Speed Six frames. All chassis were then fitted with double-spoke wheels from chassis FR2649 over the summer – again probably the result of extra strains associated with the high-performance Speed Six engine. From KR2684, one of the very last 1929 chassis, battery trays fitted inside rather than outside the frame became standard.

It cannot have surprised anyone at Cricklewood that the Speed Six should out-sell the Standard Six during the 1929 season. A total of 66 Standard Sixes were delivered for 1929, as against 69 Speed Sixes, to make a total of 135 six-cylinder chassis. That overall figure was a distinct improvement on the 99 sold for 1928, and even on the 127 sold the season before that. Meanwhile, 3-litre sales were nearly extinct, with just 8; the 4½-litre remained a strong seller with a total of 256; and the overall total for the 1929 season was 399. It was marginally below the 1928 season's overall total, but not enough to cause major concern. Also very clear was that performance still sold the Bentley brand: whenever a new and more powerful model was introduced, it found a ready market.

1929-30: a sudden collapse

That the Speed Six was grabbing all the attention was very obvious from the spread of models on the coachbuilders' stands at Olympia in October 1929 as the new season opened. There were six Speed Sixes, and just three Standard Sixes alongside three 4½-litres, one of them supercharged.

The exciting promise of 1928's Barker streamlined sports body on the 6½-litre was not followed by anything remotely similar this year. All the bodies on the Standard Six chassis were rather grand and formal. On the Bentley Motors stand, a Thrupp & Maberly Cabriolet de Ville on the longest available wheelbase represented business as usual, and the same coachbuilder had another Cabriolet de Ville on its own stand. Park Ward displayed a rather sober enclosed-drive limousine, while Gurney Nutting had a "Prince of Wales" Weymann limousine (so called after a four-light body style ordered by Edward, Prince of Wales). What nobody had been able to anticipate when preparing these show exhibits, of course, was that the end of October would see the Wall Street Crash, which would make a huge difference to the market for upper-crust motor cars such as those made by Bentley.

In practice, there would only be penny numbers of Standard Six models for the 1930 season, and the chassis of all of those would be completed by October or November 1929. Only one of them, KR2697, was actually built to 1930 specification. These final chassis probably all had Bentley & Draper hydraulic rear dampers instead of the friction types on earlier examples – a first use of such items on a production car from Cricklewood. They also had longer front springs, with the axle mounted another 1¼in further forwards to extend the wheelbase from a nominal 12ft 0in or 12ft 6in to 12ft 2⅛in or 12ft 8⅛in. Using Elektron for a number of engine castings did help to reduce weight by somewhere around 300lb, but this was not enough to make a significant difference to the performance or appeal of the 6½-litre.

The very last Standard Six chassis appears to have been KR2697, which also seems to have been the first to have a new tyre size of 33 x 6.75. But by the time it was completed, it was alone among a sea of Speed Sixes. The new high-performance derivative had taken over.

That the Speed Six had captured the imagination of customers is immediately apparent from the sales figures for the 1930 season. There were 108 Speed Sixes as against just 18 Standard Sixes. Not that Cricklewood would have seen this as a problem, because the new 8-litre model was due to be introduced in autumn 1930 to replace the Standard Six as the chassis of choice for the carriage trade.

Much worse news was that Bentley sales were slowing down altogether as a result of the economic recession. To the grand total of 126 6½-litre chassis of both types sold in the 1930 season could be added only 138 4½-litres, including the new supercharged models. That made for total sales of just 264 chassis – a massive drop as compared to what had been achieved in the 1929 season.

Driving the 6½-litre Bentley

The introduction of the 6½-litre chassis was in many ways a very significant event, because it brought real performance to the large car market. At Cricklewood, its potential must have been very clear. In the words of AFC Hillstead, writing in *Those Bentley Days*, "It was obvious from the very first that the 6½-litre Bentley would revolutionise big car performance. Not only did it possess all the good qualities of the 3-litre magnified a thousandfold, but it would carry the heaviest coach-built bodies with ease."

Right from the start, Bentley Motors made clear to the motoring magazines that the 6½-litre chassis was intended for the carriage trade and not just as another sporting chassis in the spirit

EX1 was rebuilt with a production style radiator, which tapered towards the bottom to distinguish it from the straight-sided type used on the four-cylinder cars. This style was standard on all the early 6½-litres, but relatively few examples have survived intact.

of their original 3-litre.

So when the model was announced in June 1925, *The Autocar* faithfully reported (in its issue dated 19 June) that the car "has been brought out because the firm has experienced a very great demand for a chassis which will take the heavy and luxurious type of closed body, and carry it in silence with a great degree of flexibility on top gear, and yet prove really fast when it is a question of maintaining a high average speed for long dstances."

As noted above, the only 6½-litres in existence at the time of that announcement were the two prototypes, EX1 and EX2, and neither was really suitable for use as a press demonstrator. It was probably something of a scramble to get the first production chassis completed at Cricklewood in the last few months of 1925, and the first customer cars were not delivered until March 1926. So it is no real surprise that the press were not given the opportunity for a full road test until later that year.

In fact, only *The Motor* seems to have shown an interest. Perhaps *The Autocar* felt that it had already written enough about a chassis which most of its readers would never be able to afford, when it had described its features in June 1925. Or perhaps its reasoning was that the car was already a year old by the time a demonstrator was available, and was therefore no longer newsworthy. So there is a disappointing lack of contemporary evidence to show how the cars appeared at the time.

The Motor report appeared in its issue dated 21 September 1926. The car was a short-chassis (11ft wheelbase) model with the C-type gearbox which had been new in May 1926, although its chassis number of WB2552 actually made it the second production chassis. It had done duty as a sales demonstrator and had also been used for a time by Bentley's Chairman, Woolf Barnato. The body was an unremarkable four-light saloon by the Leicester firm of Hamshaw.

Refinement of running was a key characteristic, and *The Motor* made much of this:

"The first few miles served to show that this car, in respect of silent running and general refinement, can bear comparison with any others at present available. The engine is very nearly inaudible, as is also the transmission system, practically the only sound which marks one's passage along the highway being the humming of the wind and the swish of the tyres."

The brakes, too, were smooth, and the steering very light.

However, the other most noticeable characteristic was (not surprisingly) the engine's power delivery. *The Motor* wrote of "acceleration equalled only by sports models" and of the top-gear flexibility and response from low speeds. "Once under way it is hardly ever necessary to change to an indirect ratio," they enthused. Such things mattered a great deal at a time when synchromesh gearboxes were still some way in the future and even the most able driver was apt to crunch the gears from time to time.

Nevertheless, the motoring weeklies were not the only publications who had an opportunity to try a 6½-litre Bentley. In January 1927, the *Daily Mirror* newspaper tested one, and its motoring correspondent was deeply impressed. His comments must have pleased the Bentley people greatly, because they reproduced them in the sales brochure for the car:

"After reading over what I have written it occurs to me that I have still failed to convey to you the extraordinary docility of charm and road manners of this really wonderful motor car. It combines noiselessness with power, speed and comfort in the most unusual degree. Luxurious in its true sense is the only word which describes its character. It is, in short, a great achievement."

6½-LITRE BENTLEY PRODUCTION

Note: These figures relate to "season" and not to calendar year, and the totals are not broken down by wheelbase size. They are based on the "traditional" classifications of chassis; the figures calculated by Hay in 2008 allow for a total of 362 Standard Six chassis.

1926	58
1927	127
1928	99
1929	66
1930	18
Total	368

CHASSIS NUMBERS AND BUILD DATES OF THE 6½-LITRE CARS

The chassis number of a 6½-litre Bentley can be found on the left-hand side of the chassis front cross-member.

The lists below show the blocks of numbers which relate to build sanctions. As noted elsewhere, Bentley chassis were by this time constructed in groups of 25, for which parts would normally be ordered in advance. These groups were the build sanctions, and were identified by two initial capitals.

As will be readily apparent, the numbers used ran in blocks of 25 from 2101 to 2870 (although the final HM sanction was for only 20 chassis, all of them actually Speed Six models). However, these blocks of numbers were not used in anything like chronological order. Note also that the Speed Six chassis were numbered within the main batches and had no special identifiers. The lists of Speed Six chassis are given in Chapter 3. Note that some Standard Six chassis have been reclassified as Speed Six types over the years as additional information has come to light. The totals given in this book were generally accepted until recently, but Clare Hay's book, *Bentley Speed Six*, published in 2008, suggests different totals for those cars and therefore, by implication, for the Standard Six chassis.

The build sanctions are listed below in chronological order of manufacture. The construction of bodywork typically took between two and three months, although some bodies took much longer, and there would have been other delays when Cricklewood sent a completed car back to the bodybuilder for modifications before it would issue the Five-Year Guarantee. Delivery dates shown below come from Bentley Motors records and are the dates on which the guarantees were issued.

It would be reasonable to suppose that the actual build date of most chassis was two or three months earlier than their delivery dates, but there were cars which took longer than the usual time to complete.

For a more precise dating of any individual chassis, it is advisable to contact the Bentley Drivers' Club.

Chassis numbers	Delivery dates	Remarks
EX1	(1924)	First prototype
EX2	(1924)	Second prototype
WB2551-WB2575	Mar 1926 – Dec 1926	First 1926 season car: chassis no WB2551
TB2526-TB2550	July 1926 – Apr 1928	
FW2601-FW2625	Sep 1926 – May 1927	
WK2651-WK2675	Dec 1926 – May 1928	
TW2701-TW2725	Mar 1927 – Sep 1927	
BX2401-BX2425	Mar 1927 – Sep 1927	
DH2201-DH2225	Apr 1927 – Oct 1927	
KD2101-KD2125	July 1927 – Dec 1927	
PR2301-PR2325	Oct 1927 – July 1928	
BR2351-BR2375	Dec 1927 – Jun 1928	
MD2451-MD2475	Feb 1928 – Jun 1928	
FA2501-FA2525	Jun 1928 – July 1929	
WT2251-WT2275	Oct 1928 – Feb 1930	WT 2265, a Speed Six, was the first 1929 season chassis
KF2376-KF2400	Dec 1928 – Dec 1929	
LB2326-LB2350	Feb 1929 – July 1929	
BA2576-BA2600	Apr 1929 – Dec 1929	
FR2626-FR2650	July 1929 – Jun 1931	FR 2628, a Speed Six, was the first 1930 season chassis
KR2676-KR2700	Sep 1929 – Aug 1920	
SB2751-SB2775	Oct 1929 – Apr 1931	
NH2726-NH2750	Dec 1929 – July 1930	
LR2776-LR2800	Mar 1930 – Nov 1930	
HM2851-HM2870	Apr 1930 – Dec 1930	

SPECIFICATIONS FOR BENTLEY 6½-LITRE (STANDARD SIX) MODELS

Years of manufacture
1926-1930

Build quantity
368 (later figures from Hay give 362)

Engine
6597cc (100mm x 140mm) OHC six-cylinder with four valves per cylinder
One Smith-Bentley BVS50 carburettor
4.4:1 compression ratio
147bhp at 3500rpm

Transmission
Four-speed "crash" gearbox.
BS-type gearbox (probably mainly with lighter bodywork):
3.364:1, 1.823:1, 1.278:1, 1.00:1, reverse 3.364:1.
C-type gearbox (probably mainly with heavy bodywork):
3.364:1, 1.823:1, 1.357:1, 1.00:1, reverse 3.364:1.

Final drive ratio:	Standard	3.846:1
	Heavy bodies	4.166:1

Suspension
Semi-elliptic leaf springs on front and rear axles; front axle with Bentley & Draper friction dampers; rear axle with Bentley & Draper friction dampers up to end of 1929 season, and Bentley & Draper hydraulic dampers thereafter

Steering
Worm and wheel steering

Brakes
Drum-type brakes on all four wheels, with rod operation; handbrake acting on a separate set of rear shoes. Dewandre vacuum servo standard from early in the 1928 season.

Chassis dimensions
Wheelbase:	11ft 0in (mainly intended for open bodywork)
	12ft 0in; later 12 ft 1¼in; finally 12ft 2½in
	12ft 6in; later 12ft 7¼in; finally 12ft 8½in
Overall length:	16ft 1in (standard)
	16ft 7in (optional long wheelbase)
Overall width:	5ft 8½in
Track:	56in front and rear
Weight:	32½cwt (standard)
	33cwt (optional long wheelbase)

Performance
Max. speed:	90mph approx
0-60mph:	18 secs approx
Fuel consumption (typical):	12mpg (2.64 miles per litre)

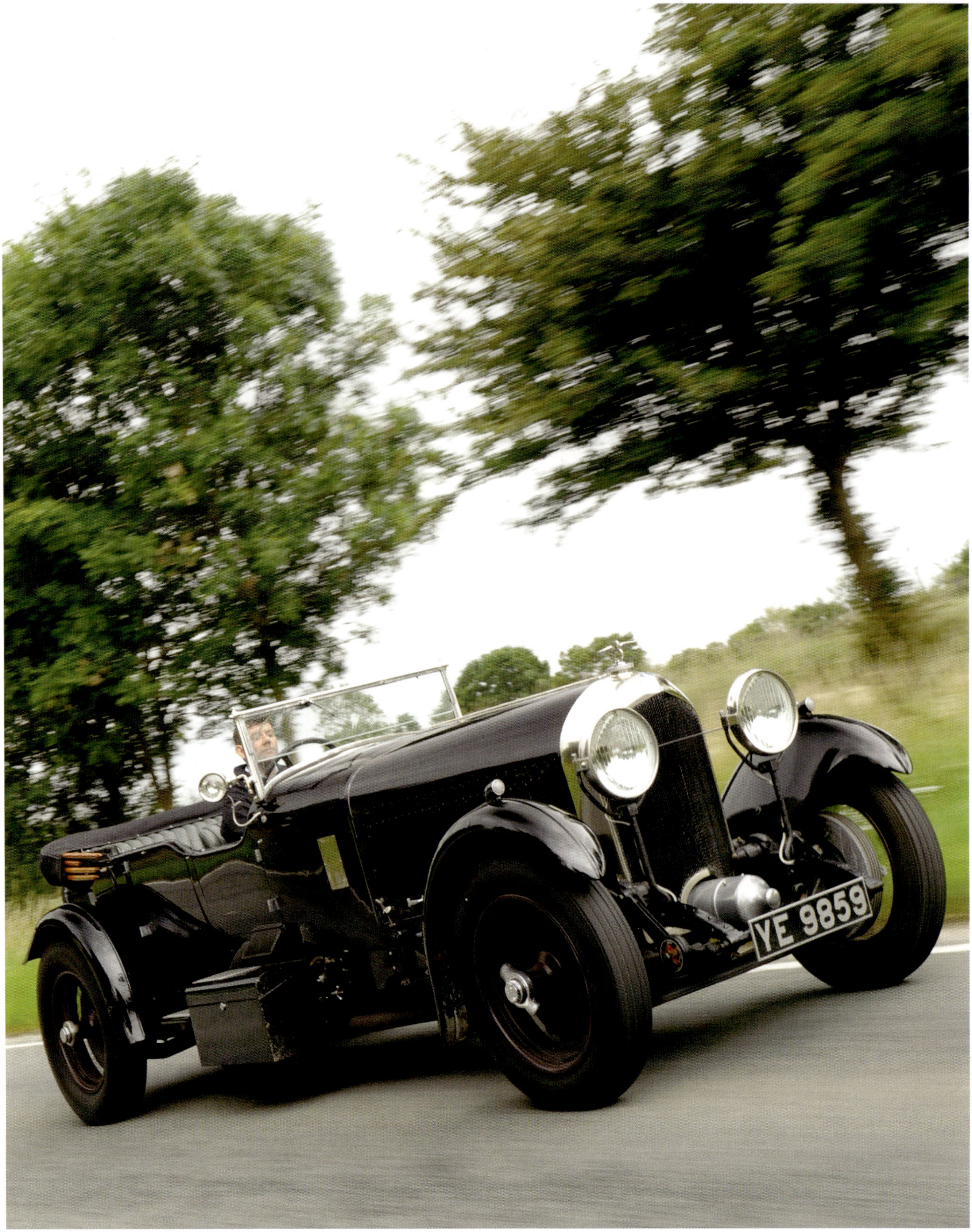
YE 9859

THE 6½-LITRE

Chassis BX2421 was built at the end of 1926 and delivered in early 1927 with this Vanden Plas sports tourer body. It was the first 6½-litre to have such bodywork, which was nevertheless not quite to standard specification. Helmet wings were the customer's choice, and so was an inside handbrake. The headlamps, too, were special. The body was panelled in aluminium and was originally grey, with black wheels. The chassis was a very early example with the push-on brakes and had the optional longer steering column. A 26-gallon tank was also part of the original specification, together with twin rear-mounted spares. The car has since been modified to carry a trunk ahead of a single spare.

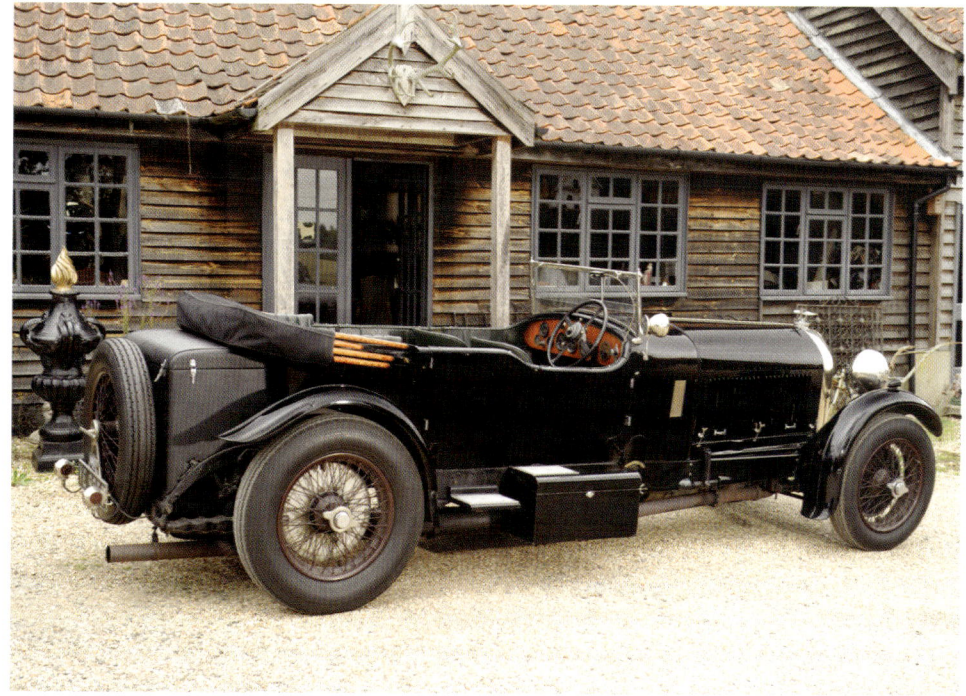

This engine was built with the single-carburettor specification, but has been modified with the twin carburettor installation associated with the Speed Six models.

The car was built with its dynamo driven from the rear of the engine, but was updated by Bentley Motors in the later 1920s with the later front-mounted dynamo.

On the left side of the engine can be seen the six spare spark plugs (on a panel that replaced the original dynamo front panel), the starter and the Autovac.

THE 6½-LITRE

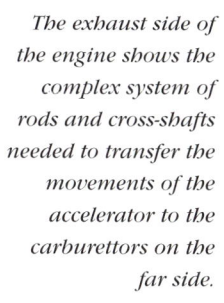

The exhaust side of the engine shows the complex system of rods and cross-shafts needed to transfer the movements of the accelerator to the carburettors on the far side.

The chassis number on the base of the steering column is evidence that this car retains its original components.

The handbrake on a Vanden Plas sports tourer would normally have been outside the bodywork. Here, it was mounted saloon-style inside the body.

The rear bench offered ample room for two passengers, and just enough for three if necessary.

Instrumentation was sparse, but sufficient, while the front seat backrests offered some side support.

THE 6½-LITRE

BX2421 was specially ordered with modified headlamp mountings to take German-made Zeiss headlamps.

The swivelling spotlight on the windscreen pillar was more useful than it looked, especially if trying to find the right address in the dark!

The switchbox also carried the chassis number, together with a warning not to leave the car with the ignition on.

The Vanden Plas "label" was attached to the inside of the front passenger door.

Chapter Three

The Speed Six

Despite the performance available from its big six-cylinder engine, the 6½-litre Bentley was not really a sporting car – not, at least, one in the same mould as the 3-litre from the same manufacturer. It was resolutely intended for the carriage trade, but with the added ingredient of much better performance than the average "large" chassis of the mid-1920s.

Nevertheless, the sporting potential of that vast engine cannot have been lost on anybody who worked at Cricklewood, or on many Bentley customers for that matter. By mid-1928, when it was becoming clear that even the new 4½-litre was hard pressed to keep Bentley among the front runners in sporting events, it was clear that something had to be done. Bentley team driver Tim Birkin was convinced that supercharging the 4½-litre was the best way forward, but WO was very much opposed to the idea. His preferred solution was to uprate the six-cylinder engine, which he knew still had plenty of development potential. Both plans went ahead, thanks to support for Birkin's proposal from the Bentley Board, and much to WO's disgust.

The plan to develop the six-cylinder engine probably took shape over the summer of 1928. Cricklewood called in intake systems specialist Harry Weslake to look at the engine, and there is little doubt that some of Weslake's ideas did make it through to production. More contentious is Weslake's suggestion that the modifications made to the engine were all his. "The truth is difficult to uncover," wrote Michael Hay, in Bentley "Old Number One".

The basic modifications made to the 6½-litre engine were the obvious ones. The single Smith-Bentley carburettor was replaced by a pair of vertical SUs, and the compression ratio was raised. As part of the change to twin carburettors, the inlet manifold had to be redesigned, and it is likely that Weslake's ideas had some impact here. In place of the elegantly curved water-heated manifold of the single-carburettor engine came a business-like box structure to carry the HVG5 carburettors. This arrangement gave 160bhp on the bench – 20bhp more than the single-carburettor engine – and the power delivery worked well with the existing C-type gearbox and the alternative 3.846:1 and 4.166:1 axle ratios.

A first chassis was running and bodied by the end of October 1928, and that car, on chassis number WT2265, became the Bentley Motors demonstrator. It was still performing that role in April 1929, when *The Motor* borrowed it for an evaluation test. The car was fitted with a Gurney Nutting Weymann saloon body – relatively light but by no means overtly sporting in nature. Whether Cricklewood had hoped to have it ready in time for the Olympia Show is not clear. No doubt they would have been pleased if they had, but, one way or another, the car was simply not ready to be seen in public by the time of the Olympia Show that month.

It seems probable that some of the other coachbuilders who worked closely with Bentley Motors had been tipped off about what to expect, too. That could explain the appearance at Olympia of the striking Barker-bodied streamlined two-seater on a 6½-litre chassis. So different in its demeanour from the grand and formal bodies that habitually adorned the 6½-litre chassis, it must have been intended as a demonstration of what Barker could do when the new chassis became available, and no doubt it would have been built on one if Barker's had been able to obtain one in time for the Show.

In all important respects, the chassis frame was the same as that of the existing 6½-litre. However, the Speed Six chassis had the 3/16in (0.188in) heavier-gauge steel from the beginning, and this was not seen until shortly afterwards on the Standard Six chassis. As for wheelbases, only the nominal 12ft size (actually 12ft 1¼in) was available in the beginning, the short-wheelbase team car which would later serve as a development vehicle being an anomaly.

Despite the intention of making the new twin-carburettor model a sporting machine, with a wheelbase of this size it was altogether too big to have the same agility that had been so much a part of the original 3-litre model's appeal. This of course had no bearing on Cricklewood's plans for special sporting derivatives – work was already in hand to take care of that – but it did mean that the new chassis was aimed at a different clientele. These were not buyers who simply wanted to go as fast as possible at sporting events such as those held at Brooklands. Instead, these were buyers who recognised the value of size in creating an elegant and imposing car – a fashion statement such as that 1928 Show two-seater from Barker.

Equally important was that the new and more powerful engine had not turned the car into a less civilised machine, and the smoothness and quietness that had always been characteristics of the 6½-litre chassis were still present. Bentley made a point of saying so in their sales brochure, where they described the new model as the Silent Speed Six. "Heralding a new era in automobile performance," they added, "the 6½-litre Silent Speed Six is the only car in the world which offers a perfect unison of Town Carriage luxuries and Sporting Car capabilities."

The chassis of course had both a plate clutch and a Dewandre vacuum servo for the brakes from the beginning, as both were now standard on the ordinary 6½-litre. Other chassis items were modified from their standard configuration, however. The new twin-carburettor engine would inevitably be more thirsty than the single-carburettor version, and so to maintain the car's touring range a larger 25-gallon petrol tank was standardised. Then to make sure this new chassis would be more readily distinguished from the model that now became known as the Standard Six, a new radiator was fitted. This had straight sides instead of the tapered sides of the parent model, and the winged B motif at the top had a green enamelled background. In addition, Lucas P100DB headlamps, distinguished by their bull's-eye lenses, were to be standard equipment.

1929: the first cars

That first demonstrator car remained the only complete Speed Six model for at least two months, and the first cars were not delivered to customers until January 1929. Like that first demonstrator, they were numbered within the standard 6½-litre chassis sequences and did not have special sequences or batch designations of their own. This was consistent with established Bentley practice: short-chassis, long-chassis, Speed and Supersports derivatives of the 3-litre had all been numbered within common sequences.

Most of the first few cars had closed body-

The Speed Six was deliberately distinguished from the Standard Six by its straight-sided radiator, as seen here on a "works" shot used for the sales catalogue. The front axle beam is the early type, without jacking-points.

Compare this "works" picture of a Speed Six engine with that of the Standard Six type. The block is still reversed from normal Bentley practice, with the inlet manifold on the left where, in place of a five-jet Bentley-Smith carburettor, there are two SUs.

The engine with the rocker box removed so that the overhead valve gear can be seen.

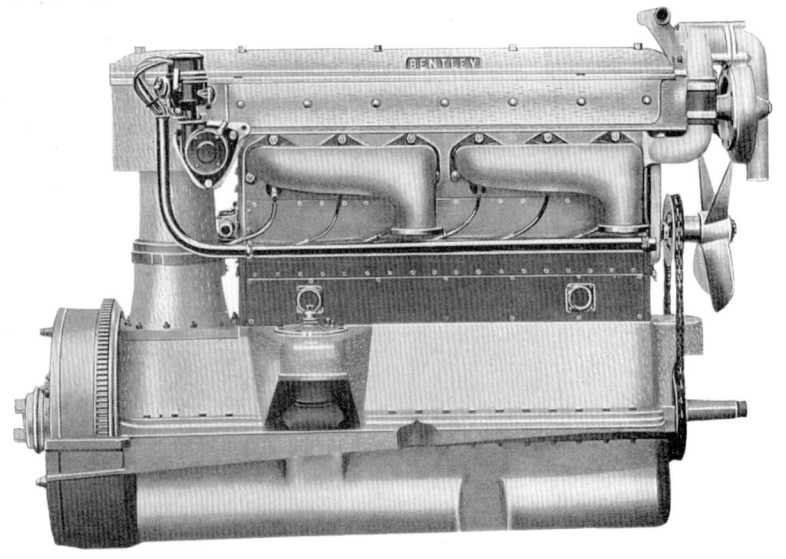

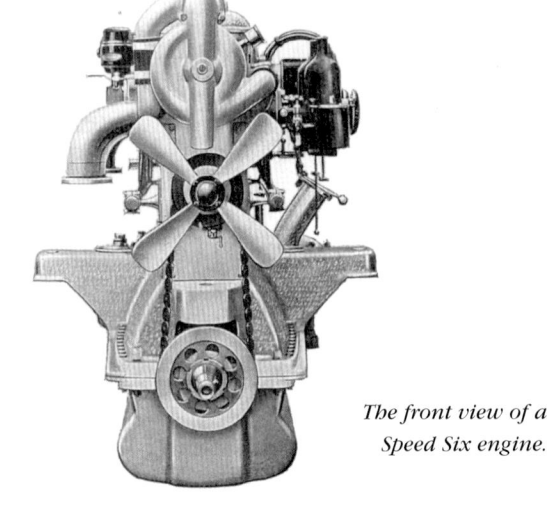

The front view of a Speed Six engine.

Again, it is worth comparing this picture with the equivalent "works" shot of the Standard Six engine. Although the layout is essentially the same, there are several detail differences.

work, although there was a leavening of open two-seater and open four-seater designs. But the new Bentley went down very well. During what remained of the 1929 season, a total of 69 chassis were delivered – three more than were delivered of the established Standard Six model. Quite clearly, Bentley had delivered what the public wanted.

The new car impressed the leading motoring magazines of the day, too. It was, said *The Motor* of 9 April 1929, "an outstanding example of British design and craftsmanship." There is more of what that magazine said in a later section of this chapter, entitled "Driving the Bentley Speed Six".

However, while public acceptance of their products was what Bentley Motors needed to stay in business, other projects were already under way at Cricklewood. After 15 cars had been built, a very special competition chassis was put together with the aim of running it at Le Mans in the summer alongside the 4½-litre team cars. This car, on chassis number LB2332, was built on the shortest chassis then available for the 6½-litre engine, which was the 11-foot wheelbase short-chassis type used only for the Standard Six. This car, which would go on to have a very distinguished career indeed, was ready by May 1929. Many of its innovations would later find their way into the production Speed Six models, but for the moment it remained unique.

By the time when Speed Six production began in earnest, the change to a single-pole electrical system had already been made on the Standard Six chassis, and so all the Speed Six models had such a system. Probably all Speed Six engines had the additional oil bath to lubricate the rockers.

Other changes during the first half of 1929 matched those on the standard models. So the new Bosch fuse box would have arrived on chassis LB2341, the first Speed Six chassis built after the recorded changeover point. The problem of heat entering the driving compartment that had afflicted earlier Standard Six models had by this stage been tamed, and Cricklewood was confident enough to eliminate the asbestos lagging that had been used on the exhausts of the first cars. It disappeared from the exhaust downpipes in April, at LB2339, and then from the silencers as well in July, at FR2632.

1930: making it work better

Although small numbers of Standard Six models were built at Cricklewood early in the 1930 season, the Speed Six had completely supplanted the earlier model in production by December 1929, and possibly earlier.

From the start of the 1930 season, the longer wheelbase (nominally 12ft 6in) was introduced alongside the original 12ft wheelbase. This came with the strut gear already seen on the long-wheelbase Standard Six chassis. The cost of a Speed Six chassis of either length also increased from £1700 to £1800. With hindsight, putting up prices at such a time was not the most sensible thing to do but the increase had probably been planned long before the Wall Street Crash in October. Its purpose was almost certainly to ease the transition to the forthcoming 8-litre model as well as to bring in additional revenue, because the new car would be more expensive still at £1850. Perhaps Cricklewood feared that a sudden jump from £1700 straight to £1850 would deter some customers.

The 1930 Speed Six chassis had hydraulic rear dampers in place of the friction type previously standard. Headlights were Lucas P100s in place of the earlier Smith's type, although special requests could always be accommodated. The 1930 chassis also had some major changes to the ignition system. Although the principle of two sets of spark plugs fired by separate electrical sources remained in place, the execution was very different. Out went the long-established twin-magneto design, and in came what sales brochures referred to as a Dual Ignition System.

Although one magneto remained in place to fire the plugs on the left-hand side of the cylinder block, a coil ignition system was used

Beautifully presented, this was the engine of SB 2761, as it appeared at the BDC Silverstone event in 2009. Quite clear here is the cross-shaft for the accelerator mechanism and the associated rod linkages to the carburettors. There are scrutineers' stickers attached at the rear of the engine bay, and the large chromed horn is a nice (but non-standard) touch.

SB 2761 again, showing the casing of the dynamo where it protruded through the radiator, and a pair of more modern driving lamps which help to compensate for the relatively poor light from the original style headlamps.

to fire those on the right-hand side. The sales brochure explained it like this:

"After lengthy bench and road tests, it was proved that two independent ignitions firing two plugs in each cylinder gave the best results. The magneto and coil are so arranged that the timing is synchronised, and further, in the unlikely event of one system failing, the engine will continue to run satisfactorily on the other. A special switch has been designed giving four positions: – (1) Off; (2) Left hand ignition; (3) Right hand ignition; (4) Both systems; and one of the most important features of this Bentley switch is that a red light appears, which warns the driver that the coil ignition must be switched off when the engine is stopped, thus preventing continuous discharge of the batteries."

This change was accompanied by a switch to a German-made Bosch FU6B magneto, which replaced the British-made ML ER6 fitted to the earlier cars. The coil ignition system meanwhile came from Delco-Remy. Both magneto and coil ignition systems were driven by a skew gear on the back of the camshaft. A further and final change to a Bosch GF6 magneto was made from chassis number LR2783.

All the 1930-season Speed Six engines had stronger connecting rods and racing-type rockers without the third rivet hole of the standard type, plus a compression ratio increased to 5.3:1. This gave a further power increase to 180bhp. Other changes were introduced in stages at the beginning of the season. First of all came a change from white metal bearings to shell bearings at engine number BA2588 (in chassis number BA2583). Then at engine number SB2759 (in chassis number KR2699) the cylinder block was changed to the single-port type pioneered on the short-chassis Le Mans car earlier in 1929. In essence, this meant that there was a single, large "slot" opening in the side of the block to bring fuel-air mixture to all the inlet valves; earlier engines had two openings or ports for each cylinder, which meant that there had been 12 ports on the inlet side of the block. The two-ports-per-cylinder arrangement was the same as that employed on the four-cylinder engines. These earlier 6½-litre blocks are variously known as "twin-port" (ie two ports per cylinder) and "multi-port" types, and the use of these different terms has led to some confusion over the years.

More engine changes followed shortly afterwards. At engine number SB2770 (in chassis number SB2760), the water jacket plates were changed from mild steel to stainless steel in order to resist corrosion more effectively. And on the very next engine, number SB2771 (in chassis number SB2763), a five-gallon sump made of Elektron replaced the original three-gallon type.

Axle changes followed. First came a new nosepiece made of weight-saving Elektron at chassis number SB2765, and slightly later a new banjo at NH2728. The very last series of engines then switched to the Bosch co-axial starter motor that was by then intended for use with the 8-litre engine. Much smaller in diameter than the earlier Smith's type, its key advantage was refinement: on the Bosch starter, the pinion slid into mesh before turning the flywheel, and this eliminated the noise so characteristic of the Smith's starter as it sought engagement with the ring gear.

However, despite the undoubted success of the Speed Six, its days were numbered. A decision had already been made to go to an even larger engine for the six-cylinder chassis, and the plan was to introduce that engine at the Olympia Show in October 1930. Perhaps to ease the transition from Speed Six to the new 8-litre, the latter part of the LR sanction chassis (from LR2790) and all except two of the final HM sanction built over the summer of 1930 were long-wheelbase cars fitted with the taller bulkhead and radiator that would be associated with the new 8-litre model. (The two exceptions were, of course, the two short-chassis works racers prepared for the 1930 Le Mans event. Although chassis HM2870 followed them numerically, these were the last two Speed Sixes actually built.)

Even though the new 8-litre was designed to give Bentley a leading position in the market, WO himself probably felt a twinge of regret that the 6½-litre engine was due to go out of production. In later years, he admitted that the Speed Six had been his favourite of all the cars produced at Cricklewood. The Speed Six had indeed done well for Bentley Motors. During the 1930 season it had been the company's best-seller, with its 126 sales just edging ahead of the 124 examples of the unsupercharged 4½-litre.

There are, however, indications that the car would not have been made in quite such large numbers if everything had gone according to plan. That final batch of 20 which formed the HM sanction (the sanctions were normally of 25 chassis) seems to have been sanctioned to keep the company going over the summer of 1930 while final preparations were made for assembly of the new 8-litre. Of these, two became the short-chassis Le Mans cars in time for the event at the end of June. Had this last

This is an early 11ft 6in Speed Six chassis, fitted with battery trays on the left-hand chassis rail. A comparison with pictures of four-cylinder chassis will show that the rods to the front brakes are no longer on the outside of the chassis frame. The fuel tank is the standard 25-gallon item. Despite its apparent sturdiness, the frame could flex a little, and strut gear was used to stiffen up later examples.

This was chassis KR 2697, pictured during its rebuild. Originally a Standard Six, it was rebuilt to a semi-Le Mans specification with Speed Six engine and oversize fuel tank, as seen here.

BENTLEY SPEED SIX PRODUCTION

Note: These figures relate to "season" and not to calendar year, and the totals are not broken down by wheelbase size. They are based on the "traditional" classifications of chassis; the figures calculated by Hay in 2008 give a total of 182 Speed Six chassis. (Hay lists nine additional Speed Six chassis and disallows four formerly considered to be Speed Six types. This modifies the total by five (nine minus four), which exactly accounts for the difference between the "old" figure of 177 Speed Sixes and the "new" figure of 182.)

1929	69
1930	108
Total	177

batch not been built, however, no doubt the two Le Mans cars would have been constructed as a "batch" on their own.

All this inevitably raises the question of why the Speed Six had to be taken out of production when it was. The car was the company's best-seller, despite a market that was beginning to shrink as a result of the shock-waves that emanated from the Wall Street Crash in October 1929. The 4½-litre and its supercharged derivative were more or less dead in the water by the summer of 1930. And yet Bentley Motors (or, at least, the company's Board) chose to stake everything on the new 8-litre model and on its rather hastily conceived 4-litre derivative for the 1931 season.

Cash was certainly very tight at the time. The Board's view may well have been that the company needed to go forward with two models in production. The 8-litre had to be one, because so much had already been spent on its development. The Speed Six could not be the other, because its price of £1800 was not sufficiently lower than the £1850 planned for the forthcoming 8-litre. The existing cheaper Bentley, the 4½-litre, was obviously not going to last much longer. So the 4-litre was brought in to fill the gap.

In effect, this means that the well-proven Speed Six was ousted from production by the completely untried 4-litre at a time when it was not only selling very strongly but had also just managed a convincing one-two victory at Le Mans. No wonder, then, that WO would be so bitterly opposed to the new 4-litre when it arrived.

POLICE CHASE CARS

Two Speed Six chassis became high-speed pursuit cars with the state police force of Western Australia. The chassis were LR2783 and LR2785, and both were delivered in July 1930. They were bodied as six-light saloons by Bolton of Perth, in Australia, carried two-way radios and remained in active use until 1947. These cars were probably the only six-cylinder Bentleys ever used by a police force anywhere in the world.

However, they were not the only police Bentleys: London's Metropolitan Police had a 4½-litre, along with another four-cylinder model which was kept at Hendon Police College for many years for driver training purposes.

These are the two Bolton-bodied cars used by the Western Australia Police. On the left is LR 2785, and on the right is LR 2783.

CHASSIS NUMBERS AND BUILD DATES OF THE SPEED SIX CARS

The chassis number of a Bentley Speed Six can be found on the left-hand side of the chassis front cross-member.

The lists below show the chassis numbers of cars known to have been built as Speed Sixes. The accepted total of Speed Six chassis has varied over the years, and the figures used in this book were generally accepted until recently. However, Clare Hay's book, *Bentley Speed Six*, published in 2008, suggests different totals. Chassis which are classified as Speed Sixes by Hay (but not previously), and chassis earlier assumed to be Speed Six types but not listed as such by Hay, are noted as such in the lists below.

All the Speed Six chassis were numbered within the build sanctions allocated to the Standard Six cars, and these are listed in Chapter 2. Note how the chassis were initially built mainly in pairs, and then gradually in larger groups until the Speed Six took over completely from the Standard Six model during the 1930 season.

The lists below show the Speed Six chassis in approximate chronological order of manufacture. The construction of bodywork typically took between two and three months, although some bodies took much longer, and there would have been other delays when Cricklewood sent a completed car back to the bodybuilder for modifications before it would issue the Five-Year Guarantee. Delivery dates shown below come from Bentley Motors records and are the dates on which the guarantees were issued.

It would be reasonable to suppose that the actual build date of most chassis was two or three months earlier than their delivery dates, but there were cars which took longer than the usual time to complete.

For a more precise dating of any individual chassis, it is advisable to contact the Bentley Drivers' Club.

Chassis numbers	Delivery dates	Remarks
WT2265	October 1928	Bentley Motors demonstrator
KF2378	January 1929	
KF2381	February 1929	
KF2384	January 1929	
KF2387-KF2388	January-February 1929	
KF2390	May 1929	
KF2393-KF2394	March-April 1929	
KF2396-KF2397	February-March 1929	
KF 2398	February 1929	Now listed as a Speed Six by Hay
KF2399-KF2400	March-July 1929	
LB2326-LB2327	February-March 1929	
LB2328-LB2331	February-April 1929	Now listed as Speed Sixes by Hay
LB2332	May 1929	Short-chassis Speed Six team car for Le Mans
LB2333-2335	March 1929	Now listed as Speed Sixes by Hay
LB2338-LB2339	April-June 1929	
LB2341-LB2343	April-May 1929	
LB2346-LB2347	March-May 1929	
LB2349-LB2350	April-May 1929	
BA2576-BA2578	May-June 1929	
BA2580-BA2584	April-November 1929	
BA2586-BA2587	May-June 1929	
BA2589-BA2595	April-July 1929	
BA2598-BA2600	July-October 1929	
FR2626-FR2628	July 1929-April 1930	FR2628 was the first 1930 season chassis
FR2630-FR2650	June 1929-June 1931	
KR2676-KR2678	September-October 1929	
KR2681-KR2683	September 1929	
KR2694-KR2696	March-June 1930	KR2694 not listed as Speed Six by Hay
KR2697	July 1930	Now listed as a Speed Six by Hay
KR2698-KR2700	October-December 1929	
SB2751-SB2775	October 1929-April 1931	SB2758 not listed as Speed Six by Hay
NH2726-NH2750	December 1929-July 1930	
LR2776-LR2800	March-November 1930	LR2791 not listed as Speed Six by Hay
HM2851-HM2870	April-December 1930	HM2868 and HM2869 were short-chassis Le Mans cars. HM2870 not listed as Speed Six by Hay

SPECIFICATIONS FOR BENTLEY SPEED SIX MODELS

Years of manufacture
1928-1930

Build quantity
177 (182 according to later calculations)

Engine
6597cc (100mm x 140mm) OHC six-cylinder with four valves per cylinder
Multi-port head on 1929 models; single-port head on 1930 models
Two SU HVG5 vertical carburettors
5.1:1 compression ratio (1929); 5.3:1 compression ratio (1930)
160bhp at 3500rpm (1929); 180bhp at 3500rpm (1930)

Transmission
Four-speed "crash" gearbox.
C-type gearbox:
3.364:1, 1.823:1, 1.357:1, 1.00:1, reverse 3.364:1.
Some cars were built with the D-type gearbox:
2.64:1, 1.63:1, 1.35:1, 1.00:1, reverse 2.64:1.

Final drive ratio:	Standard	3.846:1
	Heavy bodies	4.166:1
	Also	3.538:1
	Racing	3.333:1
	Le Mans	3.13:1
	Track cars	2.8:1

Suspension
Semi-elliptic leaf springs on front and rear axles; front axle with Bentley & Draper friction dampers; rear axle with Bentley & Draper friction dampers up to end of 1929 season, and Bentley & Draper hydraulic dampers thereafter

Steering
Worm and wheel steering

Brakes
400mm (15.7in) drum-type brakes on all four wheels, with rod operation and Dewandre vacuum servo

Chassis dimensions

Wheelbase:	11ft 2½in (Three Le Mans cars, plus one for Mrs WB Scott)
	11ft 8½in (standard)
	12ft 8½in (optional)
Overall length:	15ft 7in (standard)
	16ft 7in (optional long wheelbase)
Overall width:	5ft 8½in
Track:	56in front and rear
Weight:	32cwt (standard)
	33cwt (optional long wheelbase)

Performance

Max. speed:	90-93mph
0-60mph:	17 secs approx
Fuel consumption (typical):	12mpg (2.64 miles per litre)

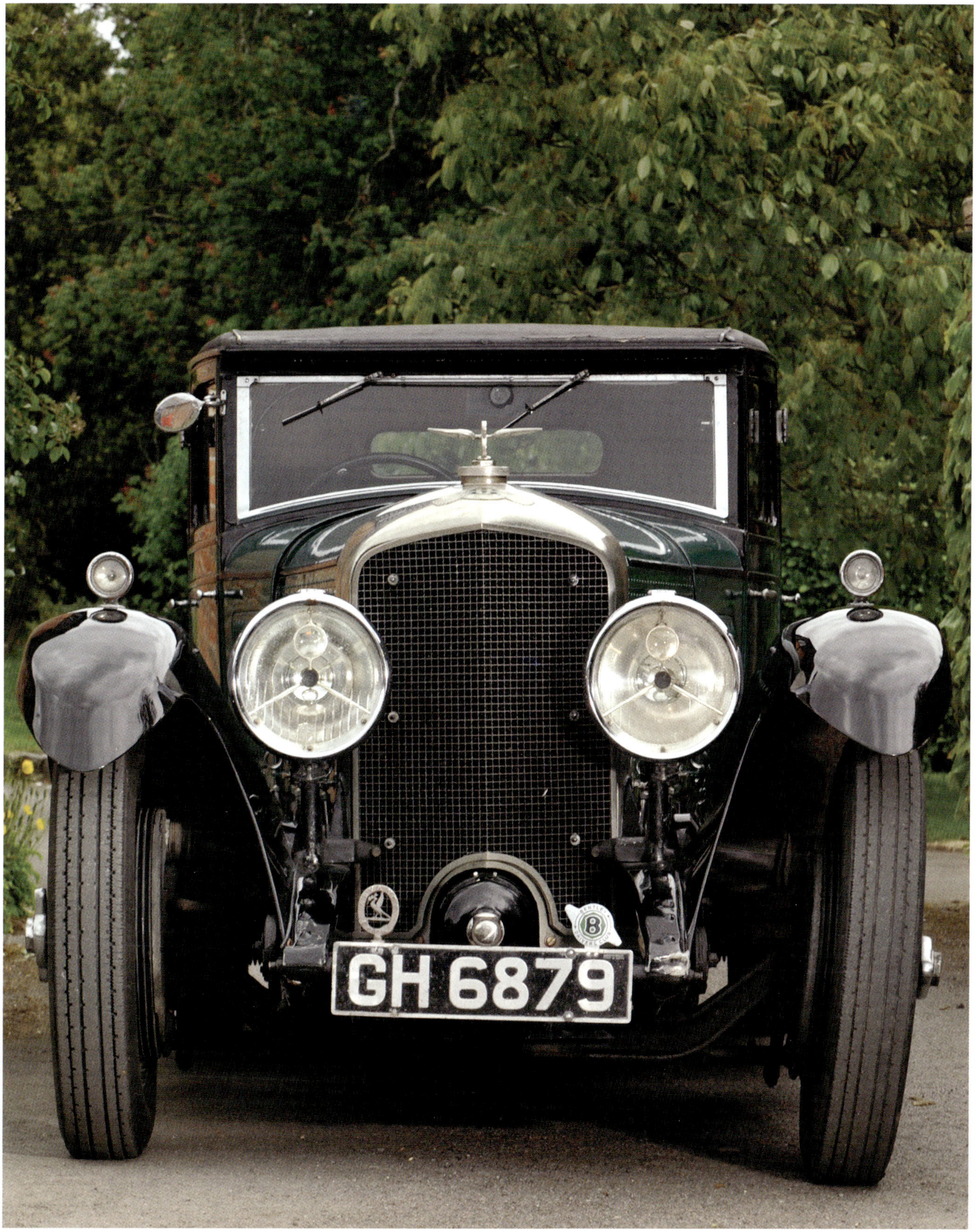
GH 6879

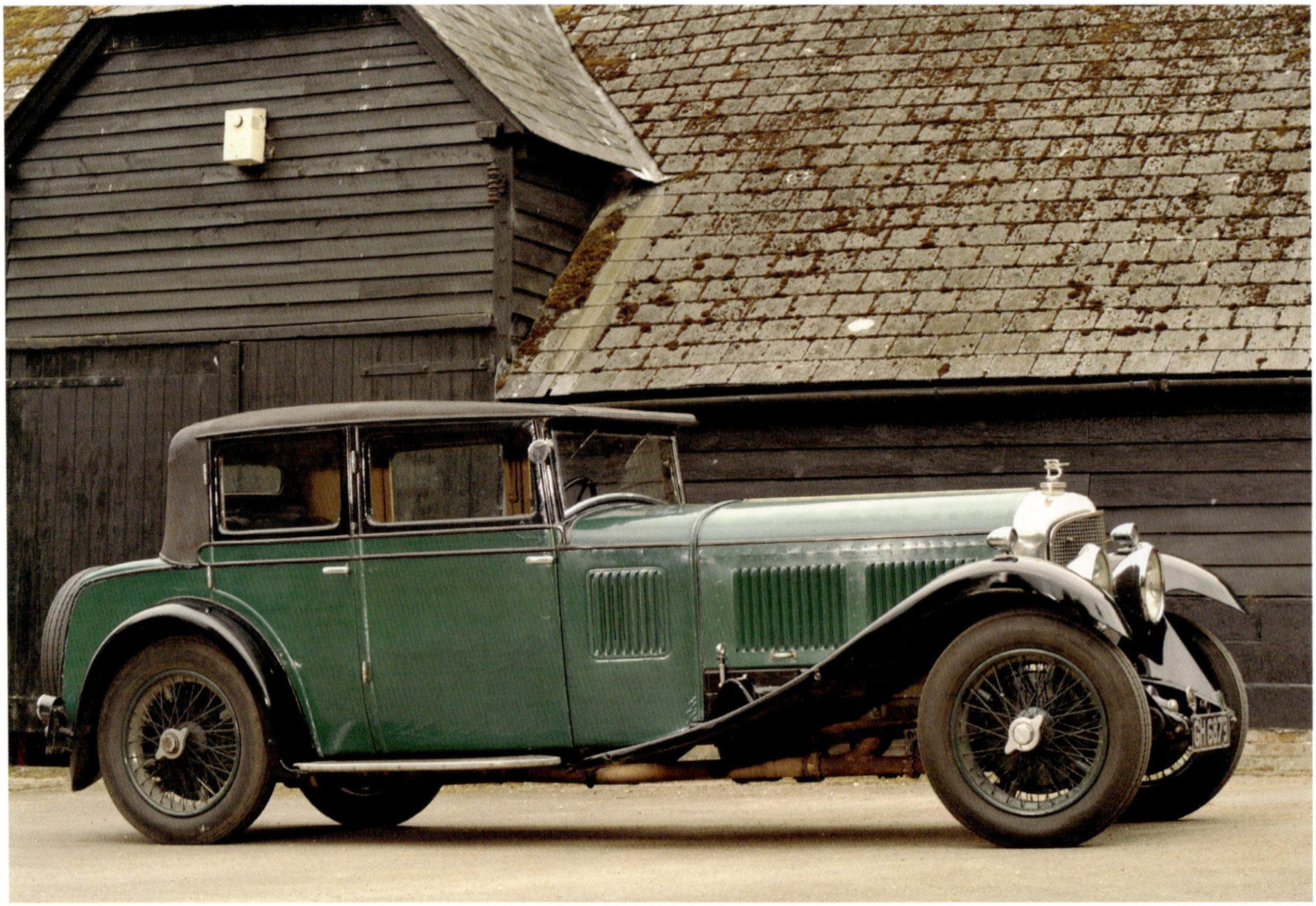

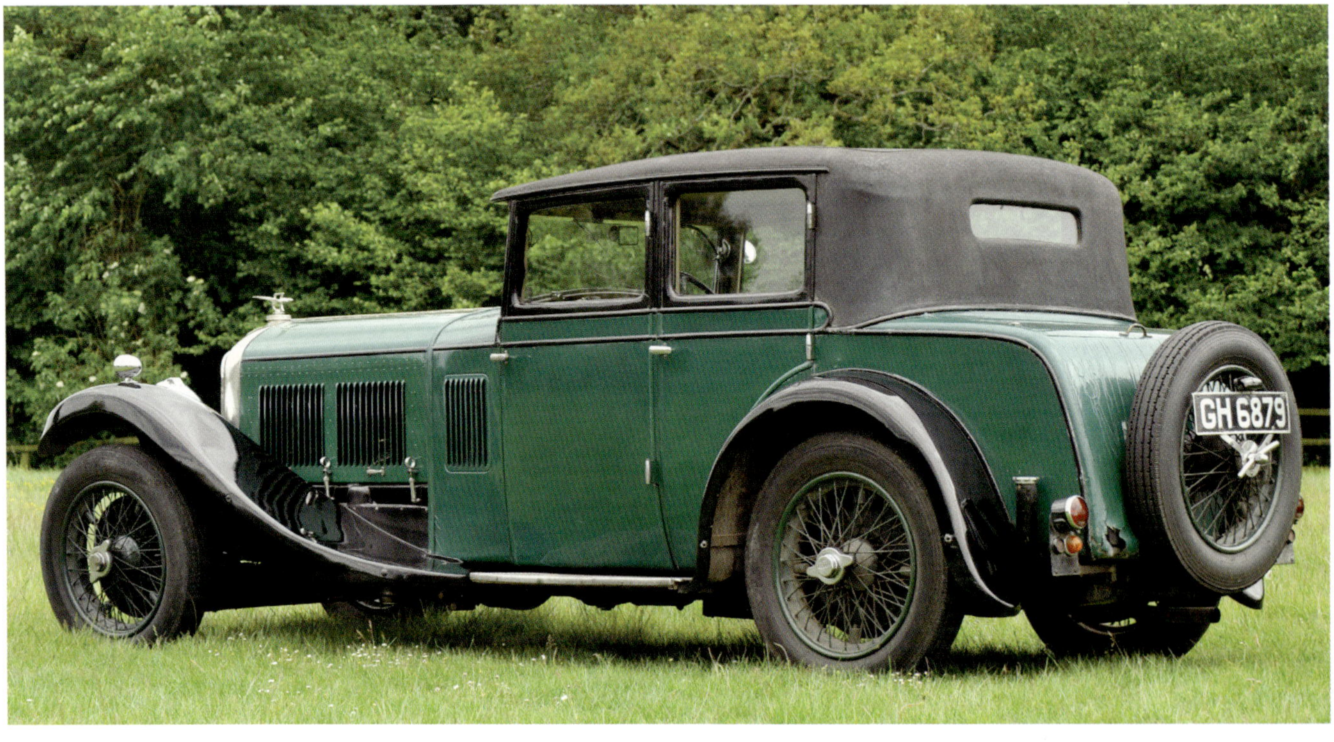
GH 6879

THE SPEED SIX

David Low's Speed Six is a 1930 model on the "11ft 6in" wheelbase chassis, with its original Gurney Nutting saloon bodywork. The car's attractive lines suggest its sporting performance, with the long bonnet blending into a deep scuttle, flowing wings and the separate step-type running-boards which were fashionable at the time. The radiator stone-guard may have been no more than a sensible precaution, but it also added to the sporting appearance of the car.

49

The twin carburettors of the Speed Six engine were on the left. Note the differences in the manifolding between this engine and the earlier 6½-litre converted to Speed Six configuration with the older, box-shaped manifold. The ignition system on this side has a Bosch magneto.

A delightful rarity is this seal applied by Bentley Motors.

This is the Autovac, which has a configuration different from that used for the 8-litre and 4-litre chassis not long afterwards.

THE SPEED SIX

The float-operated oil level indicator located on the carburettor side of the crankcase.

The Bosch dynamo was not fitted when the car was new, but was a service update in October 1930

The exhaust side of the engine shows the Delco-Remy coil ignition system; the coil is sunk into the bulkhead.

The door opening is rather narrow and the legroom not enormous, but those rear seats offer plenty of comfort.

In the fashion of the time, the windscreen was demisted by being opened on a sliding catch like this on either side.

The peak above the windscreen was a fashion of the period.

THE SPEED SIX

The front doors are traditionally trimmed in leather with wood trim and a kick-panel of carpet-like material.

There is something very inviting about that interior! In the fashion of the time, the seat backs are pleated but the cushions are in plain leather.

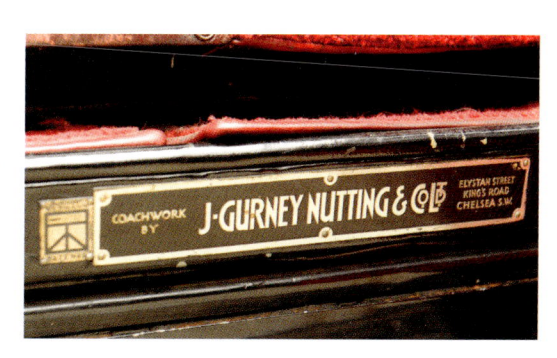

The coachbuilder's plate was in its customary place inside the door above the running-board, and that small plate on its left here acknowledges that Weymann patents were used in the construction of the body.

Footwell vents are fed by fresh air from the louvred panel on the outside of the scuttle.

53

BENTLEY SIX-CYLINDER MODELS IN DETAIL

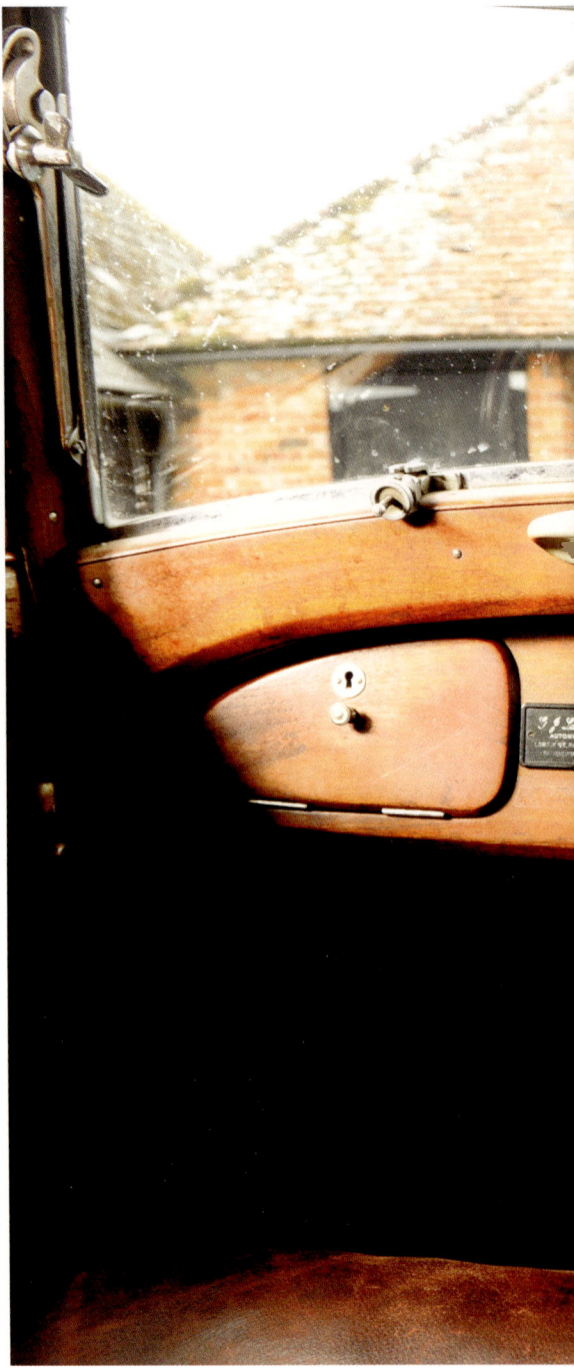

The dashboard arrangement incorporates separate lights for the instrument dials, a grab-handle for the passenger, and a dealer plaque which tells a little part of this car's history.

54

Hinged plates in the coachwork provide access to the brake adjuster on the driver's side and to the tool kit on the passenger's side.

The fuel filler was located almost discreetly behind the left-hand rear wing.

The luggage trunk was built into the back of the body in the latest fashion, and access was gained through the top. The paintwork has suffered over the years – but to replace it would be to lose some of this car's wonderful originality.

Additional lights and reflectors are modern additions but have been tastefully blended in. Some parts of the body are beginning to succumb to age more than 80 years after the car left the Gurney Nutting workshops.

The Speed Six chassis always had Bentley & Draper friction dampers at the front.

The optional winged-B radiator cap emblem overlooks the green "label" associated with Speed Six cars.

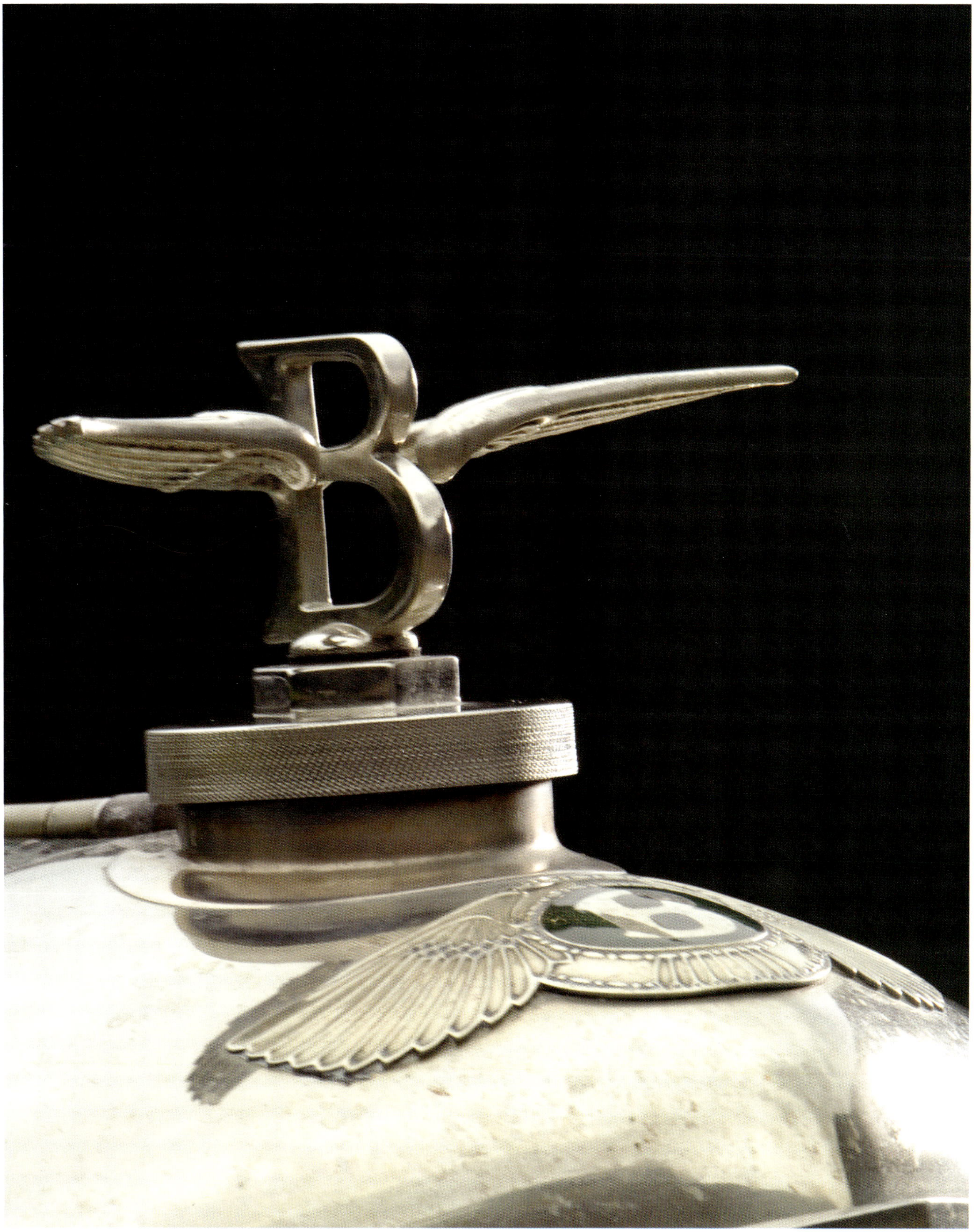

Chapter Four

Coachwork on the 6½-Litre Chassis

Strictly a "Three-quarter coupé" with a window behind the door, this body was built by Vanden Plas on an early 6½-litre chassis, number TB 2532. The upright lines and fake-wood paint probably dated quite quickly.

As had been the case from the start of 3-litre production, Bentley Motors did not themselves provide bodywork for their chassis. However, they did have informal arrangements with a number of London coachbuilders whose coachwork they had "approved" and towards whom they would steer customers who needed guidance. Notable among these were Harrisons, who had bodied Bentleys from the earliest days, and Vanden Plas, who were located right next door to the Bentley works and were particularly favoured for open bodywork. WO's own view, as expressed in *An Illustrated History of the Bentley Car*, was that "Mulliners were possibly the most satisfactory, especially for saloons, while Vanden Plas were far and away the best for open coachwork".

Nevertheless, customers were free to choose who bodied their Bentley chassis, and the result was a vast range of different bodies and styles on the six-cylinder models. At the top end of the scale were Hooper, the royal coachbuilders, whose creations were formidably expensive and enormously prestigious. Right behind them were companies like Barker and HJ Mulliner, Park Ward, Gurney Nutting, and Thrupp & Maberly. Far less prestigious, but for all that no less capable, were some of the smaller companies like Connaught and Lancefield, and some customers chose to have their bodies built in the provinces, in some cases by companies who were very little known. It all made for an exciting array of styles, and one which has been a constant source of fascination for Bentley enthusiasts and historians ever since it became apparent that the vast majority of these coach-built bodies had been consigned to history.

Today, the survival of a six-cylinder Bentley with its original coachwork is a rarity, not least because the construction of many of these bodies did not stand the twin tests of time and neglect. Fortunately, however, the historical value of surviving examples has been recognised, and there is no longer much likelihood that any of them will be discarded in favour of yet another Le Mans replica body.

The original bodies

The popular image of the 6½-litre Bentleys today is heavily conditioned by two factors. One is the glamour of the open four-seater Speed Six models which swept everything before them at Le Mans, and the other is that the vast majority of surviving examples carry broadly similar open bodywork. Unfortunately, nothing could be further from the truth of what these cars were really like in their heyday.

Right from the start, the 6½-litre chassis was intended to carry heavy bodywork of the type favoured by the carriage trade. That was its whole *raison d'être*: the six cylinders gave the engine the refined character that the customers wanted, while the increase in swept volume ensured that the performance associated with the Bentley name would not be lost when heavy and formal bodies were fitted. The Speed Six simply gave better performance than the Standard Six, and was never intended to be a sports car. The famous Le Mans cars which had the Speed Six engine were actually specially-built derivatives of the production models, and their weight-saving short chassis was just not available to ordinary Bentley buyers.

There were, of course, open touring bodies available for both types of 6½-litre chassis. In the 1930 sales brochure for the Speed Six models, an "open sporting four-seater" is illustrated as one of four samples of approved bodywork for the chassis. It is actually the cheapest of the four, at £2230 for the complete car. The two-door Weymann saloon at £2310, the four-door Weymann saloon at £2430, and the Weymann coupé de ville at £2500 are all more expensive. Bentley Motors never had an open 6½-litre of any description on their own stand at the Olympia Show in all the six years they displayed chassis of this type, and in fact the only green fabric-panelled Speed Six open tourer ever seen at Olympia was in 1929 on the Vanden Plas stand. No doubt it was there to exploit the success of the short-chassis Vanden Plas-bodied team car at Le Mans earlier in the year.

Of the 545 cars built on 6½-litre chassis, bodywork details have survived for all but seven. Original bodywork details are listed on Robert McLellan's exceptionally useful website, www.vintagebentleys.org (although there are errors), and some calculations based on those lists are very revealing. Taking Standard Six and Speed Six models together, no fewer than 334 cars – a massive 61% – were bodied as saloons. Open cars of any kind were relatively rare, amounting to just 88 (slightly over 16%) even when more sophisticated designs such as cabriolets and drophead coupés are taken into account. This of course reflects the decline in popularity of open cars as the 1920s drew to a close: those who could afford decent weather protection were increasingly inclined to insist on it when buying a new car.

Some two years later, this was Vanden Plas' idea of a coupé on Standard Six chassis WT 2263. The roofline is considerably lower, making the car look more sleek. The fabric covering for the roof and rear-quarters, plus the dummy landau irons, give a convincing impression of a drophead coupé.

TOTALS OF INDIVIDUAL BODY STYLES

Saloons	334
Four-seaters	49
Coupés	42
Limousines	38
Two-seaters	16
Landaulettes	15
Drophead coupés	10
Coupés de Ville	7
Not known	7
Cabriolets	6
Cabriolets de Ville	6
Sedancas	5
Tourers	4
Sedancas de Ville	2
Torpedos	2
Allweathers	2
TOTAL	545

Allweathers

The Allweather body was popular immediately after the Great War but declined in popularity quite quickly during the first half of the 1920s. It was essentially an open touring body but with a weatherproof canvas hood and sidescreens that took some little time to erect.

Just two 6½-litres were bodied in this style, which was really something of a throwback to earlier times. The earlier one had Standard Six chassis number FA 2509 and was delivered in July 1928, its body being by HJ Mulliner. The later example was on NH 2750, a Speed Six delivered in July 1930. This was one bodied in the UK by Gill, but to a design by Hibbard and Darrin of Paris which was considerably more sophisticated than the description "all-weather" tends to suggest.

Cabriolets

Cabriolet bodies "were effectively refined tourers", according to Ian Beattie in *The Complete Book of Automobile Body Design*. "They combined the general arrangement of touring bodies with a higher level of weather protection", so where the tourer had sidescreens, the cabriolet normally had glass windows that wound or dropped into the doors. The six known examples on 6½-litre Bentley chassis were all by the more expensive coach-builders.

There were two by Hooper (FW 2604, June 1927, and KD 2117, October 1927), two by Thrupp & Maberly (LR 2800, April 1930, and HM 2851, June 1930), and one each by Barker (TB 2539, October 1926) and HJ Mulliner (DH 2220, July 1927).

Despite modernising touches like the disc wheel covers, this 1928 coupé body by Arnold on Standard Six PR 2320 has the tall roof characteristic of earlier 1920s designs.

Cabriolets de Ville

The cabriolet de ville was a formal body with glass in its side windows, a folding fabric top over the rear compartment, and an extension to that top which could be unfurled to cover the driving compartment if required. Typically, however, the chauffeur would be exposed to the elements unless the weather was severe.

There were six cabriolets de ville on Bentley 6½-litre chassis. All were built by Thrupp & Maberly. The chassis numbers, with delivery dates, were MD 2471 (May 1928), FA 2518 (November 1928), KF 2392 (July 1929), LB 2340 (July 1929), KR 2685 (August 1930) and LR 2784 (July 1930). There is some indication that KR 2685 was shown at Olympia in 1930. Sadly, not one of these magnificent bodies has survived intact.

Coupés

There were 42 coupé bodies on 6½-litre chassis, by 16 different coachbuilders. These are listed below, with the most prolific builders first.

Gurney Nutting	9
HJ Mulliner	7
Harrison	6
Park Ward	4
Vanden Plas	3
Hooper	2
Victor Broom	2
Arnold	1
Auster	1
(Based in North London; otherwise unknown)	
Blake	1
(Based in Liverpool)	
Compton	1
(Presumably Compton & Hermon of Thames Ditton in Surrey)	
Freestone & Webb	1
James Young	1
Lancefield	1
Offord	1
Page & Hunt	1
(Based at Farnham in Surrey)	

Coupés de Ville

A coupé de ville usually had an enclosed close-coupled passenger compartment at the rear with an open driving compartment for the chauffeur. There were seven such bodies on Bentley 6½-litre chassis.

The earliest example was by Freestone &

Webb, delivered in September 1926 on chassis TB 2544. Windovers built one on WK 2651, and the Leicester firm of Hamshaw built one on WK 2672; both were delivered in January 1927. Knibbs (WH Knibbs & Sons of Manchester) delivered a coupé de ville on TW 2716 in June 1927, and Park Ward delivered one on FA 2524 in November 1928. The last two were both by Gurney Nutting, on KF 2378 and BA 2597, delivered in January and June 1929 respectively. Not a single one of these bodies is known to survive today.

Drophead coupés

Drophead coupé bodies were essentially the same thing as cabriolet types, with two doors containing glass windows, and a folding hood. Most had four seats. There were ten examples on the 6½-litre Bentley chassis.

Half of these bodies were built by HJ Mulliner, although it is impossible now to tell how many different styles there were. Those five cars were on chassis TB 2542 (delivered in September 1926), TB 2548 (March 1927), FR 2647 (September 1929), NH 2742 (March 1930) and LR 2776 (July 1930). Four of the others were built in Britain, by Motor Bodies of Newcastle (WT 2271, December 1928), Gurney Nutting (LB 2327, March 1929), Thrupp & Maberly (NH 2733, July 1930), and Lancefield (LR 2782, July 1930). The fifth was bodied in France by Saoutchik, the Parisian coachbuilder, for a customer in the USA. This was on chassis number SB 2769, and was delivered in November 1929. It is very satisfying to record that several of these original bodies still exist to demonstrate the craftsmanship of their coachbuilders.

This Martin Walter coupé body was built for chassis SB 2761 in 1930, but when pictured had been fitted to an earlier Standard Six chassis, PR 2321 from 1928.

HJ Mulliner built the fabric-panelled coupé body on this late Speed Six chassis, NH 2735 from 1930.

Another HJ Mulliner design, this time their Simplex drophead coupé on chassis TB 2542 from 1926. The car is believed to be the only surviving short-chassis 6½-litre that still retains its original bodywork.

A 1928 6½-LITRE, FA 2519, WITH BARKER BOAT-TAIL BODY

Barker's stand at Olympia in 1928 featured a genuine show-stopper – a streamlined boat-tail two-door body on the 12ft 6in wheelbase 6½-litre Bentley chassis. What must have been most apparent to those who saw it was that it had borrowed a number of styling elements from Malcolm Campbell's Bluebird Land Speed Record car, which in February that year had taken the record on Daytona Beach in Florida at a speed of 206.956mph. By the time of the Olympia Show in October, the record had again been broken, and was held by the White Triplex which had achieved 207.55mph at Daytona Beach in April. Nevertheless, to a patriotic British audience, the memory of Campbell's triumph would have been an enduring one.

The most obvious "Bluebird" features on the car were the pontoon-shaped wings, which to a recognisable degree aped the aerodynamic wheel fairings on the record car. Bluebird's wire-spoked wheels had also been made more aerodynamic with the aid of disc covers, and the Barker show car had similar covers over its wire wheels. Instead of conventional running-boards, or even the small steps that were favoured by the sporting fraternity, the car had teardrop-shaped pontoon structures, which doubled as running-boards and as storage compartments.

There were other striking features in the boat tail itself. The folding top was arranged so that it disappeared out of sight under a cover in the forward end of the rear deck, and behind it there was a wholly concealed dickey seat that could accommodate two more passengers. The spare wheel was also concealed within the long tail. All of this was finished in an eye-catching colour scheme of light yellow, with dark Oxford Blue for the wings, wheels and chassis, and burnished aluminium on the horizontal surfaces of the bonnet and rear deck. The interior was also upholstered in blue, and the use of this colour no doubt helped to reinforce the link to Bluebird – although the Land Speed Record car was in fact painted in a much lighter shade than any used on the Bentley.

To reinforce the impression of length, this car was fitted with a special extended bonnet (made for Bentley by Ewart & Sons in Camden Town). This reached from the radiator right up to the base of the windscreen, and concealed the scuttle which at the time was normally picked out as a separate feature on the car. Under the bonnet, velvet-lined tool trays were let into the scuttle just in front of the bulkhead – a somewhat flamboyant luxury touch which was really perfectly in keeping with the extravagant air of the rest of the car.

The Show car remained unique, although Barker did build a second car with many similar features on a Speed Six with the 11ft 6in wheelbase in 1929. Park Ward also copied much of its style on a July 1929 Speed Six chassis, again on the 11ft 6in wheelbase.

According to legend, this remarkable car was used as a fast refuelling vehicle by the Royal Air Force during the Second World War – although the story does seem rather fanciful. One way or another, the car survived the hostilities and still exists today.

Imagine this car in yellow with blue wings: Barker's boat-tailed body was a sensation at the 1928 Olympia Show.

Four-seaters

Of the 49 four-seater bodies found on 6½-litre chassis, it is no surprise that the majority were by Vanden Plas, whose name was on 20 of them. The company's close geographical association with Bentley Motors in Cricklewood must have been a key factor, and of course there was a certain glamour attached to the body style used by the works team. Of those 20 cars, two (HM 2868 and HM 2869, both delivered in May 1930) stood out as genuine works team cars.

The next most prolific builders of four-seater bodies on the 6½-litre chassis were HJ Mulliner, with seven, and then Gurney Nutting and Cadogan with four each and Harrison with three. Barker constructed two bodies, but the remaining nine were built by nine different coachbuilders. They were Hooper, Freestone & Webb, Park Ward, Connaught, Gill, Offord, Mann Egerton, Beadle and Caffyns. The majority were London-based, but Mann Egerton in Norwich and Caffyns in Eastbourne represented provincial input, while Beadle in Dartford were not quite far enough away from London to qualify as provincial.

Landaulettes

The landaulette body style was ideally suited to those who wanted to be seen out in their cars, and originated with royalty and aristocrats who believed their subjects wanted to be able to see them. It featured an enclosed body but with a folding hood over the rear seats, where the owners sat in the open.

Although the style was declining in popularity in the 1920s, as social attitudes changed, there was enough of the old British class structure still about for no fewer than 15 landaulette bodies to be ordered on 6½-litre Bentley chassis between 1926 and 1928, on both the standard and long-wheelbase chassis. Regrettably, not a single one of these bodies has survived to the present day, and even photographs seem to be almost non-existent.

The most numerous landaulette bodies were by Hooper, who built four. These were on chassis numbered TB 2526 (delivered in September 1926), TW 2708 (March 1927), PR 2324 (February

Seen here with weather equipment erected, this four-seater body was built by Cadogan on a 1927 chassis, WK 2656.

The Vanden Plas four-seater body on TW 2714, another 1927 chassis, has a central body beam to aid rigidity.

Vanden Plas incorporated a rear trunk on this four-seater sports body for Speed Six LB 2349 in 1929.

Though often recorded as a saloon type, the Freestone & Webb body on LB 2345, a 1929 Standard Six, is in fact a landaulette with division.

1928) and BR 2366 (April 1928). Harrison's name is attached to two more (TB 2528, August 1926, and WK 2662, December 1926), and also to a third car which they constructed under sub-contract to the coachbuilder Offord, who had probably designed it. This was on BX 2411, and was delivered in April 1927.

HJ Mulliner built two 6½-litre landaulettes (TB 2531, July 1926. and WK 2657, December 1926) and so did Gurney Nutting (TB 2529, August 1926 and TB 2530, July 1926). The remaining four came from four different coachbuilders. Connaught built the body on WB 2570, which was delivered in July 1926. TB 2527 was bodied by Alford & Alder, was delivered in September 1926 and may have been one of their last coachbuilding commissions. Maythorn built the body on WK 2668, delivered in April 1927, and Salmons & Sons bodied BX 2405, which was delivered in June 1927. The car confusingly described as a "sports saloon limousine landaulette with partition" in Michael Hay's *Bentley: The Vintage Years* was a Barker confection that appeared on the Bentley Motors stand at Olympia in 1927. However, it is generally thought to have been a limousine and is listed as such here.

Limousines

Typically, a limousine was intended to be driven by a chauffeur rather than by the owner. It was also generally larger than a saloon, with the emphasis on legroom for the rear seat passengers, and often had additional accoutrements: a duplicate speedometer for the rear-seat passengers, a clock, and a drinks cabinet were all fairly common features. Nevertheless, the borderline between a large owner-driver saloon and a limousine was somewhat fluid in the minds of the public, even if it was more clearly defined within the coachbuilding fraternity. So the 38 limousines listed here should not be seen as a definitive list, but rather as closely indicative of the true position.

No fewer than 17 different coachbuilders constructed limousines on the 6½-litre chassis. The most numerous limousine bodies were by Hooper, HJ Mulliner, and Vanden Plas, who built five each. There were three limousines each from Connaught, Gurney Nutting, and Thrupp & Maberly. Barker, Harrison, and Maythorn all built two each, and the remaining eight were built, one each, by Arnold, Arthur Mulliner, Gill, Maddox, Mann Egerton, Park

Still a limousine, but exhibiting later fashions, is the HJ Mulliner body on TW 2724 from 1927. The panels are of fabric, and the rear quarter-panels carry dummy landau irons.

Tall, elegant, and fitted with the vee screen that was then fashionable, this is the Vanden Plas limousine body on FW 2605. It was exhibited on the coachbuilder's own stand at Olympia in 1926.

Ward, Schutte, and Windovers. Schutte was an American coachbuilder, the Charles Schutte Body Company of Lancaster, Pennsylvania, and their body was on one of the few chassis sold new to an American customer.

Saloons

Much to the chagrin of those who today believe that every 6½-litre Bentley should be a Vanden Plas tourer, by far the most numerous bodies were ordinary saloons. They were not necessarily dull saloons – indeed, many were by the leading coachbuilders of the day – but they were undeniably saloons. They were also built

Saloons were the most common bodies on 6½-litre chassis, and their most prolific creator was Gurney Nutting. This is an early example from that company, on 1926 chassis WB 2567.

This is a later Gurney Nutting saloon body, on 1928 chassis FA 2504. The car was pictured at a Bentley Drivers' Club meeting.

COACHWORK ON THE 6½-LITRE CHASSIS

65

1930 SPEED SIX, HM 2855, WITH COUPÉ BODY BY GURNEY NUTTING

This striking fastback coupé was built specially for Bentley Motors' Chairman, Woolf Barnato, by Gurney Nutting, who by that time were based in the Chelsea district of London. Gurney Nutting were well established as builders of bodywork on Bentley chassis, and at the time had the formidably talented AF McNeil as their chief designer. Nevertheless, it appears that Barnato himself had a hand in the design of the body for HM 2855. Many of its features were also seen in a boat-tailed tourer that Gurney Nutting built for Barnato on a supercharged 4½-litre chassis at about the same time.

The chassis was the 11ft 8½in version of the Speed Six. The body was constructed on a lightweight wooden frame using Weymann patents, and the use of aluminium castings for the front window and windscreen pillars made it possible for these pillars to be very slim. The shallow windows reflected the "sportsman's coupé" style that was then current, but the rakishly swept fastback roof and tiny boot were highly individual features which gave the car much of its appeal. Further distinction came from the louvred chassis valances combined with styled cycle-type wings – both features which were also seen on the open body for Barnato's supercharged 4½-litre.

The sweeping roofline had one disadvantage, which was to reduce headroom in the back of the body quite severely. As a result, only a single rear seat was fitted, facing sideways across the car. The body was finished in two-tone brown, and the interior in beige with a white steering wheel. HM 2855 was delivered to its new owner on 21 May 1930, just a couple of months before Bentley Motors called in the receivers.

This car was for many years erroneously identified as the one with which Barnato had raced the Blue Train in France to win a wager. It may never rid itself of that association because the story was repeated over and over again in press articles, and was even trotted out again in 2005 in Bentley publicity for the 75th anniversary of the event, although it had long since been proved incorrect. Well-known paintings and drawings, in particular magnificently evocative examples by Terence Cuneo and Alan Fearnley, have further etched the story into the public consciousness.

Barnato did indeed race the Blue Train in a Bentley, but not in this one. In January 1930, Rover had raced "Le Train Bleu" from Cannes to Calais with its Light Six 2-litre model, and had won. Barnato, then holidaying in Cannes, wagered in March that he could go one better, and that he could reach his club in London before the train reached Calais if they both left Cannes at the same time. So on 13 March 1930, he did as he had promised to win the bet. However, the date makes clear that he could not have used the Gurney Nutting coupé because he had not yet taken delivery of it. The car he actually used has been identified as his HJ Mulliner saloon-bodied Speed Six, on chassis BA 2592.

The Gurney Nutting coupé was found in a dilapidated condition in the 1980s and carefully restored. It still exists today and is one of the most recognisable Cricklewood Bentleys to have survived.

The Gurney Nutting coupé built for Barnato was another sensational design on the Speed Six chassis.

COACHWORK ON THE 6½-LITRE CHASSIS

TW 2705 was a 1927 chassis bodied as a saloon by Freestone & Webb. The overall lines are very pleasing, but the huge trunk sounds a jarring note. Note the vee-screen and the boat-style scuttle ventilators.

The helmet-type front wings on this Weymann-bodied Speed Six saloon, BA 2563, meant that the coachbuilder had to conceal the chassis frame and visible parts of the running-gear in another way. The solution chosen by HJ Mulliner was probably the least elegant aspect of the body.

Arguably, Freestone & Webb did not get the trunk right on this saloon, either. This is 1930 Speed Six chassis LR 2790, and features the pontoon-type running-boards that were then fashionable.

Interiors of closed bodies on vintage Bentley chassis are rarely seen. This is the Freestone & Webb saloon on LR 2790. Note the deeply luxurious seats with folding front armrests and ample lounging room in the rear, the parcel net in the roof and the exquisite "sunburst" wood trim on the doors. There are tables built into the rear doors, too.

67

by a wide variety of different coachbuilders. With the most prolific first and the least prolific last, the list below shows the coachbuilders who constructed saloons on the 6½-litre chassis. There was no significant difference between styles on the Standard Six and the Speed Six chassis, and so the list makes no distinction between them. Note that one man's saloon is another man's limousine, so the totals should not be treated as definitive.

Coachbuilder	Count
Gurney Nutting	80
HJ Mulliner	62
Freestone & Webb	41
Harrison	21
Weymann	15
Park Ward	14
Connaught	9
Barker	7
Victor Broom	7
Albany	5
Arthur Mulliner	5
James Young	5
Arnold	4
Hamshaw	4
Hooper	4
Martin Walter	4
Thrupp & Maberly	4
Maythorn	3
Salmons & Sons	3
Vanden Plas	3
Windovers	3
Wylder	3
Blake	2
Cadogan	2
Connaught/HJ Mulliner	2 (Note 1)
Lancefield	2
Surbiton	2
Barker/Park Ward	1 (Note 2)
Bolton	1
Bristol Aeroplane	1
Caffyns	1
Carbodies	1
Carlton	1
Corsica	1
Howes	1
Hoyal	1
Mann Egerton	1
Phillips	1
Progressive	1
Schutter & Van Bakel	1
(Dutch coachbuilder, for a Dutch customer)	
Unknown	1
Vincent	1

Note 1
The attribution "Connaught/HJ Mulliner" suggests that both coachbuilding companies had a hand in these two bodies. Although the London firm of Connaught was a long established one, Nick Walker has pointed out that "the strong suspicion is that from the mid-twenties onwards Connaught was just a design house, with no production facilities of its own" (*A-Z of British Coachbuilders, 1919-1960*). The presumption must therefore be that Connaught designed these bodies, but that HJ Mulliner built them. The chassis were in fact consecutively numbered, being PR 2312 and PR 2313, and both were Standard Six types on the 13ft wheelbase.

Note 2
This single saloon body was on Standard Six chassis KR 2680 and was delivered in March 1930. According to Michael Hay (*Bentley, The Vintage Years*), it was a fabric-panelled saloon built by Barker that was actually mounted to its chassis by Park Ward. Quite why this should have come about is not clear.

For 1928, the Hooper body on MD 2461 made quite a statement. Helmet wings and pontoon-type running-boards, an adventurous two-colour paint scheme and wheel discs would all have caused the man in the street to take a second look.

COACHWORK ON THE 6½-LITRE CHASSIS

The Barker body on KD 2124 from 1928 was described as a saloon, but there is clearly a division and the line across the roof suggests that the rear quarters really do fold down – in which case, this was strictly a landaulette with division.

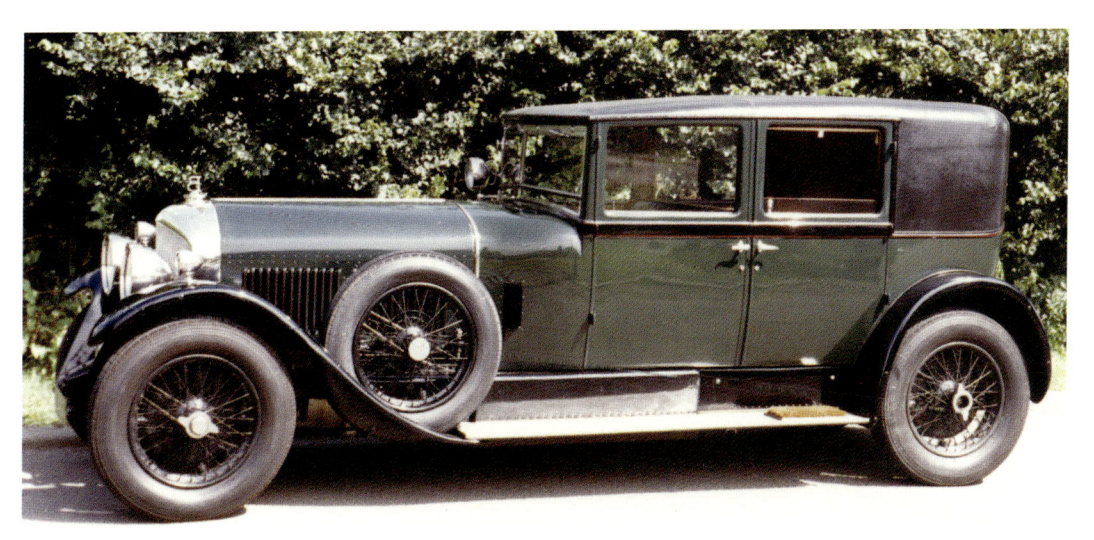

On the other hand, the Barker body on PR 2316, delivered in 1929, is definitely a saloon. The roof is solid, but covered in fabric for effect.

Speed Six BA 2591 carried a Freestone & Webb two-door body, which was right on the borderline between a two-door close-coupled saloon and a two-door coupé. The triangular rear windows are a notable feature.

The Wylder body on SB 2772 is another case of a body described as a saloon turning out to have been a de ville type, as this picture makes clear.

69

Vanden Plas built the elegant six-light saloon body on KD 2125, and showed it at Olympia in 1927.

Very different indeed is this Vanden Plas confection on WT 2260, a 1929 delivery. The rakish lines suggest that this was intended as a sports saloon, although the long chassis seems to have allowed for plenty of room inside.

Yet another sports saloon body was this one by Corsica, built on Speed Six chassis HM 2861 in 1930. Note the louvred scuttle, intended to make the bonnet appear longer and give an impression of power. The helmet wings, low roofline, and two-door configuration all add to the car's sporting look.

Gurney Nutting built this saloon body on FW 2619 for the Duke of Kent. The subtle patterning of the fabric body covering is just visible in the photograph.

Howes & Sons from Norwich built the saloon body on this early 6½-litre chassis, FW 2607.

Another lesser-known bodybuilder was Surbico, actually the Surbiton Coach and Motor Works from the Surrey town of the same name. This two-door body on TW 2713 was in the sports saloon style, with low roof and rakish lines. The car has now been restored to superb condition.

6½-LITRES TO SUIT AMERICAN TASTES

Very few Bentleys of any kind had bodywork built outside the UK, but two 6½-litre models for American customers were bodied abroad. One had a closed body by an American coachbuilder, and the other a three-position drophead coupé body by a French coachbuilder. Though destined for the USA, both cars retained their standard right-hand steering configuration: Bentley Motors offered no alternative.

The earlier of these cars was delivered in November 1929, and was on a 12ft wheelbase Standard Six chassis, number SB 2769. Its drophead coupé body was a most elegant though not unusual creation by the French coachbuilder Saoutchik in Paris. At this stage, Saoutchik was still on the way up in the coachbuilding world, and had not acquired the reputation for extravagantly flamboyant designs that would later become its trademark.

Nevertheless, the Saoutchik drophead coupé did boast the coachbuilder's characteristic use of chromed body highlights, with a line running the full length of its sweeping wings. The vee windscreen was somewhat anachronistic, but may have been used because the extra vertical bar and accompanying surround provided an opportunity for more brightwork. The car also had an attractive wooden dashboard that was a world away from the deliberately functional instrument boards in the works team cars, and rather more attractively laid out than many British coachbuilders seemed able to manage.

When new, the car probably had unadorned wire wheels. However, in preservation it has acquired wheel discs and spare wheel covers which suit its lines very well and would not have been out of keeping with Saoutchik's taste for ornamentation.

The closed body was built on chassis number HM 2854 – numerically one chassis earlier than Woolf Barnato's stunning Gurney Nutting coupé, and delivered in July 1930.

Relatively little is known about this car, which some sources describe as a saloon and others as a limousine. Built on the longest, 12ft 8½in wheelbase, version of the Speed Six chassis, its dimensions would suggest that it was at least intended as a limousine. What does seem clear is that it was ordered by an American customer, who quite understandably wanted to have it bodied by his own choice of coachbuilder. That choice fell on the Charles G Schutte Body Company, of Lancaster, Pennsylvania.

Not a great deal is known about Schutte, although the company did do production runs for the Duesenberg Model A. During the 1920s, it also bodied small numbers of Cadillac, Franklin, Marmon, Oldsmobile, Packard, Pierce-Arrow and Rolls-Royce chassis. A merger with the Blue Ribbon company of Pennsylvania in the mid-1920s led to a plan to close Schutte's Lancaster factory; shareholders objected, and eventually the company closed down. It would appear that this Speed Six was one of the company's last body commissions.

Distinctively American in appearance, with wide, heavy wings and large round tail-lights, the Schutte car appears to have had a fabric-covered roof. It is thought to be still in existence in the USA.

The Saoutchik body on Speed Six SB 2769 was an interesting combination of American taste and French practice.

COACHWORK ON THE 6½-LITRE CHASSIS

Sedanca bodies on the 6½-litre chassis are represented by this formal HJ Mulliner confection on KR 2687, a 1930 Standard Six chassis. With the roof over the driving compartment in place, the overall appearance is that of a large saloon.

Sedancas and Sedancas de Ville

The sedanca name was coined early in the 1920s by the Spanish Count Salamanca. Strictly, it described an elegant formal body style where the rear compartment was completely enclosed while the chauffeur's compartment was exposed to the elements. However, the term "de ville" was also in use for an open front driving compartment of this type, and some coachbuilders combined the two terms to produce the name of "sedanca de ville". It is doubtful whether the longer description was intended to denote anything special, and the two names seem to have been used rather confusingly as alternatives.

Sedanca bodies were most eye-catching, and it is no surprise that Bentley had such bodies on their show stand in 1926 and 1927. In 1926, the body was by Barker on chassis number FW 2617; painted grey with a wood-grain finish, it was subsequently delivered to the company's Chairman, Woolf Barnato. In 1927, the Show car was by Hooper, on chassis number KD 2119, with the body finished in crimson and black. A second Hooper-bodied car in grey and black was delivered on chassis number KD 2123 in November 1927, and a third, this time in brown and black on chassis number PR 2302, was delivered in December 1927 after doing duty on the Bentley stand at the Scottish Show.

HJ Mulliner built a most attractive sedanca de ville for the 1929 Olympia Show on chassis KR 2687, and Park Ward built one on chassis HM 2870 which was delivered in August 1930. (This chassis had earlier been KD 2124, and had carried a Barker saloon body, but was renumbered by Cricklewood and rebodied.) One customer actually went to Henri Binder in Paris to have a sedanca de ville body constructed; this one was on chassis number LR 2796 and was delivered in July 1930.

Torpedos

Strictly speaking, a torpedo was an open tourer with a body line that ran at the same height between scuttle and rear panel without being interrupted by the tops of seat backs or any other feature. It was therefore, supposedly, as smooth as a torpedo. The style was losing popularity by the mid-1920s, and just two were built on 6½-litre Bentley chassis. The earlier of these was on chassis FW 2612 by HJ Mulliner and was delivered in February 1927. The later one was by Barker on KD 2103 and was delivered in July the same year.

Tourers

A tourer body was a simple open type with four seats, and normally had a full-length folding fabric hood with detachable sidescreens. The archetypal tourers on Bentley chassis were of course those built by Vanden Plas on the four-cylinder chassis. The six-cylinder chassis was generally seen as too grand for this style of body, and so examples were rare on the 6½-litre. Just four are known to have been built.

Touring bodies remained popular, and this one was built in 1927 on BX 2421 by Vanden Plas with a number of special features to meet its owner's taste, including metal panels rather than fabric. Not visible here are the twin spare wheels mounted at the rear.

On the outside, the extra body length available for the long-wheelbase chassis is visible in the panel between the doors; on the inside, Vanden Plas managed to fit an extra pair of occasional seats to make this tourer into a 6/7-seater. The body fabric in grey contrasted pleasantly with black wings and other details. It was on WT 2264, a 1929 Standard Six.

Also built in 1929 was this sports tourer by Vanden Plas. The fabric-covered body incorporates a hinged panel to cover rear seat passengers' legs, with a windscreen mounted on it. The spare wheel treatment is interesting. The chassis is a Speed Six, number KF 2399.

Even Hooper could be persuaded to provide tourer bodywork, as on this 1920 Speed Six, LR 2793. The wheel discs do add a certain grandeur, and the dash design is delightful.

Harrison remained a supplier of bodies for the 6½-litre, and this 1928 tourer on MD 2463 was enlivened by the curved door bottoms.

Two of these were by Harrison, on chassis MD 2463 (delivered in February 1928) and HM 2863 (delivered in June 1930). The third was by Cross and Ellis, on LB 2326 delivered in February 1929. The fourth was the grandest of all, and was built by Hooper on chassis number LR 2793 for delivery in July 1930.

Two-seaters

A chassis as large as that of the 6½-litre Bentley was too large to have much appeal to those who really wanted a two-seater model, but when only two seats were required the coachbuilder could use extra length to create something out of the ordinary. In practice, most of the 16 two-seater bodies on the 6½-litre chassis were quite conventional, and several used the extra length of the rear deck for a dickey seat. Some had a special long bonnet

CARS FOR THE INDIAN NOBILITY

In the early years of the 20th century, the ruling classes in India took a great interest in motor cars, which they saw as objects of prestige and practical value. Their interest was of course in the grander types, and especially in those from Britain because of the country's close links with India. Bodywork tended towards the extravagant, mainly for reasons of prestige but also because local rulers often tried to outdo one another.

Two 6½-litre chassis were bodied in particularly extravagant style for Indian rulers. The earlier of these was on chassis number WB 2563, which was constructed by Thrupp & Maberly for the Nawab of Bhopal. It was a boat-tailed touring body with two seats plus a dickey, and wood-grained paintwork (very fashionable at the time) contrasting with an unpainted, polished bonnet. The car was intended for big-game hunting, and to that end was fitted with a pair of searchlights on stalk mounts on the long rear deck. These searchlights were attached to long cables on drums mounted on the car's running-boards, where additional batteries were also stored in boxes. When new, the car was featured in an article in *The Motor* magazine of 7 September 1926.

The later chassis was again a Standard Six, this time FA 2513 dating from September 1928. It was bodied by Barker, again with an extravagant boat-tail two-seater body finished in woodgrain paint with contrasting polished bonnet. This car was destined for the Maharaja of Bhavnagar but seems not to have been equipped with searchlights for hunting.

In 1938, the Maharja had his 6½-litre rebodied in a more sober touring style by Barker. The original boat-tailed body was acquired by Coopers, the Putney firm known for acquiring unwanted bodies and mounting them to chassis to suit customer requirements. Coopers fitted the boat-tailed body to a 4½-litre chassis, which remained in Britain. In the 1990s, the body was acquired for restoration and was initially fitted to a Standard Six chassis, number LB 2348. It has since been reunited with the original Indian chassis, FA 2513.

Research by Tim Houlding and by Rolls-Royce historian John Fasal has shown that there were three other 6½-litre cars delivered to Indian potentates. KF 2389 was a 1929 Standard Six with four-seater body by HJ Mulliner for the Nawab of Junagadh; KR 2676 a 1929 Speed Six with a Weymann coupé body by Gurney Nutting that was registered in the UK before going to the Maharajah of Indore, and LR 2778, a 1930 Speed Six with coupé bodywork by HJ Mulliner for the Maharajah of Jaipur.

Flamboyance certainly characterised the Barker boat-tailed body seen here. Originally fitted to FA 2513 in 1928, it was later removed and fitted to a 4½-litre chassis. It is seen here in "transitional" guise, on Standard Six chassis LB 2348, before being reunited with its original chassis.

COACHWORK ON THE 6½-LITRE CHASSIS

The appeal of the original 3-litre clearly carried over into this two-seater body by Jarvis, built in 1926 on WB 2553, the third production chassis. The engine of this car was removed in 1929; subsequently bored out to 7.2 litres, it was fitted into "Jumbo" Goddard's 3/6½-litre special, which later became the turbocharged 3/8-litre special.

reaching back to the base of the windscreen (and probably all made for Bentley by Ewarts) which visually elongated the lines. There was also a small number of quite exceptional bodies, where the coachbuilder made full use of the car's size.

It was Barker who produced the largest number of two-seater bodies on the 6½-litre chassis, with a total of four. At least three and probably all four of these had the then-fashionable "boat tail" styling, where the long rear deck of the car was shaped to resemble the prow of a boat.

The earliest of these cars was built on chassis FA 2513 for an Indian customer, and was signed off for delivery in September 1928. This was an astonishingly flamboyant body, as the side bar on the facing page makes clear. However, equally flamboyant, if in a different way, was FA

Two-seaters usually had a dickey seat as well, and HJ Mulliner provided one for their body on WB 2555. The instruments were neatly arranged on the dashboard and the car still survives, although now painted a darker colour.

HJ Mulliner also built the two-seater body on this Speed Six, KF 2387 from 1929. This picture shows the interesting spare wheel arrangement, normally hidden by a curved body panel.

2519, which was exhibited on the Barker stand at the 1928 Olympia Show and is described in detail on page 62. Though essentially a boat-tailed two-seat body, it was enlivened by streamlined pontoon-type wings and a delightful colour scheme of yellow with burnished horizontal surfaces, blue wings and blue upholstery.

A generally similar though less spectacular car on chassis number KF 2400 was delivered in July 1929 (and this has often been confused with the 1928 Show car), and the fourth Barker two-seater was on chassis LB 2330, delivered in March 1929.

HJ Mulliner was the next most prolific builder of these bodies, with a total of three. The first was delivered in March 1926 on chassis number WB 2555, and incorporated a dickey seat. Just a month later came WB 2558. The third body,

however, was not delivered until February 1929, on chassis KF 2387, and this time sported a boat-tailed style. That 1928 Show body by Barker had made its mark.

Freestone & Webb delivered a pair of two-seaters on the 6½-litre chassis towards the end of 1926. The earlier car was on chassis number TB 2543 in September, and the other on TW 2702 in December. Harrison was also responsible for two bodies. Of these, the earlier was on a special semi-Le Mans chassis with 11ft wheelbase, 25-gallon fuel tank and other features; on chassis TW 2722 and delivered in February 1927, this was actually a Standard Six model and was built for the Australian racing driver Bernard Rubin, who later drove for the Bentley works team. The later one was MD 2473, delivered in November 1928 and on the 12ft wheelbase.

The remaining five two-seater bodies on 6½-litre chassis were built by five different coachbuilders. The best known of these is the Thrupp & Maberly boat-tailed body on WB 2563, which was built as a hunting car for the Nawab of Bhopal in India. Featured in *The Motor* of 7 September 1926 (in which month it was signed off for delivery), it boasted such things as searchlights, polished wheel disc covers, and a wood-grained paint finish contrasting with its unpainted and polished bonnet.

Park Ward's body on FR 2637, delivered in July 1929, again bore witness to the impact of Barker's 1928 Show car, with a boat tail and pontoon wings. This car was somewhat toned down, however, by an all-black paint scheme and exposed wire wheels. Of the others, Jarvis delivered a body on WB 2553 in March 1926, Fountain delivered one on KF 2390 in May 1929, and Maythorn's FR 2633 was delivered in August 1929.

Boat-tailed bodies were not new, but became fashionable for a time on Bentley chassis at the end of the 1920s. This is the 1929 Park Ward two-seater on Speed Six FR 2637. The shapes of the wings and running-boards were inspired by Barker's 1928 Olympia Show car.

COACHWORK ON THE 6½-LITRE CHASSIS

Like so many other Bentleys of the 1920s, this 1927 6½-litre has lost its original bodywork and is now presented as a Speed Six Vanden Plas tourer with equipment as used on the Bentley works cars at Le Mans in later years. It was new in May 1927 as a Connaught limousine on the 12ft 6in wheelbase chassis, and later became a Vanden Plas tourer replica. Burned out in 1985, it was rebuilt with another replica body, and remodelled as a Speed Six on a shortened chassis. Owned by James Medcalf, it is now a superb evocation of a helmet-winged vintage Bentley as the popular imagination sees the breed.

BENTLEY SIX-CYLINDER MODELS IN DETAIL

The tall radiator and overall stance of the car are unmistakeable.... Note that just one spare wheel is carried.

Door trims the way Vanden Plas made them, complete with the embossed "B". Even the Vanden Plas coachbuilder's plate has been carefully reproduced.

Much loved – the fishtail exhaust which not only looks good but also adds to the Bentley sound.

Looking the part, this dashboard may be a replica but has the correct Le Mans-style instrumentation with a huge rev counter dominating the proceedings.

Again superbly presented, every detail of the outside handbrake mechanism is clear in this view. The tourer bodies of this style had only three doors, and the driver had to climb in from the kerb side.

On the real Le Mans cars, the back seat was most likely to be used for carrying spare parts but, as this picture shows, it was actually a rather spacious and comfortable leather-upholstered bench

Beautifully presented in every detail, this engine shows the box-shaped manifold of the early Speed Six and the elegantly-shaped SU carburettors.

The Le Mans-style petrol tank has a full stone guard: experience in long-distance racing had taught Bentley the threat of stones holing the tank. Just visible here is the Hartford friction damper. The quick-release filler cap – to a design also used for the radiator filler – is wisely padlocked in place.

This is the exhaust side of the engine, again superbly presented. Between steering column and exhaust downpipe is a modern canister-type oil filter, which has been added as a precaution. The great length of the 6½-litre engine, resulting from its space-consuming camshaft-drive arrangement, is apparent in this picture.

Twin dampers were part of the Le Mans specification.

The right-hand side of the engine has the correct Speed Six type of Delco-Remy coil ignition system. Note also the complex arrangement of rods and cross-shafts which connects accelerator pedal to carburettors – which are of course on the far side of the engine.

Chapter Five

The Six-Cylinder Cars in Competition

The large numbers of Le Mans replicas constructed on Speed Six chassis in more recent times tends to give the impression that there were many Le Mans cars. There were not; in fact, there were just three "works" cars built to a Le Mans specification for that event, and the entire Speed Six Bentley legend depends on their exploits.

By the summer of 1928, it was becoming increasingly apparent that the 4½-litre Bentley was not going to remain competitive in international motor sport events for very much longer. The biggest threat seemed to be from Mercedes, whose latest 7-litre SS model in racing trim developed 170bhp, or 225bhp with its supercharger engaged – which it could be for only short periods in order not to over-stress the engine. This was way beyond the output of a Le Mans-specification 4½-litre Bentley, and with the German company's star driver Rudolf Caracciola at the wheel, the supercharged Mercedes very quickly demonstrated its superiority.

WO had been keeping his powder dry, allowing the 4½-litre to keep Bentley in racing until there was a chance that it might become outclassed. By the summer of 1928, the 6½-litre had been in production for three years, and so WO proceeded with what for him was the next logical step. This was to develop the 6½-litre for racing, and the Speed Six model in 1928 was the first step in that direction. Meanwhile, of course, Bentley driver Tim Birkin had become convinced that supercharging – which was not only being used by Mercedes – was the way forward, and set off on his own to produce a supercharged version of the 4½-litre chassis.

At Cricklewood, those involved with the team cars had every intention of upholding the Bentley honour with a win at Le Mans in 1929 to match the win in 1928. If Mercedes entered the 1929 event with their latest supercharged car, Bentley would be in trouble; as it was, there had been formidable opposition in the 1928 event from the American Stutz Black Hawk, which had been placed second. For 1929, the Americans were likely to step up the pressure.

The Speed Six engine in standard form put out 160bhp, so the 170bhp of the bigger Mercedes engine was going to be fairly easily achievable. Much was going to depend on race tactics to overcome the additional speed that the German car could muster when its supercharger was engaged. When it became clear that there would be no Mercedes entry at Le Mans for 1929, there must have been a large sigh of relief from those in the Racing Shop at Cricklewood. They were, however, ready. As Michael Hay revealed in his book, *Bentley – "Old Number One"*, figures for the 1929 Le Mans Speed Six taken in the engine test shop showed that it was developing no less than 206bhp.

Just one Speed Six was prepared for the 1929 Le Mans event, and although Cricklewood probably had every confidence in its success, they did not put all their eggs into a single basket. The original plan was to field three team cars, the other two being 4½-litres. When it became clear that the two supercharged 4½-litres fielded by Tim Birkin (and funded by the Hon Dorothy Paget) were not going to race, two more 4½-litres were entered under the Bentley Motors name. The company also decided to use the new Double-Twelve event at Brooklands as a dress rehearsal for Le Mans. This event was to be held over the weekend of 10-11 May, which gave ample time for any problems to be ironed out before Le Mans in June.

The chassis chosen for that first Le Mans-specification Speed Six was number LB 2332, from a sanction of the usual 25 cars that was probably laid down in December 1928. Not surprisingly, an 11ft wheelbase was specified – not actually a Speed Six option as far as the ordinary public was concerned, but of course available for open bodywork with the Standard Six engine. Thus right from the start this car was not intended to be the sort of car that Bentley had used in the early days: at the time of the 1922 TT, the company had been at pains to point out that "unlike our competitors, we have not built special racing cars for this event, but instead entered three standard chassis drawn from our production stock." The 1929 Le Mans Speed Six was most definitely a special racing car.

Michael Hay did some excellent and detailed research on the car's history during the 1990s, and it is to his efforts that we owe much of what can be said about LB 2332 today. The chassis was built up in the Racing Shop at Kingsbury over the winter of 1928-1929, in the building leased from the Vanden Plas coachbuilding company right next door to the Bentley Motors site. The car's specification was drawn up by Nobby Clarke, and is given in full in Hay's book, *Bentley – "Old Number One"*. However, even the briefest of overviews makes clear how special that chassis really was.

The frame was reinforced at various strategic points, and the suspension included modified rear springs and no fewer than four racing dampers on the front axle. The brakes were not the usual 6½-litre type with Dewandre servo, but rather the "semi-servo" type from the 4½-litre, probably chosen because of the slight lag associated with the servo. These brakes operated by making use of the front axle's torque reaction under braking to increase the braking effort itself. The differential nosepiece also came from a 4½-litre because the standard 6½-litre spiral bevel gears would not have been up to the

The traditional Le Mans start: the drivers have run across the track from the right of the picture to join their cars for a quick getaway. In the foreground is Birkin in car number 1, the Speed Six Bentley that would go on to win the 1929 event. Directly behind is a 5.3-litre du Pont.

strains of racing; as there were no straight-cut gears for the otherwise stronger 6½-litre differential, those from the four-cylinder car were used, together with the accompanying nosepiece. A special propshaft had to be made up to suit.

For safety, many fittings on the chassis were held in place with slotted nuts and split-pins on their bolts. The battery, too, was moved from its standard position to a platform in the passenger footwell, to afford greater accessibility. The gearbox was a close-ratio D type with special indirects, and of course there was a truly massive fuel tank – this time holding 40 gallons – to reduce the need for pit stops during the race. It was fitted with the expected mesh and asbestos stone-guard. The wheels, too, were different from production types: they had a 20-inch diameter instead of the standard 21-inch size, the smaller size of course revolving a fraction faster at any given engine speed.

As for the engine, it differed considerably from the standard production Speed Six type. The biggest change was to a single-port induction system, although there were also special rockers, hour-glass pistons and a lightened flywheel. There was no fan or pulley, as there would be enough air-flow through the radiator at speed to make these power-sapping ancillaries superfluous. In addition, there was a racing-pattern extended oil filler accompanied by a special hinged flap in the left-hand bonnet side. Careful assembly accounted for the remaining differences, with various edges rounded off and fitting tolerances carefully checked to make sure that no fretting could occur during the Le Mans event.

Once the chassis had been prepared, it was wheeled over to the Vanden Plas body shop. Surviving documents suggest that the order was placed on 31 January 1929, and show that it was for a "Le Mans type sporting four-seater to 1927 design, with modifications approved by Mr WO Bentley". The 1927 design was the one used on the prototype 4½-litre car for that year's Le Mans, and differed from the standard production four-seater mainly by being lighter through the absence of some stiffening features. The car was complete by 24 April, when it was registered as MT 3464, and was tested and given its Five-Year Guarantee on 10 May. The new owner was logged as Woolf Barnato, the Chairman of Bentley Motors and, of course, one of the most successful racing drivers in the works team.

The 1929 racing season
That registration was achieved on the day when the car was due to run in the Brooklands Double-Twelve event. This was a new one on the calendar, and it suited the Bentley team down to the ground as practice for Le Mans because it was arranged along Le Mans lines as a two-day endurance race. It even had a Le Mans-style start, with the drivers and riding mechanics obliged to sprint across the track to join their cars when the starter's flag fell. However, rather than a continuous 24-hour race, it was run in two stints of 12 hours each because residents around the Brooklands track were not keen on the noise of all-night racing. So this first event began at 8 o'clock on the morning of Friday 10 May, and stopped for the night at 8 o'clock in the evening. The cars were then placed overnight in a secure *parc fermé*, and the second 12-hour section was run during the daytime on the Saturday.

The drivers chosen for the Speed Six were Barnato and Dudley Benjafield, another veteran team member. A handicap system prevented the sheer size of the Bentley – it was the biggest-engined car in the field – from romping away with the first place, and so the Bentley team calculated the speeds their car would need to beat its smaller-engined rivals. As always, WO did not believe in over-extending his cars, but

The Le Mans event has always been run on public roads. This is "Old Number One" at Le Mans in 1930.

rather in pacing their race very carefully.

It soon became clear that the Speed Six was far and away the fastest car in the event, and from the end of the first lap it held the lead for some four hours, lapping at a regular 92mph, or 6mph faster than the 4½-litres in the event were managing. This was most encouraging, and slick pit-work by the Bentley crew ensured that a rear wheel change did not delay Benjafield's progress by too long. However, shortly after that, things began to go wrong. Benjafield again stopped at the pits, complaining of an electrical problem with the car: the dynamo was not working.

Benjafield and his riding mechanic, Stan Ivermee, whipped off the aluminium dynamo cover and discovered that one of the arms of the drive coupling had fractured. An on-the-spot repair was out of the question, so Benjafield removed the dynamo altogether and slung it in the back of the car. The pair then shot off again and were still running well two hours later when the Speed Six was stopped by officials. Regulations insisted that the electrical system had to be in full working order, and that of the Speed Six was not. "It was a great pity," wrote Benjafield later, in his book *The Bentleys at Le Mans*, "as by the scale of the handicap, we had so much in hand that we could almost afford to have stopped for lunch and still won the race." As it was, the best Bentley could achieve that time round was second place, with Sammy Davis and Roland Gunter in a 4½-litre being bested by Boris Ivanowski's Alfa Romeo 6C 1500.

Even so, it was an encouraging start. All the signs were that the Speed Six would indeed have finished first, as Benjafield later suggested, without that mechanical failure. In the few weeks before Le Mans, the Speed Six went back into the Racing Shop for more work and was supposedly making even more power by the time it emerged ready for the Le Mans event in June.

One Speed Six was clearly expected to be enough for Le Mans, although of course it was never intended to be the sole Bentley entry. The original plan had been to back the six-cylinder car up with a pair of 4½-litres – by no means totally outclassed in international events, despite Tim Birkin's forebodings – but in the end Cricklewood actually entered four 4½-litres. Birkin had entered a pair of his supercharged cars, but was forced to withdraw them at the very last minute because of problems. So Bentley Motors filled the gap with two more of their own cars.

The original plan for who would drive what was altered at the same time. Birkin was paired with Woolf Barnato in the Speed Six, so giving the car the drivers who were probably the very best that Bentley could muster. WO may also have smiled secretly that Birkin was going to find out just how much better the Speed Six was than his own supercharged creation. As he noted in *My Cars and My Life*, "the final choice for the team was always mine".

As already noted, the supercharged Mercedes were not present at Le Mans in 1929. Nor were any French-manufactured cars – and that in an event run on French soil. Instead, the main threat to the Bentleys came from America. There were two Chryslers, a Du Pont straight-eight, and three Stutz Black Hawks, of which one was supercharged. The rest of the field was made up of the usual variety of smaller-engined machines. The regulations required that they should all carry ballast equivalent to the weight of three passengers, that the driver must carry out all repairs (no riding mechanics were carried), and that the number of spare wheels and tyres used should be strictly limited. This year, to the drivers' relief, there was no requirement to run with the hood up for several laps, and so the Barnato-Birkin car ran without a

Barnato powers the Speed Six through the corner at Mulsanne in 1929.

hood at all to save weight.

Wearing race number 1, and with Birkin at the wheel, the Speed Six got off to a rapid start and had established a formidable lead by the end of the first lap. While the other Bentleys experienced various problems – especially the two which had been entered at the last minute – the six-cylinder car simply thundered on relentlessly. It seems that its bonnet was not raised at any time during the race. Dudley Benjafield's recollection, in *The Bentleys at Le Mans*, was that the Speed Six led the field from start to finish, but Sammy Davis's report in *The Autocar* claimed that the Glen Kidston-Jack Dunfee 4½-litre actually took over for a couple of laps.

One way or another, the new Bentley absolutely dominated the race. Twelve hours in, it was so far in the lead that WO gave orders to slow down to a fast touring speed. Ten hours after that, he gave similar orders for the remaining 4½-litres to slow down as well. As always, his aim was to ensure that the cars were not over-stretched, especially when they did not need to go all-out to win. The main thing was to keep going.

Just before the four o'clock finish, the Speed Six and the remaining three 4½-litres formed up in team order on the Mulsanne straight just before the pits, finishing in the first four places just over one lap later. It was Birkin at the wheel, Barnato claiming an aversion to the final laps of a major race after his experience at Le Mans a year earlier, when he had had to nurse his ailing 4½-litre into first place, fearful all the time that it might not make the finishing line. That same car, with Glen Kidston at the wheel, followed the Speed Six across the line in second place at the 1929 event.

This was Bentley's third successive win at Le Mans. The Speed Six, reined in considerably for the second half of the race, returned an average speed of 73.62mph, and Bentley Motors also went home with both first and second places in the Index of Performance. It was the first time any manufacturer had won both awards.

For the rest of the 1929 season, and well into the 1930 season as well, LB 2332 remained the only race-prepared Speed Six. It was entered for a number of additional events over the summer of 1929, and it must have been during this period that it acquired its nickname of "Old Number One" – an allusion to the number it had carried in the 1929 Le Mans event. This practice of giving the team cars names was standard Bentley stuff: the 1927 Le Mans-winning car had become "Old Number Seven", and the prototype 4½-litre had become "Old Mother Gun".

In previous years, the Six Hours Race at Brooklands had been used as Bentley's dress rehearsal for Le Mans. For 1929 it had been displaced, both in the calendar and in Bentley's planning, by the new Double-Twelve. Now moved to a later date of 29 June, it was still an important event in domestic motor racing, and Cricklewood entered a team of cars.

It would have been an exciting spectacle for

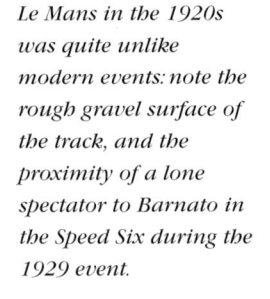

Le Mans in the 1920s was quite unlike modern events: note the rough gravel surface of the track, and the proximity of a lone spectator to Barnato in the Speed Six during the 1929 event.

Bentley followers in Britain, as the Bentley entries were headed by the Le Mans-winning Speed Six, driven by Barnato and Jack Dunfee. A second Cricklewood entry was one of the 1929 Le Mans 4½-litres, though not with its Le Mans crew, and in addition Tim Birkin was there with a supercharged 4½-litre. Two more privately-entered 4½-litres made up the full complement. This time, the Bentleys were up against a pair of supercharged Mercedes, too, although both were privately entered by British drivers.

This event was run with a complicated handicap formula. The winning car was to cover 175 laps of the Brooklands circuit. Handicaps were allocated according to engine size, and so the 7-litre Mercedes, as the largest-engined cars there, had no handicap. The Speed Six, with its smaller engine, was granted an eight-lap credit, which meant that it had to cover 167 laps. Cars were given a target lap count and distance, those for the Speed Six being 73.25mph and 439.49 miles. As had earlier been the case at Le Mans (though not this year) cars had to run with their hoods erected for a set number of laps.

Barnato immediately took the lead with the Speed Six and remained at the head of the pack when he pulled into the pits to lower the hood after ten laps. In fact, the car remained in the lead right through the race, gradually eating away at the credit laps allocated to the smaller-engined cars so that it was lying in third place overall after four hours. Its average speed gradually increased, from 73.45mph in the first hour to 75.76mph at the end of five hours, and by this time it had made up all the handicaps of the small cars and had a clear lead. One hour later, with Jack Dunfee at the wheel, Old Number One was declared the winner with an average speed of 75.88mph. An Alfa Romeo was placed second, and the 4½-litre Le Mans Bentley came in third.

For its next two events over the summer of 1929, Old Number One was in Ireland. On 13 July it was entered in the Irish Grand Prix in Dublin, a two-day event in which the first day was reserved for cars of 1500cc and under. In this event, there was a supporting cast of six other Bentleys (although one private entry was a non-starter) which included two supercharged 4½-litres. This time, WO selected Glen Kidston to take the wheel of the Speed Six.

Once again, the Bentley was up against a supercharged Mercedes driven by a British driver, but that was not the only serious opposition. Most of the thrills in the race came from a duel between Ivonowski's supercharged 2-litre Alfa Romeo and the Speed Six after the Mercedes had retired with a blown head gasket. Birkin, who had been lying second to the Mercedes, briefly took the lead but his supercharged 4½-litre overheated and he slowed, to be passed by Kidston who then claimed fourth place on handicap. Speeding up to overcome that handicap, he was achieving speeds of 110mph on the straights, but the tarmac surface was beginning to melt in the heat and Kidston once spun the big car right round and then nearly overturned when he slid into a grass bank. Another slide caused a rear wheel to buckle when it hit a grass bank and, even though the wheel was rapidly changed in the

The Speed Six passes a slower entrant in the 1929 Le Mans.

Victory! Tim Birkin in car number 1 finishes the 1929 Le Mans, with Glen Kidston in the 4½-litre, "Old Mother Gun", right behind him in second place. Could the Speed Six have had a better introduction to the world?

Modifications: the quick-release radiator cap used at Le Mans in 1929 was often copied for later competition Bentleys.

pits, this mishap cost Kidston the race. He came second, with an average speed of 79.8mph and just 14 seconds behind Ivanowski's Alfa Romeo.

The second Irish event was in the north. Run on 17 August, the Tourist Trophy race was held on the Ards circuit near Belfast. Again there were five Bentleys entered, one being a privateer's 4½-litre, three being Birkin's supercharged cars, and the fifth the Speed Six with Glen Kidston again at the wheel. Handicaps on the bigger-engined cars ensured that they remained low in the placings for the early part of the race, but Rudolf Caracciola in the supercharged Mercedes and Kidston in the Speed Six set some very fast times.

It was the circuit's bends which really decided the race. While Caracciola was able to keep his car fully under control, Kidston found himself sliding about all over the road. On a damp surface at Bradshaw's Brae, where the road passed through a treacherous S-bend, Kidston lost the car. He nearly regained control after missing a telegraph pole and a warning sign by a whisker, but as he got the car back on to the road a broadside skid developed and the car thudded to a stop half on the road and half off it, with all four wheels in the air.

The left-hand front had suffered severe damage, but neither Kidston nor his riding mechanic was injured, and they set off to walk back to the pits. Caracciola won with an average speed of 72.82mph, and of the remaining Bentleys the best place was achieved by Birkin (with none other than WO as his riding mechanic). It was a disappointing 11th on handicap – although on speed he was a close second behind Caracciola.

The last race for which Old Number One was entered in 1929 was another Brooklands event, this time the 500 Miles on 12 October. The regulations for this event allowed the car to be used in a much more stripped-out form, and so in September, Vanden Plas fitted a new body. This was of lightweight aluminium construction with a stubby, rounded tail enclosing a 42-gallon fuel tank.

The Speed Six was of course not intended to be the sole Bentley entered for the 500 Miles event, and Cricklewood entered a 4½-litre for Frank Clement and Jack Barclay, also stripped out and now fitted with a special long tail. Tim Birkin entered a supercharged car, also rebodied by Vanden Plas as a lightweight two-seater, and there were two privateer entries in 4½-litres.

WO wanted to try another set of drivers on the six-cylinder car, but he had some trouble finding anybody who would take the job on. With its lightweight body, the Speed Six was capable of lapping at well over 120mph, and the prospect of such speeds in such a heavy car on the bumpy surface of the Brooklands circuit discouraged volunteers. Fortunately, Clive Dunfee allowed his arm to be twisted, and on the morning of the race, WO buttonholed Sammy Davis (who was there to report for *The Autocar*) and persuaded him to make up the other half of the crew.

Davis wrote entertainingly about his experience in his book, and the experience itself was an entertaining one for him because he had never driven the car before. Taking a few laps to work out where some of the controls were and how the car behaved at speed, he then settled down to lap the Brooklands circuit at indicated speeds as high as 128mph. His best lap was clocked at 126.09mph, and that was also the fastest lap of the day by any car in the event. However, tyres did prove to be a problem, wearing very quickly under the twin onslaughts of a heavy car and a rough surface.

None of that prevented the car achieving an overall average speed of 109.4mph, being beaten into second place on handicap by the smaller-engined 4½-litre of Clement and Barclay which posted a 107.32mph average.

There was some talk of taking the car to Montlhéry later in the year to attack some records, much as had been done on several occasions in the past with specially-prepared four-cylinder Bentleys. Sammy Davis mentioned that such an event was being considered in *The Autocar* of 29 November, but nothing came of it.

Perhaps this was one of the early effects on Bentley Motors of the Wall Street Crash, which had occurred in October. Certainly, any business manager with an eye on the economic situation would have drawn breath rather sharply at the suggestion of spending money on such an escapade at a time like this – especially as the Bentley brand was still basking in the glory of its third Le Mans win earlier in the year.

The 1929 Double-Twelve entry
Chassis no   LB 2332
Registration   MT 3464
Race no   2
Crew   Woolf Barnato and
                  Dudley Benjafield

Note: There were also four 4½-litre Bentleys running in this event. Two were entered by privateers, and two by Bentley Motors. The best result was achieved by Sammy Davis, who came second with Roland Gunter as co-driver in a works team car.

The 1929 Le Mans entry
Chassis no   LB 2332
Registration   MT 3464
Race no   1
Crew   Woolf Barnato and Tim Birkin

The 1929 Brooklands Six Hours entry
Chassis no   LB 2332
Registration   MT 3464
Race no   3
Crew   Woolf Barnato and Jack Dunfee

The 1929 Irish Grand Prix entry
Chassis no   LB 2332
Registration   MT 3464
Race no   4
Crew   Glen Kidston

The 1929 Tourist Trophy entry
Chassis no   LB 2332
Registration   MT 3464
Race no   73
Crew   Glen Kidston

The 1929 Brooklands 500 Miles entry
Chassis no   LB 2332
Registration   MT 3464
Race no   35
Crew   Sammy Davis and Clive Dunfee

The 1930 racing season

For the 1930 season, Cricklewood prepared two brand-new Speed Six team cars, and also comprehensively rebuilt "Old Number One" on a new chassis frame, with a new engine, new differential and multiple other items. The two new team cars were bodied as tourers by Vanden Plas, using essentially the same style as had been fitted to the first car.

It was those two cars which represented the Bentley works team at the Double-Twelve event on 9 and 10 May, which Cricklewood once again chose to use as its dress rehearsal for Le Mans. Both were fitted with new Zeiss headlamps, to see how they would stand up to the rough Brooklands track and whether they would therefore be suitable for use at Le Mans. Old Number One was kept at home, perhaps in reserve. One of the Speed Sixes was driven by Barnato and Clement, the other by Sammy Davis and Clive Dunfee; and, of course, the Bentley contingent in the race was swelled by no fewer than three of the supercharged 4½-litre cars from the Birkin stable. There was also a privately-entered unblown 4½-litre.

On the first day, it was Glen Kidston in a supercharged 4½-litre who initially led the Speed Sixes, but he was forced to retire with a broken valve. Frank Clement then took the lead in the number two car, with Sammy Davis behind him in the other Speed Six. Their lead over the rest of the field was such that despite a pit stop to fix a broken valve spring, Davis was still able to retain his second place. The two Speed Sixes were still first and second when racing closed down for the night.

Practice before the race at Le Mans in 1930: this is the Davis-Dunfee Speed Six, running as number 3.

The Saturday saw the Speed Sixes still comfortably in the lead. The other two supercharged cars were now out with mechanical problems. Sammy Davis's car broke another valve spring and, later, an oil pipe as well – but once again both were rapidly fixed in the pits and he did not lose his second place. WO imposed his usual discipline on the cars, slowing them down to reduce the risk of failures while keeping them comfortably ahead of the opposition. In fact, the Clement-Barnato car was running slowly enough to oil a plug, which had to be changed near the end of the day's racing.

Good pit-work saw to that, and even heavy rain during the afternoon did not alter the lead that the two Speed Sixes had achieved. The two cars romped home with average speeds of 86.68mph and 85.68mph. It had been a further convincing demonstration of the Speed Six's potential, and of the value of well-orchestrated pit work as well. For WO, it had probably been a rather satisfying demonstration that his big-capacity six-cylinder engine had been the right way to go in racing, and that his concerns about the supercharged 4½-litre engine had been well-founded.

All the signs were good, but Le Mans was going to need a special effort. The field of entries was considerably reduced for the 1930 event, but the 19 cars that entered included a pair of straight-eight Stutz models, together with smaller cars from such as Alfa Romeo, Talbot and even MG. The biggest threat, however, came from Mercedes, who had decided this year to enter their star drivers, Rudolf Caracciola and Christian Werner, in a single supercharged car. Careful calculations based on the performance of the Speed Six at the previous year's event had suggested to them that they should be able to win in 1930.

The Bentley team were under no illusion about the severity of the threat from the German car. Even though they had three Speed Sixes on the works team, plus a further two Bentleys in the shape of Tim Birkin's supercharged cars, they could not expect to overwhelm the Mercedes by sheer numbers. So a more careful strategy was developed. It was well known that the Mercedes supercharger was designed to be used only in short bursts of around 15 seconds at a time, in order not to over-stress the engine. So the strategy had to be to keep the German car under pressure, to force its drivers to use the

THE SIX-CYLINDER CARS IN COMPETITION

The Davis-Dunfee car corners hard ahead of the Barnato-Kidston entry during the 1930 event, with Earl Howe's Alfa Romeo behind.

supercharger in the hope that mechanical failure would result. Birkin willingly complied with this plan: his main concern was that his cars should retain a chance of winning once the Mercedes was out of the race, and should not be used sacrificially for the purpose of achieving the German car's retirement.

The three works Speed Sixes were to be driven by Wolf Barnato with Glen Kidston, who would have the rebuilt Old Number One; Frank Clement with Dick Watney, in the number two car; and Sammy Davis and Clive Dunfee in the number three car. The race strategy involved Tim Birkin in a supercharged 4½-litre harrying the Mercedes in the beginning, keeping his other team car in reserve for later. And so it was played out.

Caracciola in the Mercedes got away first, with Birkin right behind him and pressing him hard. A burst of speed saw Birkin pass the Mercedes despite losing the tread from a rear tyre; the Bentley kept going and went on to set the lap record for that year's event. He managed another lap, but the shredded tyre forced him to slow down and head for the pits. Sammy Davis in the Speed Six then took station behind the Mercedes, again pressing the German car harder and harder. After a driver change, the two cars were again in first and second places until Clive Dunfee in the Bentley misjudged a corner and ended up in the ditch with a bent axle.

The Barnato-Kidston car now moved up to pursue the Mercedes, and during the hours of darkness the two cars diced with one another, swapping the lead until, shortly after 2 o'clock on the Sunday morning and 85 laps into the race with the Speed Six in the lead, the Mercedes pulled into its pit and was clearly not going to rejoin the runners. The official explanation was a battery problem, but the real diagnosis was more serious. WO remembered the incident very clearly in *The Cars in my Life*: "I went round to the Mercedes pit at once to express my sympathy, noticing at the same time that there was water pouring from the car's blown gasket, and had a word with Caracciola. He was very disappointed, of course, but was his usual generous, friendly self. They had not expected to be so hard pressed as they had been, he told me."

From that point on, WO slowed his Speed Sixes down to a fast tour, with instructions to keep their first and second places. The Barnato-Kidston car had been averaging 81mph; from now on it was slowed so much that the average dropped to 72mph. Right behind them were the two supercharged Birkin cars, the Stutz threat having evaporated many laps earlier. Although the two supercharged 4½-litres both retired with mechanical problems, the lead gained by the

THE THREE WORKS SPEED SIXES

The first works team Speed Six was on chassis number LB 2332, and its chassis was built up over the winter of 1928-1929. The body was ordered from Vanden Plas on 31 January and became their order number 1589. The coachbuilder's records show that it was a "Le Mans type sporting 4-seater to 1927 design, with modifications approved by Mr WO Bentley". The fabric panels were to be "cellulosed to match Parsons Napier Green", and the hood, tonneau cover and hood cover were also to match that colour.

The 1927 design of body was that which Vanden Plas had built on the prototype 4½-litre Bentley, "Old Mother Gun", for that year's Le Mans. In practice, there were differences, of course. The wheelbase on the Speed Six was more than a foot longer, and in place of the 4½-litre car's high, narrow wings joined by running-boards, the Speed Six had a minimal mudguard over each wheel and no running-boards. But the body tub was essentially the same, with two doors on the left but only one on the right, and a cutaway for the driver's elbow where his door might otherwise have been.

The second pair of cars were built in the early spring of 1930, and both received their Five-Year Guarantees in May. Both were again on the short 11ft chassis otherwise used only for Standard Six models, and both again had Vanden Plas bodies – "Le Mans Racer as previous year", as the coachbuilder's order book has it against each one. They were of course again finished in green. Chassis number HM 2868 was given body number 1664 and was completed by Vanden Plas in April; chassis number HM 2869 had body number 1665 and was completed by the coachbuilders in May.

HM 2868 received the registration number GF 8507 and became the number two car in the team, Old Number One retaining its status as the number one car. HM 2869 was registered as GF 8511 and became the number three car.

Both of these cars survive today in essentially original condition, although HM 2868 was rebuilt on a new chassis frame in May 1934.

A pit stop for the Mareuse/Silko Bugatti as Kidston takes the flag at the wheel of Bentley number 4.. Right behind is car number 2, the Speed Six driven by Clement and Watney.

Le Mans 1930: the car known familiarly as "Old Number One" after its 1929 victory thunders past the pits.

THE SIX-CYLINDER CARS IN COMPETITION

Again the lack of spectator protection at Le Mans is apparent as Kidston in car number 4 prepares to overtake a slower Bugatti Type 40 at Pontlieue. The Bugatti was shared between Marguerite Mareuse and Odette Siko, and the two French ladies eventually claimed seventh place, 47 laps behind the winning Bentley.

two Speed Sixes proved completely unassailable, and they went on to take first and second places on the Sunday afternoon. Glen Kidston took Old Number One across the line in first place, with the Clement-Watney car right behind him. It was not only a race win, but also a one-two in the Index of Performance. The Barnato-Kidston car had returned a race average of 75.88mph, and the Clement-Watney car an average of 73.73mph.

It was, of course, a huge triumph for Bentley. This was their fourth successive win at Le Mans, and they had beaten off the threat from the formidable supercharged Mercedes. For Barnato, it was a major personal success as his third successive Le Mans win. As a demonstration of the performance and durability of the Bentley Speed Six, it could not have been more convincing. Back at Cricklewood, a post-race stripdown revealed that both cars could have continued for another 18 hours at race speeds without mechanical problems.

It was not, however, quite an unqualified success. Bentley Motors' financial problems were closing in, and both Cricklewood and Barnato announced their withdrawal from racing shortly afterwards.

The 1930 Brooklands Double Twelve entry

Chassis no   HM 2868
Registration   GF 8507
Race no   2
Crew   Woolf Barnato and
                  Frank Clement

Chassis no   HM 2869
Registration   GF 8511
Race no   3
Crew   Sammy Davis and Clive Dunfee

The 1930 Le Mans entries

Chassis no   HM 2868
Registration   GF 8507
Race no   2
Crew   Frank Clement and Dick Watney

Chassis no   HM 2869
Registration   GF 8511
Race no   3
Crew   Sammy Davis and Clive Dunfee

Chassis no   LB 2332
Registration   MT 3464
Race no   4
Crew   Woolf Barnato and Glen Kidston

BENTLEY BOYS – THE SPEED SIX DRIVERS

There were no fewer than nine drivers associated with the works Speed Six cars in their two-year career from 1929 to 1930. In alphabetical order, they were Woolf Barnato, Dudley Benjafield, Tim Birkin, Frank Clement, Sammy Davis, Clive Dunfee, Jack Dunfee, Glen Kidston and Dick Watney. Their names are legendary, but their careers neither began nor ended with the Speed Sixes. Most of them had been driving for Bentley for several years before the twin triumphs of 1929 and 1930, and most carried on careers in motor sport afterwards, though often switching to other marques.

These, and a small côterie of others who had driven the four-cylinder cars for the works team, were known as the Bentley Boys. Their public image was of a wealthy, flamboyant, hard-partying group of essentially amateur sportsmen who were nevertheless specially talented in motor sport. Some of them certainly lived up to that image, but it was not really an accurate description of all of them. As Dudley Benjafield explained it in *The Bentleys at Le Mans*, "the Bentley Boys" was "a term manufactured by the press. I, for one, was proud to be associated with the Bentley team, but we did not altogether appreciate being described as 'The Bentley Boys'".

Woolf Barnato

Joel Woolf Barnato was the son of a man who had made his fortune from the South African diamond and gold mines, and he inherited a second fortune from an uncle. He served as an artillery officer in the British Army during the Great War, rising to the rank of Captain, and was an all-round sportsman with a taste for the high life.

His mansion, Ardenrun, near Lingfield in Surrey, became known for its extravagant parties, usually featuring the rest of the Bentley Boys. Barnato was a successful motor boat racer (his boat, *Ardenrun V*, was powered by a Bentley engine), bred racehorses, and between 1928 and 1930 he played county cricket for Surrey as wicket-keeper.

Barnato bought his first Bentley, a 3-litre, during 1925, and used it successfully at Brooklands. When Bentley Motors was desperate for new investment at the end of that year, it was Barnato whom they approached, and the following summer he acquired the business, becoming Chairman. Although there was no doubt that he called the shots in the business, he happily submitted to team discipline when driving for the works team.

As a driver, he was exceptionally good. WO believed he was the best of them all, and Barnato's results certainly did not disappoint. He won Le Mans three times, twice (in 1929 and 1930) at the wheel of a Speed Six.

Dudley Benjafield

Dr Dudley Benjafield – Benjy to those who knew him – was a leading bacteriologist with a consultancy at St George's Hospital in London and a practice of his own in London's Wimpole Street. His wife belonged to the family which owned the Savoy Hotel in London, among other properties, and so he was able to indulge in such sporting pastimes as boats and fast cars. He had bought his first Bentley, a 3-litre, in October 1923.

During 1924, he visited the works at Cricklewood to have some work done on his car. By his own account, he allowed himself to be talked into spending an afternoon at Brooklands as a passenger in a car driven by Bertie Kensington-Moir, then head of the Service Department. Gingerly getting more closely involved with motor racing in his own car over the next few months, he found himself asked to drive for the works team at Le Mans in 1925.

Benjy drove for Bentley at Le Mans every year after that, culminating in the team's last appearance in 1930. He also drove for the Bentley works team in other events. He recorded his time with the team in an excellent book called *The Bentleys at Le Mans*.

Tim Birkin

Tim Birkin was actually Sir Henry Ralph Stanley Birkin (Bart), from a wealthy Nottinghamshire family which had made its money in lace manufacture. He was a flamboyant character who nevertheless suffered from severe self-doubt; some have described him as manic depres-

Surrounded by the customary victors' garlands, Barnato and Birkin pose for photographs after the 1929 Le Mans race..

sive. He was absolutely fearless as a driver, which made him very hard on his cars.

Birkin served in the Royal Flying Corps during the Great War, serving in Palestine where he contracted the malaria which would cause him problems for the rest of his life. He first showed an interest in motor racing with a Brooklands entry in 1921, but withdrew from the sport as a result of family pressure and business commitments. He returned to Brooklands in 1927 with a 3-litre Bentley, graduated to a 4½-litre, and became a Brooklands regular. For 1928, he was invited to drive a 4½-litre in the Bentley team at Le Mans.

Convinced that supercharging was the way to go, he gained financial backing from a sportswoman, the Hon Dorothy Paget, and in 1928 set up his own workshop to develop a supercharged 4½-litre Bentley. WO was less than impressed when he found that he would have to build 50 such cars to meet regulations if Birkin was to be allowed to race, but Birkin secured backing from Barnato, Bentley's Chairman, and the supercharged car went ahead.

When Birkin's own supercharged cars were not ready in time for their planned entry at the 1929 Le Mans, Barnato invited him to be his co-driver in the Speed Six. The pair won that year's event. Birkin's entry in the 1930 event saw both his supercharged cars eliminated by mechanical problems.

After the demise of Bentley (and the withdrawal of funding by Dorothy Paget), Birkin continued racing. In 1931, he won Le Mans in an Alfa Romeo with Earl Howe, and in 1932 he took the Brooklands Outer Circuit lap record in his single-seater Bentley. However, in 1933 he burned his arm badly on a hot exhaust pipe during the Tripoli Grand Prix and died a few weeks later, either because the wound turned septic or because it provoked another malaria attack.

Frank Clement

Frank Clement joined Bentley at Cricklewood in 1920 as head of the Experimental Department. He had already been a prominent racing driver before the war, and that experience led to him becoming the company's racing and demonstrations driver in the early years. In the 1923 and 1924 Le Mans, he was riding mechanic for John Duff, and he was a driver in every subsequent Bentley entry at Le Mans up to 1930.

Clement's family were wealthy jewellers, but Clement himself was a quiet man, not at all like the more flamboyant members of the Bentley Boys.

Sammy Davis

Sammy Davis (Sidney Charles Houghton Davis) was probably best described as an occasional member of the Bentley Boys, as he drove for other teams as well in the late 1920s, notably coming second at Le Mans in 1926 with a Sunbeam. Nevertheless, there was no doubting his commitment to the works team when Cricklewood asked him to drive.

Davis had been an apprentice with Daimler in Britain before becoming a journalist and illustrator for *Automobile Engineer* magazine. He first met WO and his brother HM Bentley in this period, as they shared a love of motor sport. Davis served with the Royal Naval Air Service during the Great War, where he again came across WO. On demobilisation, he joined the staff of *The Autocar*, and it was he who wrote the first published assessment of the 3-litre Bentley in January 1920. His normal job was as the magazine's sports editor, and he wrote under the name of Casque – which is French for "helmet".

Davis was invited to drive for Bentley at Le Mans in 1927 and, as he explained in his book, *Motor Racing*, "I felt at once at home, everyone in the team having been a personal friend for quite a long time." His 1927 drive ended in victory, and it was no surprise that he was asked to drive for the team again. Though not among Bentley's Le Mans drivers in 1928 or 1929 (he drove an Alvis in the 1928 event and did not participate in 1929), he shared a Speed Six in the 1930 event with Clive Dunfee.

Clive Dunfee

Clive Dunfee (Beresford Clive Dunfee) was the younger brother of Jack Dunfee, who also drove a Speed Six for the Bentley team. They were the sons of a City financier.

Clive Dunfee drove a Speed Six for the first time in 1929, and was selected for the works team at Le Mans in 1930. He promised to give up motor racing when he married, in December 1930, but two years later his wife granted him a dispensation to drive with his brother at Brooklands. The car they drove was Old Number One, the 1930 Le Mans Speed Six that now belonged to Woolf Barnato and had been fitted with an 8-litre engine. Sadly, Clive was killed when the car clipped the top of the banking and left the track.

Jack Dunfee

The older of the Dunfee brothers, Jack Lawson Dunfee, had been a friend of Woolf Barnato and was already a noted Brooklands driver when he was invited to join the Bentley team.

Jack Dunfee drove a 4½-litre for the works team at Le Mans in 1929, and at that event, when instructed by WO to slow down to a fast touring speed, memorably asked the boss whether he would like him to get out "and push the ruddy thing!". He drove a Speed Six later that year in the Brooklands Six Hours event, but was not asked to drive at Le Mans in 1930, where his younger brother shared a Speed Six with Sammy Davis.

Jack Dunfee gave up motor racing after his brother Clive was killed in a Bentley at Brooklands in 1932.

Glen Kidston

Glen Kidston (George Pearson Glen Kidston) came from an very wealthy family, and was one of the four core members of the high-living Bentley Boys who had flats on the south-east corner of Grosvenor Square in Mayfair (the others were Barnato, Birkin and Rubin).

Kidston held a commission in the Royal Navy, and had served with distinction during the Great War on both surface ships and submarines. He had been an early pioneer of naval flight, and was a long-time competitor in motor sport with both motorcycles and cars. He owned and raced the first Bugatti in the UK.

His first drive for the Bentley works team was in 1929, when he shared a 4½-litre with Jack Dunfee. He drove Bentleys in a number of events later in the 1929 season, but his moment of glory was as co-driver of the winning Speed Six at Le Mans in 1930.

Kidston died in a flying accident over South Africa in 1932. He had just set air records to Cape Town and was returning in a borrowed plane which broke up in mid-air over the Drakensberg mountains.

Dick Watney

Richard Watney was another Brooklands driver who came into the orbit of the Bentley Boys. His high placings in the events he entered after 1928 suggested that he might be of value to the works team, and for 1930 he was offered a drive in the Speed Six alongside Bentley veteran Frank Clement. The pair achieved second place.

Watney's day job had been in the motoring industry with the Rootes Group, and he was subsequently recruited to become Managing Director of LG Motors, the new name chosen for the makers of Lagonda cars. Here, he joined WO Bentley on the Board of Directors, and was widely credited with conceiving the LG45 Rapide model of 1936.

We did it again! Glen Kidston draws on a well-earned cigarette as he and Barnato pose with the winning car. Standing alongside the car are Dick Watney and Frank Clement, drivers of the second-placed Speed Six.

Chapter Six

The 8-Litre

To someone involved with today's motor industry, where decisions about future products are invariably heavily influenced by accountants and market analysts, there are always clearly identified reasons for developing a new car. Back in the 1920s, however, things were very different. The engineer was king; he knew better than anybody else what could be achieved; and, if he was good at his job, he also had a pretty shrewd idea of what sort of product would sell well. If somebody had asked WO Bentley why he had developed the 8-litre model, the great man would probably have found the question an odd one. The chances are that his answer would have been something along the lines of "because we could".

A more rational possibility is that WO was well aware that time was marching on. The wealthy young blades who had survived the Great War and were anxious to spend their money on fast and exciting sports cars were not being replaced as potential customers by more of the same; society and its attitudes were beginning to change. So if Bentley Motors were to keep the custom of those same buyers, it had to move on with them. As they grew older and got married, so they wanted more sober family transport, and that was the 6½-litre; and as they reached the top of their professions, so they wanted grander and more luxurious machinery. But those who had been fascinated by speed in their younger days were never likely to lose the taste for it, and the 8-litre was for them.

Nowhere in WO's own writings is there any clear explanation of where the idea of the 8-litre model came from. However, what does come across quite clearly is that he saw each new model as an improvement on the one before, and so from his point of view the 8-litre was simply the next logical step after the Speed Six. Nevertheless, when we look more closely at the few available facts, it is difficult not to reach the conclusion that WO was also aiming to go one better than his rivals in the motor manufacturing business.

He was quite clearly a very competitive individual, even though his wealthy middle-class and English public-school background persuaded him to keep that side of his nature very much under wraps. For confirmation of it, though, we need only look to his great enthusiasm for competitive motor sport, and to his immediate acceptance of the challenge from the prototype Rolls-Royce Phantom while he was in France testing the prototype six-cylinder Bentley in 1924. WO had intended his original 3-litre to be the best chassis of its type, and from that moment on he must have constantly kept an eye on what other manufacturers were doing. With the 8-litre, his aim was to go beyond what everybody else had achieved.

In that, it is arguable that he was successful. The 8-litre Bentley was one of the truly great cars of the period, and has often been compared to the Hispano-Suiza H-series, the

Rolls-Royce Phantom, and even the huge Bugatti Royale that its creator hoped to sell exclusively to royalty. However, the 8-litre was really doomed from the start because it was the wrong product at precisely the wrong time. When announced in the autumn of 1930, it was launched into a world where even the very wealthy were tightening their belts as the economic depression started by the Wall Street Crash in October 1929 began to bite. It was the most expensive Bentley chassis yet, with a price of £1850 before the cost of the body was included, and in such conditions it was never going to sell well.

In fact, the 8-litre was largely responsible for finishing off an already struggling Bentley Motors. It simply did not sell, and the company had no other products on the market to keep itself afloat. Relying on an inevitably small-volume product was not a sensible business decision even if, as WO pleaded in mitigation in *An Illustrated History of the Bentley Car*, it was "by far the most profitable car we ever made." The 4-litre derived from it and intended to give the company a better-selling, lower-priced product, came too late. It was, in any case, flawed – although, as Chapter 8 makes clear, not as badly flawed as many commentators have suggested. So the fact that Bentley Motors managed, eventually, to find buyers for 100 of their magnificent 8-litre chassis is actually something for which enthusiasts should today be grateful. Had it come from a lesser manufacturer, the model would probably have sunk without trace.

Design and development of the 8-litre
Exactly when design work began on the 8-litre is open to question, but it was probably some time around mid-1929. By this time, the design department of Bentley Motors was limping somewhat in the absence of FT Burgess, the Chief Designer who had been at WO's side since the very beginning. Burgess had fallen ill and was unable to work for long periods; he died at the end of November, leaving WO without the down-to-earth common sense and consequent restraint which had been among Burgess' greatest assets. So the 8-litre was very largely developed under a new Chief Designer. This was Lieutenant-Colonel Thomas Barwell Barrington, a former Naval officer who was recruited from Rolls-Royce and before that had worked for Napier. His appointment was announced in early December, but was made retrospective to the start of November.

Work on the 8-litre had of course begun before Barrington arrived, and the first experimental engine was being bench-tested at Cricklewood by February 1930. Michael Hay's researches show that it was based on a late-series 6½-litre engine, numbered HM 2870. So inevitably it had the single-port block and combined magneto and coil ignition which characterised the 1930-model Speed Six engine, and these features would be carried over to the production engines.

We know that the first prototype engine was tried out in EX2, the second 6½-litre prototype which was familiarly known at Cricklewood as "The Box" or "The Coffin" on account of its remarkably ugly square-rigged body – "hideous" was the word WO used in *An Illustrated History of the Bentley Car*. This was a saloon type from an unidentified coachbuilder, but it had the advantage of being a lightweight design with Weymann-type fabric panelling. "It was," said WO in that same book, "a very fast and delightful car which did a prodigious mileage, including once solo from Dieppe to Cannes in one day without my having to put the lights on."

Testing on French roads was of course a regular feature of Bentley prototype work, and this car did its fair share. In the same book, WO remembered that it was used to try out an experimental method of engine cooling. "All big cars at this time were suffering from the complaint of boiling on long ascents," he explained. This experiment involved steam-cooling, with an auxiliary tank mounted between the front dumb-irons of the chassis. "It worked very well, too, but did result in a rise in noise, which we could not of course tolerate with this car. The radiator people did the job for us by designing more efficiently cooling radiators."

The engine itself was very much a development of the later Speed Six type, and used the same cylinder bore centres. However, the earlier six-cylinder engines had all had their carburettors on the left-hand side and their exhausts on the right, and for the 8-litre Cricklewood returned to the pattern established by the four-cylinder engines of carburettors on the right and exhaust on the left. Exactly how the engine was installed in EX2 without the carburettors fouling

THE 8-LITRE

The cylinder block of an 8-litre engine undergoing overhaul. This is the exhaust side, showing the twin exhaust ports for each cylinder and, below them, the holes for the spark plugs on this side of the engine.

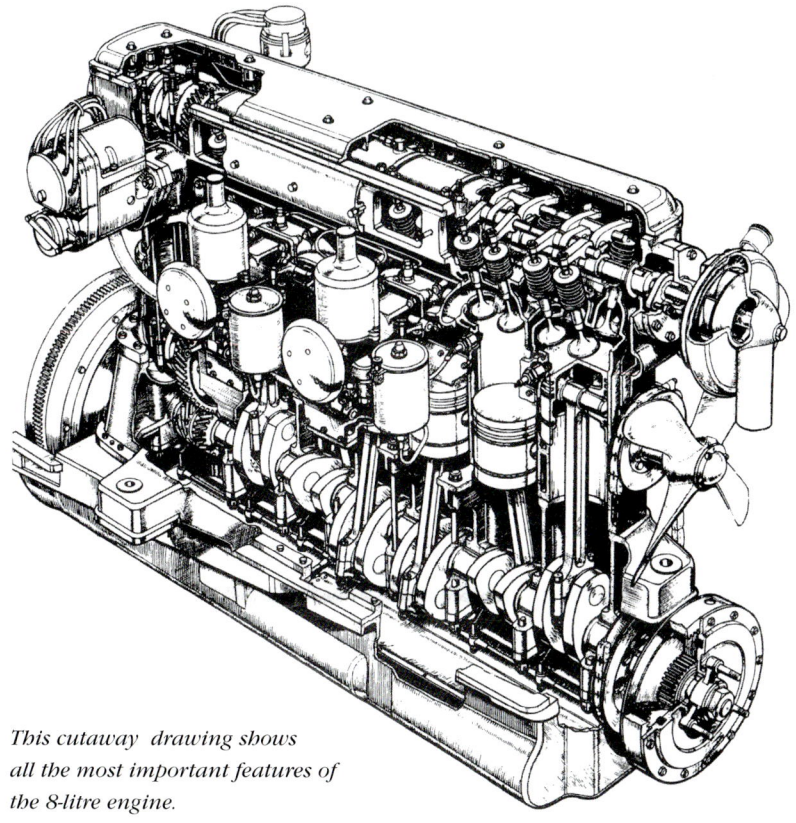

On the inlet side of the engine, the single-port block design is clear (the "port" is the large opening above the spark plug holes).

This cutaway drawing shows all the most important features of the 8-litre engine.

the steering column – which was why they had changed sides on the 6½-litre engine – remains unexplained. On the production engines, the carburettors were a pair of vertical "square-throat" SUs which, at two inches, were larger than those used on any previous Bentley model.

It is most interesting to examine why WO chose the bore and stroke dimensions that he did for the 8-litre engine. His aims were to retain and if possible improve on the refinement that the 6½-litre had achieved, while adding enough power to ensure that the new car delivered effortless performance at all speeds even when fitted with the heaviest of bodies.

His eventual choice was to retain the 140mm stroke of the 6½-litre engine and to bore the cylinders out to 110mm. Retaining the existing stroke dimension at least offered the possibility of incorporating some readily available production components into the new engine, and if the first prototype had turned out to be wanting in some way, a next stage might well have been to try a longer stroke. The previous 3-litre Bentley engine, of course, had had a 149mm stroke.

The 110mm bore size deserves comment. That 10% increase over the bore diameter of the 6½-litre was all that the retention of the existing bore centres would safely allow. It also, indisputably, allowed a large number of components from the late-series 6½-litre engines to be used in the 8-litre with little or no modification – and that, of course, saved the costs of new tooling and rationalised the spares situation to a degree. There is, however, an interesting aspect to Bentley's decision to quote the swept volume of

This is the bottom end of the 8-litre engine fom YF 5001 during its restoration. The massive connecting rods are visible above the top of the crankcase, and bolted below that is the sump. The three-throw camshaft drive is here hidden under plastic sheeting.

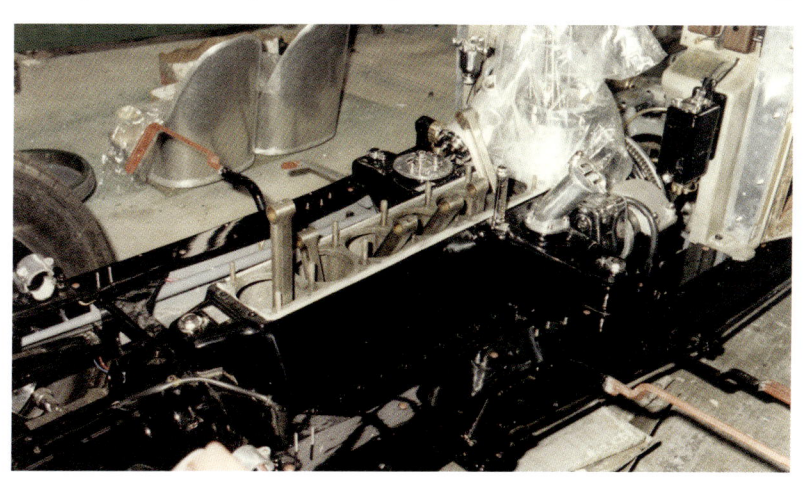

101

BENTLEY SIX-CYLINDER MODELS IN DETAIL

The Instruction Book showed the exhaust side of the engine like this:. The cylinder block is the dark section in the centre, and everything else is bolted to or around it.

Despite the massive dimensions of the engine when viewed from the side, it was characteristic of its times in being tall and narrow when seen from dead ahead or directly behind.

This illustration from the Instruction Book helps to understand how the engine was built up. In this view of the inlet side, the carburettors and inlet manifold have been removed.

their new engine as 7983cc. The enormously well-respected six-cylinder engine in the contemporary Hispano-Suiza H6C models had the same 140mm stroke and 110mm bore as the new 8-litre Bentley engine, and the size of that engine was usually quoted as 7981cc or 7982cc. So perhaps the extra cubic centimetre in the Bentley description suggests a little subtle one-upmanship was abroad.

There was another and very valuable publicity benefit to developing an 8-litre engine, and that involved competition with Rolls-Royce. That company's Phantom chassis, already an obvious competitor with the 6½ litre Bentley, had a 7.7- litre (7668cc) six-cylinder engine. An 8-litre, even to somebody who did not understand such things as power outputs, was obviously and indisputably bigger at a time when such things mattered. One-upmanship may have reared its head again here.

However, it would be very wrong to accuse WO and his team of designing their new engine solely to score points off rival manufacturers. Much more important was to make the engine more refined and more powerful, and in that they succeeded admirably. Its additional capacity ensured that it did not have to work as hard as the smaller-capacity six-cylinder Bentley engine to deliver its performance, so reducing noise levels. As for power, the production engines delivered a minimum of 200bhp in their least powerful form, and a maximum of 230bhp. These were huge power outputs for their time: a 10hp family saloon of 1930 usually produced rather a lot less than 30bhp, and half a century later, the 6½-litre V8 engine in a Bentley Mulsanne still produced no more than 200bhp.

The new engine was only part of the 8-litre story, of course. Whether it had been apparent that a new chassis frame would be needed before the prototype engine was installed in EX2 is not clear. One way or the other, however, Cricklewood clearly decided that a new frame would be needed. Its most important function would be to provide the absolute rigidity needed to eliminate the flexing that caused squeaks and rattles in bodywork, and to that end it would have to be stronger than the existing 6½-litre frame.

So the new frame was drawn up with deeper side-members than those on any earlier Bentley. These were downswept between the axles to a greater extent than on earlier cars, in order to give a lower floor level so that the overall height of the car could in turn be lower. A consequence of this was that the bottom flanges of the side-members hung closer to the ground than on earlier Bentleys, and that ground clearance as measured under the battery-box was reduced by an inch and a half as compared to a Standard Six, and by half an inch as compared to a Speed Six. The side-members were of course also strengthened by the presence of the familiar Bentley strut gear on their undersides. Between them were positioned one pressed steel cross-member and five massively sturdy tubular cross-members, together with smaller tubular cross-members connecting the dumb-irons at the front and the rear. The rear springs were mounted on outriggers, as for the 6½-litre chassis, and the whole assembly was quite extraordinarily rigid for its time.

It was also quite extraordinarily heavy, and a complete 8-litre rolling chassis weighed around 37cwt (4144lb, 1880kg) – as much as a complete 4½-litre Bentley with its closed bodywork in place. It was indeed heavy, acknowledged WO in *An Illustrated History of the Bentley Car*. If production had lasted longer than it did, "we would, first of all, have worked to reduce the weight without any loss in refinement and

The 8-litre chassis was a massive affair, with stout tubular cross-members to ensure rigidity. The side-members of the frame swept up over the axles, allowing coachbuilders to construct bodies with lower overall height.

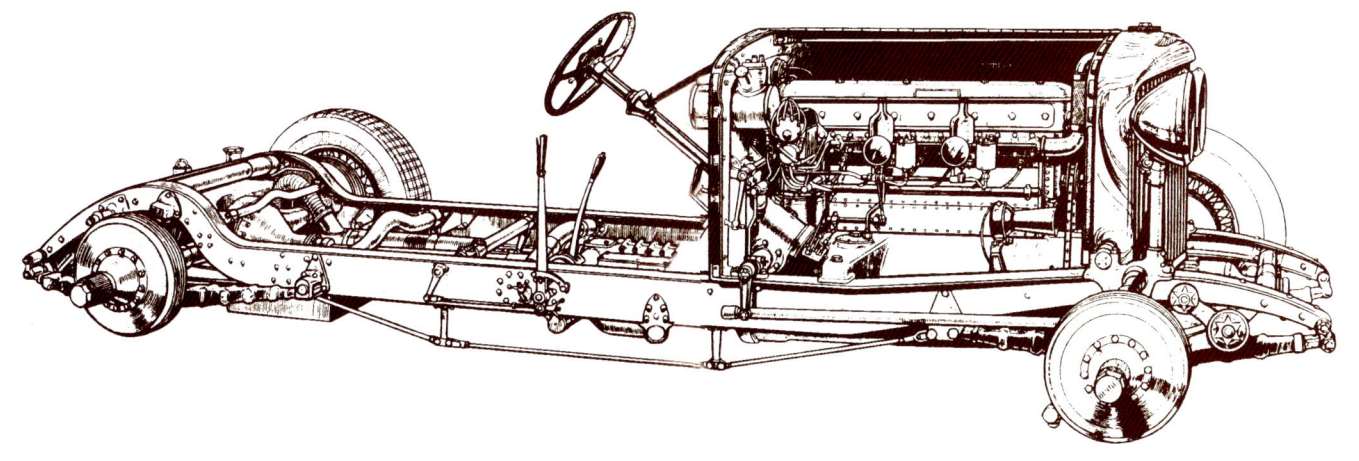

The lower centre section of the frame demanded a hypoid-type rear axle, seen here on chassis YF 5016 and in side view in the 8-litre Instruction Book.

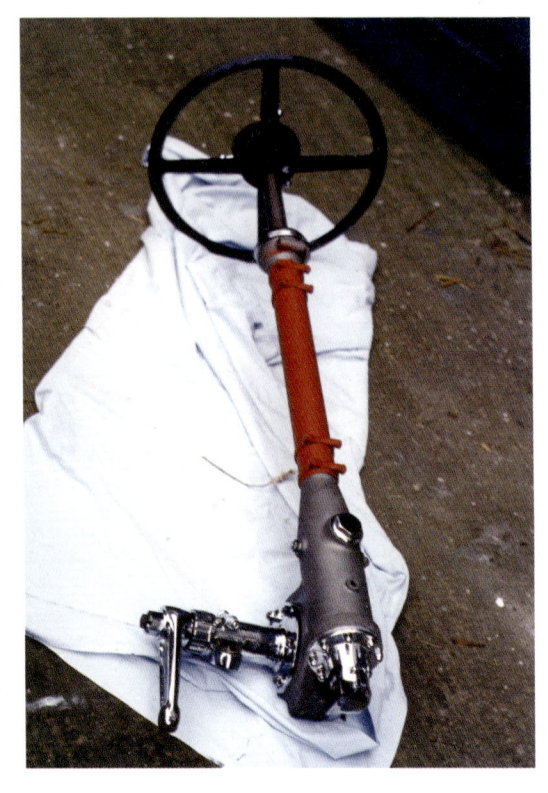

Everything was massive about the 8-litre, and that included the steering column.

silence". At this stage, however, the extra weight was of no real consequence because the new engine was more than up to the job of moving an 8-litre Bentley with a heavy, formal body at speeds of 100mph. It was only later, when the 8-litre chassis was pressed into service for the considerably less powerful 4-litre car, that its weight became an issue.

While designing this new frame, WO took the opportunity to play with some of its dimensions, and once again it is interesting to try to understand the reasons why. A few inches here and there would of course have been welcome to the coachbuilders, and the 8-litre sales brochure acknowledged that they had been consulted during the design phase: "The design of the frame has been completed in close co-operation with leading coachbuilders, and it is therefore in every way suitable for the construction of first class coachwork strong enough to give satisfaction throughout the long life of the chassis."

However, the overall width of the 8-litre's chassis remained at the 5ft 8½in which had been considered good enough for every Bentley since the first production 3-litre. It was the wheelbase that changed. The odd dimensions of the 6½-litre and Speed Six chassis disappeared in favour of a 12ft size for the standard wheelbase and a 13ft size for the optional long wheelbase. A relevant consideration here may be that the Rolls-Royce Phantom came with alternative wheelbases of 12ft and 12ft 6in. By offering a 13ft wheelbase, Bentley Motors were again going one better.

The 8-litre chassis was the first one to be assembled from its component parts at Cricklewood; earlier chassis had been fully assembled by their manufacturers, Mechans of Glasgow. It also incorporated a number of additional features that were new to Bentleys. The most obvious visually was a redesigned gearbox, known as the F-type, which had a two-piece casing with the left-hand and right-hand halves held together by a row of bolts around the centre-line; all other Bentley gearboxes had essentially been a box with a flat "lid" that was bolted in place. The most important internal feature of this gearbox was that it had bearings between each gear in order to reduce noise – or, as WO rather quaintly put it in *An Illustrated History of the Bentley Car*, "to increase the silence". These bearings also made the gearbox more expensive to manufacture, as he was at pains to point out. The redesign had in fact resulted in rather longer gear throws than on earlier Bentley gearboxes, but the difference was not great enough to be of concern.

The propshaft running from that gearbox led to another feature that was new to Bentleys, in the shape of a hypoid rear axle. In a hypoid axle, the drive pinion is located below the centre-line of the ring-gear in order to reduce the height of the driveline so that the floor level can remain low, and it was precisely for this reason it had been specified for the 8-litre. As the hypoid axle was not used on the 4-litre derived from the 8-litre, the larger-engined car remained the only Cricklewood Bentley to have one. The car's size and weight also led to other unique design features, and the wheel hubs on both axles were made larger than those on any other Bentley. In addition, there were wider 7.00 x 21 tyres in place of the 6.75 x 21 size used on the Standard and Speed Six models.

The brakes on the 8-litre also ended up being different from those on any earlier Bentley chassis, but mainly because of a change in the law rather than because of any advance in Bentley engineering. The law had originally required that the handbrake should operate on a completely separate ancillary system to that operated by the footbrake. A change in requirements enabled Cricklewood to use single shoes for the rear brakes in place of the separate shoes for handbrake and footbrake on earlier chassis. The rear brakes were now operated by cables rather than by rods. Front axles were also of a modified design which incorporated jacking

A Dewandre vacuum servo was standard equipment, and is seen here in the illustration from the 8-litre Instruction Book

The Dewandre brake servo is again seen in this picture: it is behind the gearbox and has an oval brass plate on its lid. The gearbox was new for the 8-litre, and readily identifiable by its vertically split casing. This is YF 5001 again, during its restoration.

BENTLEY SIX-CYLINDER MODELS IN DETAIL

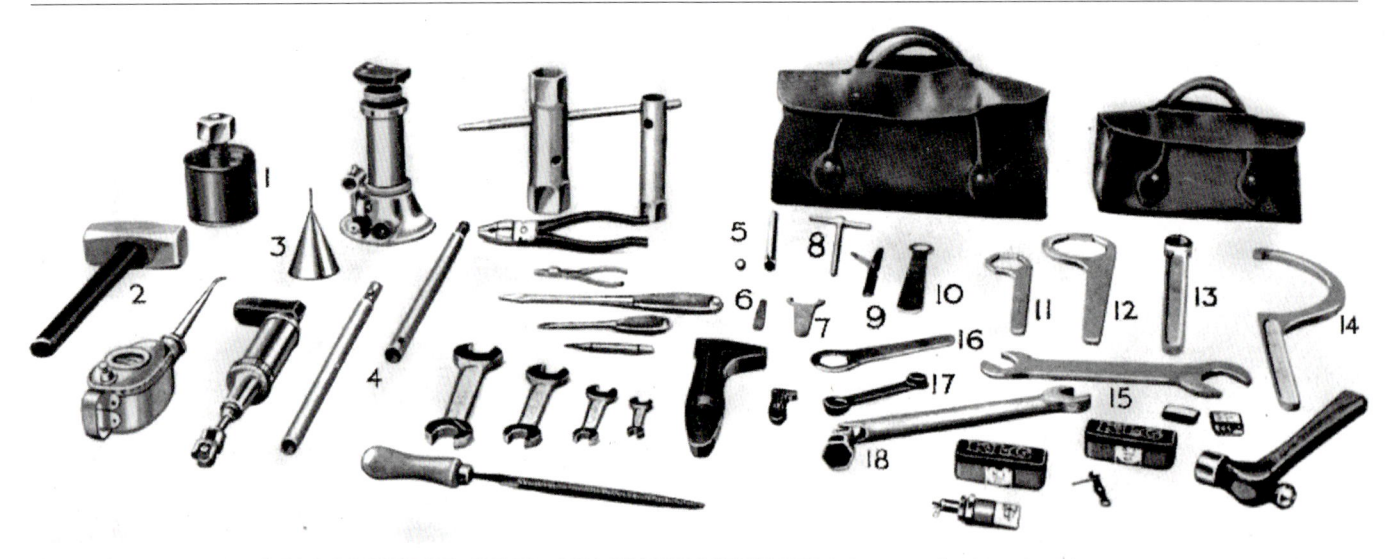

Fig. 45. KIT OF TOOLS PROVIDED WITH THE EIGHT LITRE BENTLEY. The Numbered parts are: 1, Hub drawer; 2, Wheel locking ring removal hammer; 3, Small funnel for filling; 4, Jack handle; 5, Ball removal tool for relief valve; 6, Tappet key; 7, Rear shock absorber adjusting spanner; 8, Tappet adjusting key; 9, Feeler gauge .004 and .006; 10, Ring spanner for tappet adjusting; 11 and 16, Spanner for removing draw plugs; 12, Hub cap spanner; 13, Cylinder nut spanner; 14, "C" Spanner for camshaft drive housing; 15, Fan adjusting spanner; 17, S.U. carburettor spanner; 18, Sparking plug spanner.

Every 8-litre chassis was supplied with a comprehensive tool kit, but it was up to the coachbuilder to decide where those tools should be located on the completed car. Harrison's solution for YR 5076 was neat.

pads (although it is possible that these axles were fitted to the very last Speed Sixes as well.)

A particular concern during the design stage had been to reduce the maintenance requirement, and to that end small details had been improved; the Autovac, for example, was now installed with its filler pointing towards the outside of the car. New to Bentleys was the centralised chassis lubrication system made by Tecalemit. Topping-up a single reservoir was all that was needed at specified intervals; pressing on a foot pedal then pumped lubricant through a series of small-diameter tubes to five points on the chassis which would otherwise have had to be lubricated individually. These included the spring shackles, which were totally enclosed by metal dust covers attached to the gaiters. The result was that the springs were completely enclosed and protected from road dirt and water, while remaining correctly lubricated.

The 8-litre chassis also had a much more sophisticated electrical system than earlier Bentleys. Although the 6½-litres had depended on a pair of 6-volt batteries, the new model went back to a single 12-volt type, as used in the four-cylinder cars. There were now two fuse boxes, as well, both mounted on the left-hand side of the dash within the engine compartment. Between them they contained no fewer than 10 fuses, six in one box and four in the other. As on the 6½-litres, the dynamo was mounted between the front dumb-irons and driven from the nose of the crankshaft; either the 2 DAC5 shared with the 6½-litre or a 2 DAC3 type was used on production chassis. Bosch supplied the starter motor, which was a BNE 2/12 RS2 type that had been tried out on the final series of Speed Six engines, and also the magneto. Three different magneto types were used in production, the FU6B shared with the Speed Six, a GF6A or an SR/6, and in all cases the 8-litre was fitted with a dual ignition system with a Delco-

Remy MRS12 coil.

A final refinement on the new chassis was a set of thermostatically controlled radiator shutters. It hardly needs to be said that this was very much a case of keeping up with the Joneses – or rather, keeping ahead of the Phantoms, which had used a hand-operated radiator shutter system since 1925. WO pointed out in *An Illustrated History of the Bentley Car* that they were "expensive to make and fit: they were also a boon and a blessing." The benefit of the shutters was that they remained closed while the engine was cold, so shutting off cooling air to the radiator and allowing the engine to reach working temperature more quickly. Once it had done so, the thermostatic control opened the shutters to restore normal airflow to the radiator matrix. The automatic shutters were housed in a typically Bentley tall radiator frame, surmounted by a large winged-B motif with a blue enamelled background. Meanwhile, the radiator itself was not integral with its outer shell, as on earlier Bentleys, but rather a separate block bolted to the shell.

1930-31: the 8-litre on sale
As far as Cricklewood was concerned, the new 8-litre model was the future and, by the time it was announced to the public, production of other models was already at low levels. Nevertheless, when the motoring press were briefed about the new model – *The Motor* gave preliminary details in its issue of 16 September 1930 and reported that rumours of the new Bentley had been around for some weeks – the official word from Bentley Motors was that their 1931 programme included the 4½-litre, supercharged 4½-litre, 6½-litre and Speed Six. That impression was confirmed when the 8-litre was introduced at the Olympia Show in October. The new chassis was certainly the big news, but other models were still around: the Bentley stand had a Speed Six, a 4½-litre and a supercharged 4½-litre, the Gill stand had a 4½-litre and the Vanden Plas stand had a supercharged car. It looked like business as usual, with the added fillip of the new model.

Besides the two wheelbases, Bentley gave their customers the usual choice of power and performance options. So there were no fewer than four choices of engine compression ratio, and three different axle ratios – although a Bentley salesman's job was to make recommendations about which would be the most appropriate for any given car. The choice of these options was included in the chassis price of £1850, which was a flat rate that applied to both wheelbase sizes. Perhaps again reflecting that element of one-upmanship that seems inseparable from the story of the 8-litre, this price was slightly higher than that of a Rolls-Royce Phantom II.

Production of the 8-litre probably started some time around August, and at least nine chassis had been built by the time of the Olympia Show. All had been bodied in suitably grand style, and six of them were on display. The Bentley stand had an HJ Mulliner saloon on the 12ft chassis; Freestone & Webb had a Weymann saloon on the 13ft chassis; Gurney Nutting had a Weymann coupé and a Sedanca de Ville, both on the 13ft chassis; Park Ward's contribution was a saloon on the 12ft chassis, and Thrupp & Maberly displayed a drophead coupé, also on the 12ft chassis.

Neither of the first two chassis was on display, as both had been retained by Bentley Motors. The very first one, on a 13ft wheelbase and bodied by HJ Mulliner as a saloon, became the company's demonstrator. The second, another HJ Mulliner saloon but this time on a 12ft wheelbase, became WO's personal transport. However, it was neither of these but another car, YF 5007, the Gurney Nutting coupé delivered to long-standing Bentley customer Nigel Holder, that alerted WO to a problem with the 8-litre. As he explained it in *An Illustrated History of the Bentley Car*:

There were friction dampers on the front axle, and the road springs were encased in gaiters and fed with oil from the Tecalemit one-shot lubrication system. This is YF 5001, pictured some time after its restoration.

"Forward of the scuttle the 'prongs' of the frame by unhappy chance were set up, like a tuning fork, on the wrong frequency at certain high speeds. In the earlier cars when this periodicity, or 'tramp', set in the whole frame gave because it was not nearly so rigidly made. In the 8-litre, at just 80mph, really wicked tramp would set in. If you happened to be on a bend, control of the steering instantly ceased…. I was…. alarmed by the implications of this discovery. The big car had been well and truly launched. We had a number of orders for it. And our financial position was in its usual delicate state…. I don't want to over-exaggerate this crisis, and in any case it applied only to cars with very heavy bodies…. We had to delay deliveries for some weeks while we worked to cure the trouble. We did so in the end by mounting the body unrigidly attached to the dash through bolts passing through rubber bushes, thus breaking up the wrong frequency vibrations."

That, at least, was the way WO remembered it, but it appears that another modification was made at the same time. The first 8-litres, all fitted with the new and longer springs devised for the chassis to improve the stability which had given trouble on the long-chassis 6½-litres, had the springs shackled at the front. Those shackles were very swiftly switched to the rear, where they had been on earlier Bentley chassis. Perhaps that, too, had contributed to the tramp problem that had so alarmed WO. One way or another, the tramp must have been eliminated by the end of November, because WO's own 8-litre was lent to representatives of *The Autocar* and *The Motor* for road test and the reports were published in the first week of December. However, none of the Olympia Show cars – including, of course, YF 5007 – was delivered to a customer before December 1930. No doubt they were all modified at the works.

The 8-litre had the distinction of being the largest-engined car then made in Britain, and at one time that alone would have attracted a number of wealthy customers. But the flamboyance of the 1920s had been dealt a fatal blow by the Wall Street Crash. Orders for the 8-litre were by no means abundant, and the first sanction of 25 cars seems to have been slow to sell. Assembly of the second-sanction chassis at Cricklewood probably began some time around February 1931, and even if all of the first-sanction chassis had found buyers by then, five months to find customers for 25 chassis was not an encouraging sign. Things seem to have picked up a little after that, though, with the third sanction following a month or so later and the fourth sanction two months after that.

However, there were to be no more than these four sanctions – 100 cars in all – because the Receiver was called in to Bentley Motors during July 1931. Many cars were still incomplete: there were chassis still in build at Cricklewood, and there were very many cars still out with coachbuilders which had not yet returned to be signed-off and given their Five-Year Guarantees. In fact, the majority of 8-litres were probably delivered to their first owners after Bentley had gone into receivership. New chassis were still finding first owners as late as 1933.

There were almost no running changes to the 8-litre during its brief production run. During spring 1931, right at the end of the second production sanction, a reinforced crankcase was introduced. This arrived on engine number YR5099, which went into the chassis with the same number. The actual changes were thicker walls and strengthened radii.

Most of the 8-litre chassis were built with the longer 13ft wheelbase, the actual total being 65 of the 100 built. All the remaining 35 were on the 12ft wheelbase, and there were no special-order short-chassis or competition derivatives. The 8-litre was always strictly a grand car and, as Chapter 7 shows in more detail, very few were bodied as the sort of open tourers that today's Bentley enthusiasts so admire.

The 8-litre Bentley on the road

By date, the first road test of an 8-litre Bentley was the one published in *The Motor* of 2 December 1930, but in practice the test in *The Autocar* dated 5 December was published at the same time. Both magazines were lent WO's own car, chassis number YF 5002, which had an HJ Mulliner saloon body on the 12ft wheelbase.

The Motor summarised its impressions by saying, "this new model combines in an exceptional manner a capacity for high speeds with refined and flexible running". It also recorded that "the car runs very quietly, is docile and flexible in traffic, holds the road admirably and is possessed of exceedingly good brakes…. The suspension system is comfortable but firm, so that one gains the impression that all four wheels are definitely biting the road and are likely to continue to do so... on a bend taken fast there is no side sway or roll."

A key finding was that the 8-litre would run at any speed between 6mph and an indicated 104mph in top gear, and the magazine noted that the big engine would be turning at just 200rpm at the bottom end of that scale. "Cruising at 75mph is so effortless as to be deceptive," and yet "hard braking from high speeds does not cause the slightest tendency to swerve".

There was just a hint of criticism about the steering, which "has a higher ratio than normal for a big car, this having been selected to provide a very moderate steering-wheel movement such as is desirable at high cruising speeds for quick control. Nevertheless the effort required is by no means tiring." Overall, "it is difficult to convey in words the extreme confidence with which the 8-litre Bentley inspires the driver and passengers."

The Autocar report was much more effusive, beginning by pointing out that Bentley Motors' attempt to present the car as a town carriage failed to do the car justice because "the dominant note of the new Bentley is its tremendous performance, and on that performance alone it stands right in the forefront as an equal, at least, of any other car in existence." No doubt the Rolls-Royce people sat up and took notice of that!

The 8-litre's flexibility impressed *The Autocar* as much as it had their rivals at *The Motor*: "this car can be driven really softly in its high top gear as slowly as a man walks, and can accelerate from that without snatch and without difficulty." The magazine reported a "sense of great latent power" in the car, and pointed out that its ride and handling were very far ahead of the levels they had reached in the 6½-litre models: "the new car is steady with easy riding springs and so puts the earlier model entirely in the shade.... It seems to have no side sway whatsoever on a fast corner."

There were no more road tests in Britain's specialist motoring magazines, but there was an interesting test of an 8-litre as a used car in *The Autocar* for 6 November 1936. At that stage, the test car was five years old and had 40,000 miles on its clock, so it was still representative of the 8-litre in its heyday. The magazine borrowed it from the Bentley Service Station in Cricklewood, which at that time was still maintaining, refurbishing and even selling used examples of the "WO" models.

The car in question was perhaps rather special, even among the illustrious ranks of 8-litre Bentleys. Built on chassis number YR 5095 and delivered new in June 1931 to Bentley Chairman Woolf Barnato, it was a special two-door, four-seat tourer by Vanden Plas. *The Autocar* liked it so much that they put 450 miles under its wheels during their test, including a maximum-speed run at the Brooklands track which achieved 100mph "on a bad day".

The car needed some acclimatisation, not least because it had been built to suit Barnato, who was a big man, and *The Autocar* tester clearly was not of the same physical stature. However, once cushions had been added to the seat so that the driver could actually see the road ahead, "the car was as great a joy to drive as can be imagined". The tester revelled in its "sweeping, thrilling acceleration", and could find only one fault. That was with the steering which, although "really accurate", was "not light, especially on a sharp turn at low speed."

CHASSIS NUMBERS AND BUILD DATES OF THE 8-LITRE CARS

The chassis number of a Bentley 8-litre can be found on a ledge on the left-hand side of the bulkhead.

The lists below show the 8-litre chassis in approximate chronological order of manufacture. The construction of bodywork typically took between two and three months, although some bodies took much longer, and there would have been other delays when Cricklewood sent a completed car back to the bodybuilder for modifications before it would issue the Five-Year Guarantee. Delivery dates shown below come from Bentley Motors records and are the dates on which the guarantees were issued.

It would be reasonable to suppose that the actual build date of most chassis was two or three months earlier than their delivery dates, but there were cars which took longer than the usual time to complete.

For a more precise dating of any individual chassis, it is advisable to contact the Bentley Drivers' Club.

Chassis numbers	Delivery dates
YF 5001 – YF 5025	Oct 1930 – Sep 1931
YR 5076 – YR 5100	Apr 1931 – Sep 1931
YM 5026 – YM 5050	May 1931 – Sep 1932
YX 5101 – YX 5125	July 1931 – Dec 1932

SPECIFICATIONS FOR BENTLEY 8-LITRE MODELS

Years of manufacture
1930-31

Build quantity
100

Engine
7983cc (110mm x 140mm) OHC six-cylinder with four valves per cylinder; single-port head
Two SU 2-inch vertical "square-throat" carburettors

5.1:1, 5.3:1, 5.5:1 or 6.1:1 compression ratio; most cars had 5.1:1 or 5.5:1
200bhp at 3500rpm (5.1:1 compression);
225bhp at 3500rpm (5.3:1 and 5.5:1 compression);
230bhp at 3500rpm (6.1:1 compression)

Transmission
Four-speed "crash" gearbox.
F-type gearbox:
3.243:1, 1.792:1, 1.345:1, 1.00:1, reverse 2.926:1.

Final drive ratio:	Standard	3.533:1
	Heavy bodies	4.071:1
	Light bodies	3.310:1

Suspension
Semi-elliptic leaf springs on front and rear axles;
front axle with Bentley & Draper friction dampers;
rear axle with Bentley & Draper hydraulic dampers

Steering
Worm and wheel steering

Brakes
Drum-type brakes on all four wheels, with Dewandre vacuum servo.
Rod operation of front brakes, cable operation of rears.

Chassis dimensions
Wheelbase:	12ft 0in or 13ft 0in
Overall length:	16ft 9¾in (12ft wheelbase)
	17ft 9¾in (13ft wheelbase)
Overall width:	5ft 8½in
Track:	56in front and rear
Weight:	37cwt

Performance
Max. speed:	100mph
0-60mph:	18 secs approx
Fuel consumption (typical):	11-12mpg (2.42-2.64 miles per litre)

WO admired HJ Mulliner as a builder of closed bodywork, and it was Mulliner's who built the saloon body on his own 8-litre. Chassis YF7002 had the shorter, 12ft, wheelbase and is now preserved by Bentley Motors at Crewe.

BENTLEY SIX-CYLINDER MODELS IN DETAIL

Seeing this in the rear-view mirror would have produced the same reaction in most drivers of the 1930s as a modern Bentley does today – and rightly so, as the 8-litre was a 100mph car.

The Zeiss headlamps specified for this car were not a standard feature. Interestingly, WO seems to have preferred them to the standard type.

Every 8-litre came with a comprehensive tool kit in its own box. The trunk is more spacious than it appears in this picture.

112

THE 8-LITRE

The knife-edge creases in the rear wings helped to slim the car from the rear. A separate luggage trunk was characteristic of the times.

This is the correct arrangement for the cooling fan, driven by a linked belt from the nose of the crankshaft.

The winged-B emblem was fitted to the top of the fuel tank, but was the only marque recognition badge on the rear.

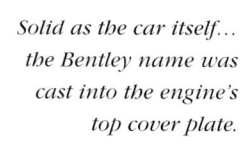

Solid as the car itself... the Bentley name was cast into the engine's top cover plate.

The instruments were not always laid out in the same way, even on two bodies by the same coachbuilder. Compare the arrangement here with that on the dashboard of the HJ Mulliner limousine YM5038.

The sliding windows in all doors were an interesting feature.

As always on a WO Bentley, the steering wheel boss incorporated adjustment levers for the ignition and fuel systems.

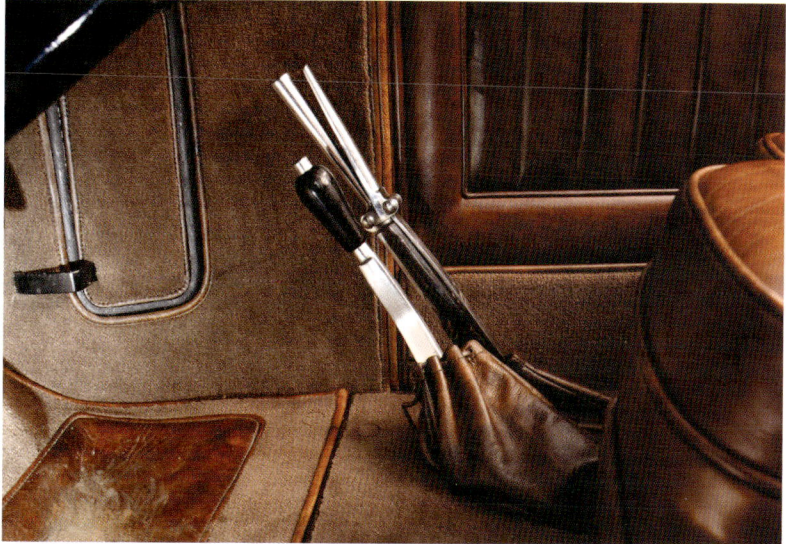

The very gear lever and handbrake that WO once used himself... visible on the left is the footwell vent which allowed cool air into the car when required.

Chapter Seven

Coachwork on the 8-Litre Chassis

The Bentley 8-litre was first shown to the public at the Olympia Show in October 1930, but that was its only appearance there. By the time of the 1931 show, Bentley Motors was in receivership and was in no position to advertise its products to new purchasers.

The range of bodies on display at that 1930 show nevertheless reflected both the optimism of the company in introducing this new flagship model and the types of body for which it was most likely to be suited. On their own stand, the company had an HJ Mulliner Weymann saloon on the shorter of the two wheelbases. This was on chassis number YF 5006, the sixth production chassis.

Of the five other 8-litres on display at Olympia, two were also saloons. Freestone & Webb had a Weymann metal-panelled saloon (later owned by Woolf Barnato) in an elegant combination of light and dark grey, with a tan interior featuring Dunlop air cushion seats and figured walnut woodwork. This was again on the 12ft wheelbase chassis, this time number YF

One of the most attractive bodies ever built on an 8-litre Bentley was the Gurney Nutting coupé on YF 5007, which was displayed at Olympia in 1930. Sadly, the car was later lost, supposedly falling into the sea while being loaded aboard a ship. This is a careful replica, created over a period of 43 years from 1961 for John Rees. It sits on chassis YM 5043, which originally had a Carlton sedanca de ville body.

5009. The third saloon was on the Park Ward stand, again on the 12ft wheelbase and finished in black with green wheels, green leather upholstery and what may have been stainless steel exterior fittings. This was on chassis number YF 5008 and later became a demonstrator.

Gurney Nutting had two 8-litres on their stand – nobody else had more than one – and showed two very different body styles. On the long-wheelbase chassis, YF 5004 carried a formal Sedanca de Ville body in dove grey with a black top, black leather for the chauffeur to sit on and grey cloth for the owners, and a chrome-plated waistline strip running from the radiator grille right around the back of the body. This feature made the car look even longer than it really was. On the 13ft wheelbase chassis was YF 5007, fitted with Weymann close-coupled saloon bodywork which has also been described as a coupé type. Variously described as finished in biscuit and black or cream and black, it had stylishly curved running-boards which stopped just short of the spare wheels stowed alongside the bonnet, and was a most attractive creation.

The final 1930 Show car was yet again on the 12ft wheelbase chassis, and this time on the Thrupp & Maberly stand. On chassis number YF 5005, this was a drophead coupé with a fully disappearing head over its two-seat passenger compartment and a long rear deck which may have contained a dickey seat. The low roof height and narrow windows combined with louvres in the scuttle to suggest power and speed. Finished in black and pastel blue, with enclosed wings, separate running-boards, and wheel discs to suggest modernity, it was another extremely attractive and imposing design.

All of these bodies were designed to impress, both with their appearance and fittings, and all were from the top echelon of coachbuilders. Yet not one of them suggested that the coachbuilders planned to break new ground with their creations for the 8-litre chassis. All were essentially conventional, stainless steel fittings and stylishly curved running-boards notwithstanding. For the moment, the key advantage of the 8-litre was that it added a new level of performance to large and heavy cars. There were no new dimensions, or differently shaped front panels, to prod the coachbuilders in the direction of something new.

Nor did the sales brochure for the 8-litre suggest that anything radically new might be in the wind. Brochure no 35, issued in February 1931, showed just four illustrations of complete cars, two being coachbuilt in the traditional way and the other two having "panelled Weymann coachwork".

Of the two coachbuilt cars, one was an enclosed-drive limousine (that is, the chauffeur's compartment was incorporated within the bodywork rather than separate from it, as in "de ville" types). The coachbuilder was not specified, but this six-light design had no particularly distinctive features and was very much what a conservatively-minded customer of the time might have chosen.

The other car was described as a "Fixed Top Cabriolet de Ville", a term which is not altogether easy to understand! The body was essentially that of a sedanca de ville, with blind rear quarters and no roof for the chauffeur's compartment. Again, this style would have appealed to conservative customers, not least because the de ville fashion was on the wane by 1930, but it did incorporate some modern touches in its two-piece running-boards and metal wheel covers. The catalogue illustration was probably based on YF 5003, bodied by Gurney Nutting in a very similar fashion to the Olympia Show car, YF 5004. The brochure illustration nevertheless grafted the distinctive twin steps of the Show car onto the side view of the other, and "lost" its large rear trunk.

The Weymann-panelled "Two-door Close-Coupled Saloon" was quite clearly based on the Gurney Nutting body fitted to YF 5007, with its elegantly curved running-boards. The use of a lighter colour for the doors and passenger compartment may have reflected the way the car appeared on the show stand, or could have been intended to represent a possible way of giving the car a distinctive appearance.

The final car illustrated in the brochure was simply described as "a 100mph Saloon", but was very clearly an HJ Mulliner design and is likely to have been based on the lightweight four-door body built for WO's personal use on chassis number YF 5002.

The way they were
Of the 100 cars built on the 8-litre chassis, bodywork details have survived for all but two. The very last chassis, YX 5125, was bought as a spare for a second 8-litre Bentley by Captain Vivian Hewitt of Anglesey when he heard that

Bentley Motors were going under. It was carefully maintained but not used, and after more than 20 years in storage was sold and fitted in 1952 with a four-seater touring body by the London firm of Dottridge Brothers, who were better known for building hearses.

TOTALS OF INDIVIDUAL BODY STYLES ON THE 8-LITRE CHASSIS

Saloon	45
Limousine	13
Coupé (incl. close-coupled saloons)	7
Sedanca and Sedanca de Ville	7
Drophead coupé	7
Tourer	5
Four-seater	5
Cabriolet	3
Not known	2
Coupé de Ville	2
Landaulette	1
Two-seater	1
All-weather	1
Chassis only	1
TOTAL	100

As is immediately clear, the majority were saloons – grand saloons, maybe, but saloons nevertheless. Though the 8-litre chassis certainly lent itself to limousine bodywork, there were relatively few such cars built. Such formal styles were beginning to go out of fashion at the time, and this also explains why there were so few sedancas (and sedancas de ville), cabriolets de ville, coupés de ville and landaulettes. Fewer and fewer owners now employed a chauffeur to drive them around, and so there was no need for the bodywork to make a visual distinction between the servant out in the open at the front and the owners snug in their own compartment at the rear.

Also very apparent is that open bodies, including drophead coupés, accounted for only just over 20% of the coachwork built on 8-litre chassis. Most of these were more elaborate and sophisticated than the archetypal open touring body that is still overwhelmingly associated with Bentleys of the period, and of the sparse Vanden Plas touring body that had been developed for the Le Mans cars there was not a sign.

All-weathers

All-weather bodies were very much out of fashion by the time of the 8-litre, and it is surprising to find that one chassis was bodied in this style which would have been much more appropriate on a 3-litre Bentley of five or six years earlier. Nevertheless, HJ Mulliner was prepared to oblige the buyer of chassis number YX 5123 by creating a two-door body in the All-weather style which, it must be said, looked distinctly crude on a chassis as grand as the 8-litre. The completed car was delivered very late, in February 1932.

Cabriolets

The three cabriolets on 8-litre chassis all had the 13ft wheelbase. These bodies should perhaps be counted along with those classified as drophead coupés, as the two styles were essentially the same and the choice of description was really a matter of taste: "cabriolet" tended to look to the past, while "drophead coupé" looked to the future.

All three were in the YR series of chassis, and all were delivered in 1931. YR 5090 and YR 5098 were both by Thrupp & Maberly and had delivery dates of May and June respectively. The third chassis, YR 5096, was bodied by Kellner in Paris and was delivered in September.

Chassis only

The last 8-litre chassis, YX 5125, was delivered without bodywork to the owner of YX 5119. As noted above, the car remained unbodied for more than 20 years. It was finally given a "period" body in the early 1950s.

Coupés and close-coupled saloons

The dividing-line between close-coupled saloon and fixed-head coupé was another blurred boundary in the early 1930s, both types having just two doors and rather less room for rear-seat passengers than would be provided by a saloon. Typically, however, a fixed-head coupé might present the appearance of a drophead coupé, with blind rear quarter-panels featuring false landau irons, and sometimes a fabric roof covering as well even though the actual roof underneath was a solid panel.

As noted above, an illustration of the Gurney Nutting body on chassis number YF 5007 was used in the 8-litre sales brochure, where Bentley Motors described it as a close-coupled

COACHWORK ON THE 8-LITRE CHASSIS

The description "coupé" meant very different things to different people. Altogether more conventional than the Gurney Nutting body, but no less imposing, was this one by Freestone & Webb on YF 5021.

saloon. YF 5007 was on the 13ft wheelbase and was delivered in December 1930. Some 18 months later, in June 1932 the penultimate 8-litre chassis was delivered with a two-door closed body by Mayfair. YX 5124 was on the shorter 12ft wheelbase. Again, this body featured side glass in the rear quarters behind the doors and might justifiably be called a close-coupled saloon.

Examples of the fixed-head coupé proper were the two Freestone & Webb bodies on YF 5021 and YR 5081, delivered in June and April 1931 respectively and both on the 12ft wheelbase. Bodies also described as "coupés" were delivered on one other 12ft chassis and on two other 13ft chassis. The 12ft chassis was number YR 5083 and was bodied by HJ Mulliner for delivery in March 1931. The two 13ft chassis were YR 5084 and YX 5101. The former was bodied by Binder in Paris and was delivered in August 1931; the latter was a Gurney Nutting creation delivered in October 1932.

This was Mayfair's idea of a coupé body style, built on YX 5124. The wheel discs certainly add to its more modern appearance. The picture was taken in 1977 at a Bentley enthusiasts' event.

119

THE FIRST 8-LITRE

The first production 8-litre chassis, YF 5001, had been completed by October 1930 but was not displayed at the Olympia Motor Show. Instead, it was prepared as a demonstrator for Bentley Motors, and that may explain why it had the longer 13ft wheelbase; all the other early cars were on the shorter 12ft wheelbase, including the saloon that WO used as his personal transport.

The car was bodied by HJ Mulliner as a four-light chauffeur-drive saloon with a partition. It featured Weymann-patent construction but with metal rather than fabric panels. The body was finished in maroon with black wings and roof, and the rear quarters carried the dummy landau irons which were the latest fashion. The front compartment was upholstered in black leather for the chauffeur, but the rear was in light tan leather, the large blind rear quarters allowing those on the bench seat to sink back and away from the public gaze.

After its duties as a demonstrator were over, the car was sold to Jack Buchanan, a hugely popular stage and screen star of the day who was known for his portrayals of "typical Englishmen" (although he was actually Scottish by birth).

The car was restored to the highest possible standard in 1986-87 and is today one of the finest examples of what WO had in mind for his flagship model at its launch in 1930.

YF 5001; pictures taken at BDC Silverstone, 2009.

Coupés de Ville

Two 8-litre chassis were bodied as coupés de ville, both of them on the shorter 12ft wheelbase. The earlier one was YF 5085, which was bodied by Murphy in the USA and was delivered in February 1931. The Murphy company was based in Pasadena, California, and was best known for its bodies on Duesenberg chassis, but also bodied Cadillac and Rolls-Royce models.

The second car has sometimes been described as a four-seater, and sometimes as a sedanca coupé, and this highlights very well the confusion about naming body styles in this period.

COACHWORK ON THE 8-LITRE CHASSIS

Park Ward were known for their elegant drophead coupé styles, and this one was built on YR 5093.

Chassis number YF 5023 was bodied by Vanden Plas, and despite being numerically earlier than the Murphy-bodied car and bodied by a domestic coachbuilder, was not delivered until July 1931. The car certainly seems to have had four seats, with a fixed roof section (featuring the dummy landau irons popular at the time) over the rear bench. However, the front seats appear to have been covered by a removable solid panel, which probably explains why the name "sedanca" came into the equation. From a distance, with the front section of the roof in place, the car must have looked more like a drophead coupé than anything else!

Drophead coupés
As noted above, the term drophead coupé was used more or less interchangeably with the older "cabriolet" and for most purposes the two body styles can be considered the same. Thrupp & Maberly's single creation on a 12ft chassis (YF 5005) has been described as a drophead coupé, while two of their bodies on 13ft chassis are usually described as cabriolets. A fourth car with similar characteristics, however, also on the 13ft chassis, has sometimes been described as a tourer!

YF 5005, as noted above, was on the coachbuilder's stand at Olympia in 1930. It was not actually delivered until July 1931. Of the other six 8-litres described as drophead coupés, two were bodied by Gurney Nutting. YF 5020 and YF 5024 were both on the 13ft wheelbase chassis, and were delivered in March and April 1931 respectively. YX 5106, which is the car sometimes called a tourer, was delivered in May 1932 with two-door coachwork by Thrupp & Maberly that featured a disappearing folding top; with winding windows in the doors, it was certainly correctly described as a drophead coupé.

Windovers accounted for the only other 13ft drophead coupé, which was YR 5080, delivered in June 1931. The remaining two cars were on the 12ft chassis. Park Ward built the body on YR 5093, also delivered in June 1931, and Vanden Plas took responsibility for YR 5097, delivered a month later.

This unusual drophead coupé body was built by Vanden Plas on YR 5097 for Lord Brougham and Vaux. The tiny folding roof helped the car look larger and more powerful, but the lines of the body were far more attractive when the roof was folded away.

121

YR 5095 AND YX 5122: 8-LITRES WITH VANDEN PLAS FOUR-SEATER BODIES

This pair of essentially identical bodies by Vanden Plas on the 8-litre chassis shows how the execution of the four-seater body was changing in the early 1930s. The description that once suggested the Spartan, open bodywork fitted to a Le Mans car now embraced an altogether more refined style which was in many respects close to the drophead coupé type.

Creating such a body for a chassis as large as the 8-litre Bentley was no small challenge, especially when its owner wanted no more than two doors. However, Vanden Plas made a success of it, with a style that in many ways anticipated the roadster style found on mid-1930s sports cars from the likes of MG and Singer. The effect was to make the car appear smaller than it really was, and its true size became apparent only when somebody stood alongside the car or sat in it.

The earlier body was on chassis YR 5095, recorded as completed by Vanden Plas in May 1931 and signed off at Cricklewood for delivery to Woolf Barnato the following month. To the coachbuilder, whose order number 1731 it was, it was a "special 2-door, 4-seater Sports with Copper moulding" to their sketch number 624. It was finished in grey. The second one, on YX 5122, was ordered by HD Spratt of the pet food manufacturing company and was finished in black. The Vanden Plas order book notes that this one used "silent bloc" construction – which meant that the body was isolated from the chassis through bonded metal-and-rubber bush mountings. It had order number 1736, was completed at Vanden Plas in January 1932 and signed off for delivery at Cricklewood in February that year.

Both cars survive today, the Barnato car in original condition and the Spratt car with an attractive repaint in two colours.

High sides characterised these two Vanden Plas four-seaters. Barnato's chauffeur poses with his car when it was new; the other picture shows the Spratt car after its repaint in two colours. Note the minor dimensional differences between the door bottom and the running board.

COACHWORK ON THE 8-LITRE CHASSIS

Despite the modern-looking wheel discs and fashionable side steps, the Windover drophead coupé body on YR 5080 carried the square lines of an earlier age.

Four-seaters

Five 8-litre chassis seem to have been bodied as four-seaters, but it is important to recognise that the description was a fairly broad one, and not all of them may have been the open sports tourers that the term implies.

Three were on the 12ft wheelbase, and of those, two were bodied by Vanden Plas. These were YR 5095, which was delivered to Woolf Barnato in June 1931, and YX 5122, delivered in February 1932. Both had the same two-door design with a folding hood, sweeping wing-lines and low-set running-boards which helped to make the body look low and sleek. The third 12ft chassis was YX 5121, which was bodied by Corsica for delivery in March 1932.

The other two four-seaters, both on the 13ft wheelbase, were built on chassis numbers YR 5076 and YM 5036. The earlier one was bodied by Harrison and delivered in April 1931; the later had coachwork by Wylder and was not delivered until June 1932.

Landaulette

There was one single landaulette body on the 8-litre chassis. This was by Thrupp & Maberly, on YM 5041, which was a 13ft chassis. The car was delivered in March 1932.

Limousines

The 13 limousines on 8-litre chassis make this the second most common form of body on this model of Bentley. As might be expected, the 13ft wheelbase was the dominant size, and only one limousine was built on the shorter 12ft wheelbase. There were four by Freestone & Webb, three each by Thrupp & Maberly and HJ Mulliner, two by Park Ward, and a single example by Letourneur et Marchand in France. As in other areas of coachwork, there were some grey areas around the definition of a limousine, and not every example had six windows and seven seats, even if that was the stereotype. Nevertheless, any large saloon fitted with a division probably correctly qualified for the description of a limousine.

It was Freestone & Webb who were responsible for the only 12ft limousine, which was built on chassis number YF 5010 and delivered in May 1931. The same company built three other limousines, all of course on the 13ft chassis, and these were YM 5028 and YM 5032 (delivered in July and June 1931 respectively), and YM 5042 that was delivered in September 1931.

HJ Mulliner built this limousine body on YM 5038, a 13ft chassis, in early 1932.

123

A LIMOUSINE FOR BARNATO

As Chairman of Bentley Motors, Woolf Barnato could order more or less whatever he liked for his own personal use, and a good number of very interesting Bentleys passed through his hands. Not all were exotic, of course, although all were undoubtedly expensive, even by Bentley standards.

One of his 8-litres, YF 5010, carried an interesting example of an early 1930s limousine body. Based on the 12ft wheelbase chassis, it was delivered new in May 1931 with a D-back body by Freestone & Webb. Photographs show an imposing-looking six-light body, with a division to separate chauffeur from passengers. Notable is that there was neither luggage boot nor folding grid for a trunk: cars like this were for passengers only, and their owners would send their luggage on separately.

Barnato still had the car in 1933, at the time of his second marriage (to the American, Jacqueline Claridge Quealy). In accordance with an old custom, he was pulled home to his country mansion, Ardenrun, in the car by a number of friends hauling on ropes. YF 5010 has since disappeared, and is believed to have been damaged beyond repair during bombing in the 1939-1945 war.

Freestone & Webb built the body on YF 5010, which has been described as a saloon but is clearly a limousine. The division is visible in the front view of the car with Barnato at the wheel. The rear view shows the D-back style and the absence of a luggage boot so typical of limousines.

COACHWORK ON THE 8-LITRE CHASSIS

Limousines sometimes had blind rear quarters to improve the privacy of their occupants, as did this one by Park Ward on YM 5037.

The space available in the rear compartment is more obvious in this limousine body, which was built by Freestone & Webb on YM 5032. Typical of the period is the peak over the windscreen.

Park Ward again, this time with a six-light limousine body on YF 5022.

125

BENTLEY SIX-CYLINDER MODELS IN DETAIL

Saloon bodies came in all shapes and sizes. This one was by HJ Mulliner on YF 5006. Note the built-in luggage boot and dummy landau irons. The additional louvres in the scuttle make the bonnet look longer and add to the sense of size and power.

Conservative lines from Windovers on this saloon are again matched by modern touches such as the wheel discs and side steps. The chassis was YR 5087.

The Thrupp & Maberly limousines on 8-litre chassis were YF 5016 (delivered in April 1931), YR 5086 (delivered the same month), and YR 5094 (delivered in May 1931). HJ Mulliner built the bodies on YM 5027 and YM 5033 (both of July 1931), their third example being on YM 5038 in March 1932. Park Ward's two were on YF 5022 of March 1931 and YM 5031 of July the same year.

Very little is known of the chassis bodied by Letourneur et Marchand, YR 5082, except that it was registered for use in the UK and that its first owner had what sounds like a French surname. Letourneur et Marchand were based at Neuilly-sur-Seine, near Paris, and were better known for their coachwork on French Delage and Bugatti chassis. This appears to be the only Bentley chassis on which they worked.

Saloons

Saloon bodies came from an array of different coachbuilders in the usual way, although far and away the most prolific were HJ Mulliner, who accounted for 17 of the 45 known to have been built. Freestone & Webb came next, with just six bodies, while Gurney Nutting and Thrupp & Maberly were right behind with five each. Most saloons were built on the longer 13 ft wheelbase – 27 of them against 18 on the 12ft wheelbase. Just one saloon body was built

126

outside the UK, and that was by the Parisian coachbuilder Saoutchik.

WO's opinion was that HJ Mulliner were "probably the most satisfactory" builders of closed bodies, and no doubt customers in the market for a saloon were steered towards this company by a Bentley salesman. Right from the start of 8-litre production, the company's endorsement of HJ Mulliner's work was apparent because, as already explained, it was an HJ Mulliner Weymann-bodied saloon that introduced the new chassis to the world on the Bentley stand at Olympia in 1930. In fact, HJ Mulliner bodied three of the first six 8-litre chassis as saloons, the very first chassis being on the 13ft wheelbase and the other two on the 12ft wheelbase. In total, Mulliner's built nine saloon bodies on the longer wheelbase and eight on the shorter, the last one being on 13ft chassis number YX 5120, delivered in August 1932.

This Freestone & Webb saloon on YF 5025 incorporates interesting modernising elements: the front wings are cut short of the running-boards to give a helmet effect, and the shape of the luggage boot follows that of the rear wings.

Freestone & Webb were nothing if not versatile, and this is yet another saloon style on the 8-litre chassis. YM 5045 might have been considered a sports saloon with its rakish lines and low roof. The car was fitted with a Leyland diesel engine in the 1950s, which must have reduced the fuel consumption but can have done nothing for refinement.

A very different saloon style from Freestone & Webb was mounted on YR 5089. This was on the 12ft wheelbase and the large luggage boot reduces the space available for the rear compartment considerably. This body had clearly won some prizes, and the coachbuilder's official photograph was set up to commemorate the fact!

BENTLEY SIX-CYLINDER MODELS IN DETAIL

HJ Mulliner bodied this very early 12ft chassis as a saloon for the 1930 Olympia Show. The scuttle louvres add to the impression of length, and the dummy landau irons lend a sporting air to YF 5006.

Though among the lesser-known coachbuilders, Gill could create an elegant saloon. This is one they built for YM 5040.

Though often described as a saloon, the Gurney Nutting body on YR 5088 is clearly a Sportsman's Coupé. This magnificent car has been fully restored and has taken prizes at Pebble Beach

128

Freestone & Webb built three saloons on the 12ft chassis and a further three on the 13ft chassis. The earliest was on YF 5009, delivered in December 1930, and the last on YM 5049, delivered in July 1932. The saloons that were built by Gurney Nutting were predominantly on the longer wheelbase; there were four of these, and just one on the 12ft chassis. Thrupp & Maberly's five saloons were also divided into four on the long chassis and one on the short chassis.

All three Vanden Plas saloon bodies were on the 12ft wheelbase, while all three by Arthur Mulliner were on the 13ft chassis. Park Ward built one on each size, the longer one on YM 5037 sometimes being described as a limousine. Carlton's two were on the long wheelbase, and so was the single body by Gill. The Saoutchik body was on the 12ft chassis.

Sedancas de Ville

All of the seven sedanca or sedanca de ville bodies built on the 8-litre chassis were built on the longer 13ft wheelbase. Two were built right at the start of production, which rather suggests that the coachbuilders saw the 8-litre as ideally suited to such formal bodywork, and of these, one was displayed on the Bentley stand at Olympia in 1930. Nevertheless, it is evident that the fashion for such bodies was already on the wane.

Of those first two, YF 5003 was bodied by Thrupp & Maberly, and was finished in blue with black wings and black above the waistrail. It was a formidably expensive car, for which the total bill worked out at £3039 10s 0d, the body having cost £1189 10s 0d on top of the £1850 for the chassis. The second car was on YF 5004, was bodied by Gurney Nutting, and (as already

These two views show YF 5004, a sedanca by Gurney Nutting which was among the 1930 Olympia Show exhibits. Steps instead of running-boards were a fashion of the time. With the chauffeur's compartment closed against the elements, the car looks far more modern than in open "de ville" form.

BENTLEY SIX-CYLINDER MODELS IN DETAIL

Gurney Nutting built the tourer body on YX 5102, seen here with the rear apron and screen in position.

noted) was displayed on the coachbuilder's stand at Olympia in 1930. Both were actually delivered to their purchasers in February 1931.

The other five were all bodied by different coachbuilders. Barker was responsible for the

8-LITRES BODIED OUTSIDE THE UK

An interesting trend to have Bentley chassis bodied outside the UK was becoming discernible by the time the 8-litre entered production. Four chassis were definitely bodied overseas, and a fifth was probably bodied overseas, although this cannot be confirmed. The chassis were:

YF 5013   Saoutchik (Neuilly-sur-Seine, France); saloon, delivered April 1931; this was Bentley Motors' "continental demonstrator", which suggested that the company itself was beginning to look overseas
YF 5085   Murphy (Pasadena, USA); coupé de ville, delivered February 1931
YR 5082   Letourneur et Marchand (Neuilly-sur-Seine, France), delivered August 1931
YR 5084   Binder (Paris, France); coupé, delivered August 1931
YX 5014   Unknown coachbuilder, presumed Belgian.

As Chapter 4 shows, the trend had actually begun with the 6½-litre, and four of those six-cylinder chassis are known to have been bodied overseas. Those four represented a tiny proportion of the 545 6½-litre chassis, of course – a figure of just over 0.7%. Although the total of four, and possibly five, overseas bodies on the 8-litre chassis does not initially sound greater, those four or five represent 4% or 5% of the total 8-litres built. Proportionally, this is an increase of between 571% and 714%, which is quite massive.

Exactly why this should have occurred is hard to say. It may have been simply that those who were wealthy enough to afford an 8-litre felt that a wider choice of options was open to them, and that those options included overseas coachbuilders. There would certainly have been welcome additional prestige associated with the ownership of a car which had been bodied overseas.

body on YR 5078, delivered in April 1931, and HJ Mulliner built that on YM 5034, whose guarantee was issued in August. YM 5043 was by Carlton, delivered in May 1932; Arthur Mulliner built the sedanca body on YM 5050 for April 1932 delivery; and YX 5109 was constructed by Freestone & Webb, with a delivery date of May 1932.

Tourers

The description of "tourer" was another one that could be applied to a variety of very different bodies. Those on the 8-litre chassis embraced no fewer than four different types, the common feature being a lack of weather protection other than a hood.

One type was the Le Mans-style, four-seater, fabric-covered, open body, and Vanden Plas built one such body on chassis number YX 5119. This car was also fitted with an outside exhaust and an extra-large fuel tank, and its buyer later also bought the last 8-litre chassis (YX 5125) as a spare in case he ever had a problem with it.

The second type was the dual-cowl tourer, with four doors and a bulkhead between front and rear seats. A second windscreen was mounted on this to give some wind protection for the rear seat passengers, and there was a folding fabric top but without sidescreens. Lancefield built one such body on 13ft chassis number YM 5044, which was not delivered until May 1932. Gurney Nutting also built one on a 13ft chassis, in this case number YX 5102 which was delivered the same month.

Altogether more formal was the two-door touring body that Vanden Plas built on a 12ft chassis, number YX 5111 that was also delivered in May 1932. The general appearance of this body suggested it was a drophead coupé, but without side windows or sidescreens, it qualified for the description of tourer. The fourth tourer was a refined-looking four-door body by Gurney Nutting on 12ft wheelbase chassis number YF 5011, delivered in April 1931.

Two-seater

Just one two-seater body was built, a boat-tailed type by Barker on 13ft chassis YR 5099. Delivered in July 1931, it featured pontoon wings and pontoon-shaped running-boards, with these items in black to contrast with the light colour of the bodywork. It was a strict two-seater, though

COACHWORK ON THE 8-LITRE CHASSIS

Harrison had also built minimalist tourer bodies on earlier Bentleys, but by the early 1930s customer expectations had changed. This is YR 5076, seen both open and with hood and sidescreens in place. The driving compartment is also remarkably sophisticated by earlier standards.

This Vanden Plas four-seat tourer on YX 5111 was a far cry from the minimalist bodywork associated with earlier Bentley tourers. Once again, louvres in the scuttle add to the impression of size and power. The body is high-sided, in the early '30s Vanden Plas idiom, with a deep cut-out for the driver's elbow.

a subsequent owner had the rear deck modified to incorporate a dickey seat. Strangely, perhaps, the coachbuilder minimised the car's length rather than emphasising it, fitting a standard bonnet and scuttle rather than the long bonnet which would have been available to order from Cricklewood.

Unknown bodies

The bodies on just two 8-litre chassis are not known. YX 5104 was a 13ft chassis delivered to Belgium, and was presumably bodied there. YX 5118 was another 13ft chassis. It was delivered in May 1932 with a body by Mayfair, but the type of bodywork remains unknown.

The sheer size of an 8-litre Bentley is apparent in these pictures of an HJ Mulliner limousine on 13ft-wheelbase chassis YM 5038, delivered in March 1932 and now owned by Jens Pilo.

COACHWORK ON THE 8-LITRE CHASSIS

The tall radiator of the 8-litre tended to make the car look high and narrow from the front, but the rear view gave a better impression of the true proportions of the HJ Mulliner body.

The trunk was, quite logically, a removable item that was carried on a grid rather than built into the body. It was finished to very high standards, just like the body itself.

133

The nearside of the 8-litre engine was the exhaust side. Note the six spare spark plugs, neatly arranged on the bulkhead, the distributor for the plugs on this side of the engine, the massively deep crankcase and the engine foot. The plastic cooling fan visible just behind the radiator is a modern precautionary addition.

The imposing radiator grille with its thermostatically controlled shutters was delivered with the chassis; the shutters are closed in this picture, to allow the engine coolant to warm up as quickly as possible. The headlamps are by Lucas.

With carburettors on the right of the engine, the complications of the cross-linkage used on the 6½-litre engines were not necessary. Clear here are the single magneto and the Autovac with its filler turned to face the outside of the car.

Two winged-B emblems adorn the radiator surround of this car.

The front compartment was beautifully trimmed, even though it was only for the chauffeur. Handbrake and gear lever are outboard of the driver, and the seat cushion is cut away to give clearance. The two large turnwheels under the dashboard are for adjustment of the Telecontrol dampers, and an owner has added a plate giving guidance on speeds on each gear.

Comprehensive instrumentation included a fuel gauge marked in gallons and litres, a water temperature gauge, oil pressure gauge, ammeter, speedometer with trip counter, and of course a clock.

COACHWORK ON THE 8-LITRE CHASSIS

The lower lever on the door is for the rapid-drop door glass – much needed in the days when hand signals were the standard means of warning other drivers that the driver intended to turn.

The coachbuilder's plate was proudly displayed in its usual place just above the running-board and inside the door shut. This body incorporated Weymann construction patents; the spelling of "License" is French rather than American.

137

Behind the partition, there was real lounging room in the rear, which was upholstered in Bedford cord rather than the leather used in the front. Occupants could sink back out of the public gaze behind those deep quarter-panels, and even raise the rear window blind if they wished. There are ashtrays in the fronts of the armrests, and one of the occasional seats has been deployed here. Just visible is the winding handle for the glass in the division.

There was a companion set in each rear quarter, with a mirror and an ashtray. When not in use, the mirror was concealed behind the hinged panel seen open here. Note also the ornate hanging strap and, at the join with the roof, the cord that controlled the rear window blind.

The chassis number plate was screwed to the nearside of the bulkhead on the engine side. The Dymo label from 1968 has been left in place as part of the car's history.

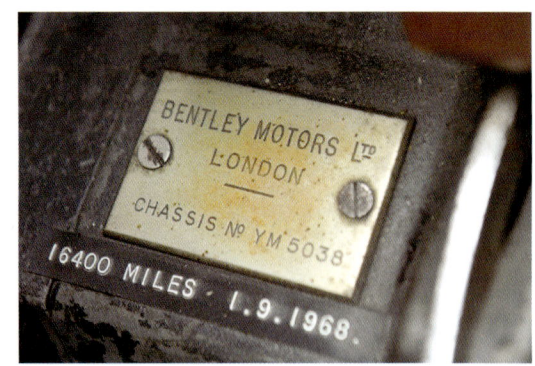

Rear door trims were upholstered to match the seats in the back, and featured pockets for the paraphernalia of travel.

BENTLEY SIX-CYLINDER MODELS IN DETAIL

Twin spares were part of the essential equipment at a time when tyre technology was not what it has since become. Punctures were quite common. 8-litre hubs were the largest on any Bentley chassis.

The twin reservoirs for the Telecontrol shock absorbers, and above them the reservoir for the Tecalemit centralised one-shot chassis lubrication system.

The road springs were outrigged from the chassis, as is clear from this picture. A leather gaiter was standard equipment. The paired lights would not have been original, but are period items that have been added to comply with modern regulations and to make the car more readily visible on the road.

The Telecontrol dampers could be adjusted from the dashboard, and depended on a hydraulic system whose pipes are clear in this picture.

140

Chapter Eight

The 4-Litre

Just as the last of the four-cylinder Cricklewood-era Bentleys, the supercharged 4½-litre, proved controversial, so did the last of the six-cylinder cars. In fact, the 4-litre model that was built for just a few months during 1931 has undoubtedly been the most controversial of all the Bentleys built before the company was sold to Rolls-Royce. The supercharged 4½-litre may not have been one of WO's own creations, but it has been forgiven for that by Bentley aficionados over the years because it did have a glamorous – if frustratingly unsuccessful – sporting career. The 4-litre, by contrast, did not. WO himself professed to hate it, his staff at Cricklewood did the same, and so few were made that the car never had a chance of attracting much support from enthusiasts.

To understand how the 4-litre Bentley came about, we have to look at events in the third quarter of 1930. The 4½-litre model, good though it had been, was dying on its feet; Bentley Motors were still prepared to take orders, but it was obvious that the car could not remain in production for much longer. Production of the 6½-litre was effectively over, although a small number of chassis were still passing through the works to fulfil late orders. The company's future therefore depended almost entirely on the success of the new 8-litre that had been announced at the Olympia Show in October – and that was simply not selling. The records suggest that no more than 10 had been sold by the end of the year, and of those several had not yet been delivered because the chassis were still out with coachbuilders.

On a broader front, the UK was feeling the knock-on effects of the recession that had hit America a year earlier. As demand for exports dwindled, those whose wealth depended on manufacturing industries reined in their spending. Luxury cars were among the casualties. So it is not hard to understand why the Board of Bentley Motors worked itself into something approaching panic towards the end of the year. Their latest product was not selling; demand for their old products was dying; and their traditional customers were in any case not spending money. The company had always been in a precarious financial situation anyway, and there were no reserves to keep it going through a difficult period. Worse, there was no telling how much longer the situation might last.

At this stage, the Board consisted of Woolf Barnato, the Marquis de Casa Maury, Ramsay Manners, JK Carruth, H Pike and WO himself. Barnato was spending a great deal of time in the USA and seemed to observers to have lost interest in what was happening at Bentley Motors. Whether his more active participation would have made a difference is hard to say, but it seems unlikely. So it was the rest of the Board who reached the conclusion that Bentley Motors needed a new and less expensive product to tide them through the difficult times ahead. This was a not unreasonable conclusion: Rolls-Royce had reached a similar one when an

BENTLEY SIX-CYLINDER MODELS IN DETAIL

This was the 4-litre chassis, immensely sturdy because of its close relationship to the larger 8-litre. Clear in this picture is that the front brake rods were outside the chassis frame.

A source of some grumbling from the shop floor: the 8-litre chassis side members had to be modified in the beginning to allow the fitting of a rubber-mounted sub-frame that carried the engine. The rubber reduced the transmission of engine vibrations to the chassis, so adding to refinement.

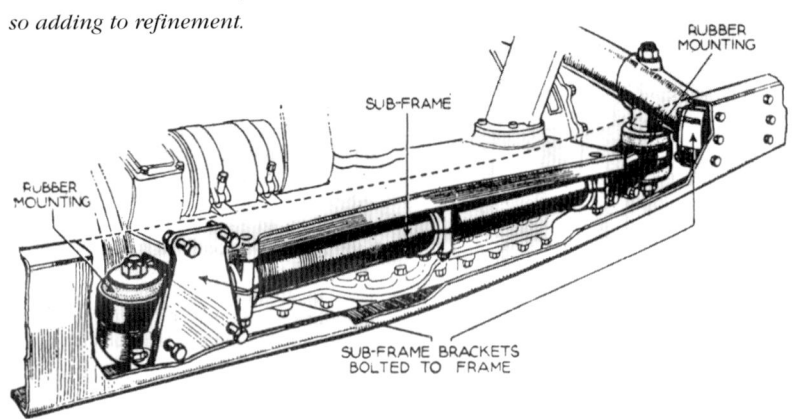

economic depression had followed the end of the Great War, and they had introduced a less expensive model to sell alongside their flagship 40/50hp Silver Ghost. The less expensive car, the 20hp, had been a huge success.

The next stage was to decide on the form this less expensive Bentley should take. The general consensus was that it should be designed to compete with the current "small" Rolls-Royce. This was the 20/25, a further development of the original 20hp, and it had a 3.7-litre six-cylinder engine. So the proposal focussed on an engine of 4 litres – bigger than that in the Rolls-Royce and no doubt intended from the start to offer better performance. As there was nothing on the Bentley drawing-boards that would fit the bill, the engine would have to be drawn up specially. That implied expenditure of time and money, and so the Board wanted an engine that was both simple in design and inexpensive to manufacture.

Then there was the question of a chassis to carry that engine. It might have made sense to resurrect and perhaps to modify the old 4½-litre chassis, which at least had the advantage of being well proven, and might have suited the power output from this new and simpler 4-litre engine. However, the Board decided instead to use the latest 8-litre chassis as a starting-point. Again, it is possible to understand their thinking. First, the 8-litre chassis embodied the latest Bentley design. Second, there were several of them lying around at Cricklewood, awaiting customers. If they could not be sold as 8-litres, they could be used for the new 4-litre car.

There was a great deal of logic to this, but it was not the logic of engineers. Indeed, WO was the only engineer on the Board, and his fellow Directors seem to have taken no notice of his arguments that the new car would be unlikely to have the performance expected of a Bentley. Performance was not really an issue as long as the new car was quicker than the Rolls-Royce 20/25 with which it would compete. As that car was no ball of fire, with a top speed somewhere around 75mph, they probably did not foresee difficulties.

WO must have been deeply unimpressed – hurt, even – by the insistence on a less complicated and cheaper engine than the ones he had spent the last decade designing. He decided to have nothing to do with the new engine, which was again understandable from his point of view. However, this was not going to help Bentley Motors out of the crisis which the rest of the Board could see staring them in the face. So, if their Chief Engineer was not going to design the engine they wanted for the new model designed to save the company, they would get somebody else to do the job.

Developing the 4-litre

When WO came to write his autobiography just over a quarter of a century later, the episode still smarted. That much is abundantly clear from the way he described the instructions he had been given from the Board. He remembered being told:" We must have something to compete with the small Rolls – a car that will undersell it. It doesn't matter about performance, so we'll use the 8-litre chassis, there are plenty of those hanging around the works; and we don't want any of WO's expensive cylinder heads, with four valves per cylinder. Push-rods will do."

The new engine was drawn up by consulting engineers. Wally Hassan,who was closely involved with Bentley engines throughout the company's heyday, told Elizabeth Nagle: "it was a very good engine. Three or four people were called in to design it: Watmough [incorrectly shown as "Watno"], Ricardo, Weslake were certainly three of them; and the best of everything was taken by the design staff and turned into the engine... it was marvellously smooth and it lasted forever."

One of the keys to any engine's success is the design of its combustion chamber, and those three engineers were considered to be the "big three" specialists in combustion chamber design at the time. Wilfred Whatmough would later become involved with Coventry Climax engines, Harry Ricardo was already famous for his pioneering work on combustion chamber design, and Harry Weslake was a cylinder head specialist. By common consent, however, the finished result owed most to Harry Ricardo. The engine he drew up for Bentley had all the Ricardo characteristics of compactness and a combustion chamber that induced turbulence in the petrol-air mixture. To keep the design simple, he used a single inlet valve in the cylinder head above the combustion chamber, and a single exhaust valve in the side of the block, both of them slightly angled. This inlet-over-exhaust design was certainly not new, but it was not common in car engines the time, and many other manufacturers would go on to copy it during the 1930s.

It was not only the valve layout that was totally unlike previous Bentley practice. So was the fact that the engine had a removable cylinder head. In truth, the monobloc design of the earlier Bentley engines did not reflect the latest thinking, and also made maintenance tasks such as decoking very much more difficult than separate-head designs; but for WO this wholesale move away from what he considered to be best practice must have been anathema. An additional drawback was that the inlet-over-exhaust design did not allow the head to be skimmed, so reducing the possibilities of tuning the engine.

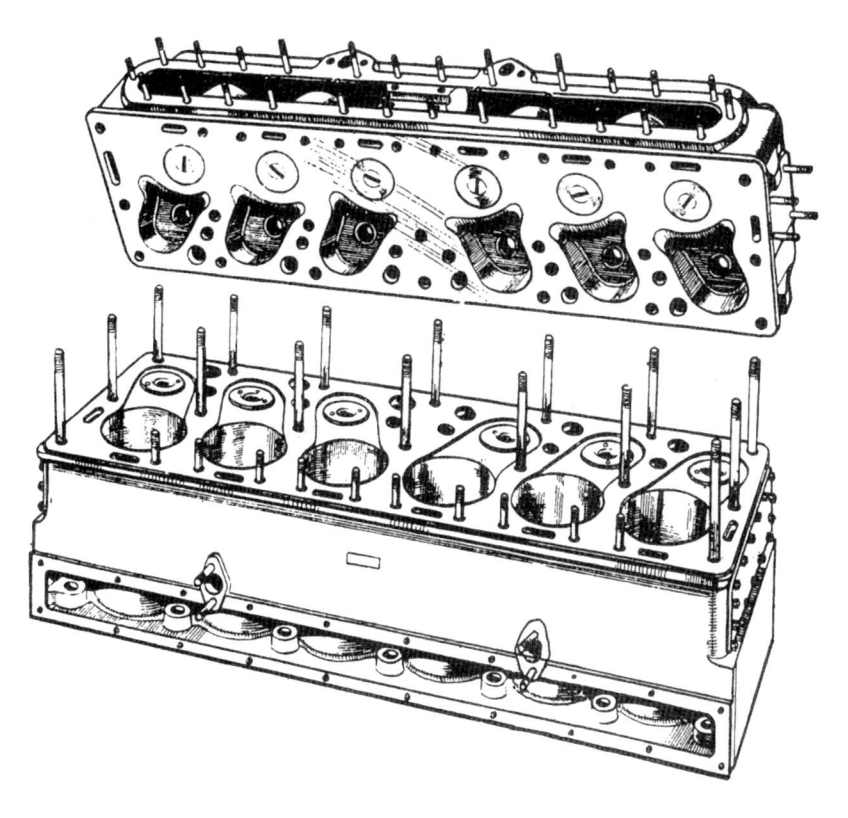

Both cylinder head and cylinder block of the new engine were made of cast iron, but the removable crankcase was cast from lightweight Elektron magnesium alloy and had especially tough supports for the bearings. There were seven of these – earlier Bentley six-cylinder engines had eight. The crankshaft itself was so designed that there was some overlap between the main bearing journals and the crankpins. This made for a forging so rigid that there was no need for a vibration damper. Even so, the risk of engine vibration disturbing the new car's serene progress was minimised by mounting the engine on a pair of longitudinal members that were rubber-mounted to the main frame.

There were seven bearings for the camshaft, too, which was located within the crankcase. It operated the exhaust valves through tappets and the overhead inlet valves through push-rods and rockers. It took its own drive from gears at the

The 4-litre engine was quite unlike earlier Bentley engines, all of which were based to some extent on the original 3-litre drawn up in 1919 by WO and Burgess. The 4-litre had overhead inlet and side exhaust valves, only two valves for each cylinder, and a detachable cylinder head. That cylinder head had a single-port design, as is clear here.

Comparing this underbonnet picture with those for earlier models of Bentley, it will be immediately obvious that the engine was considerably smaller than earlier six-cylinders. There was no "tunnel" containing the three-throw cam drive to make it longer, and there was a lot of space between the top of the engine and the underside of the bonnet. No doubt the impression that the engine was "lost in its own engine bay" provided ammunition for its detractors. The colour picture shows the engine bay of VA 4088.

front of the engine, which were far less complicated than the elegant three-throw arrangement used on the six-cylinder engines that WO had designed himself. Those gears were also used to drive engine auxiliaries.

With a 5.5:1 compression ratio, the 4-litre engine delivered 120bhp at 4000rpm, which actually compared rather favourably with the 110bhp at 3500rpm of the late 4½-litre four-cylinder with a 5.3:1 compression ratio. As a six-cylinder it was of course much smoother in operation than the older engine. So, in itself, it was quite an achievement, not least because of the short time-scale of a few months established for its design and development. That it was to be used with a radiator that had thermostatically-controlled shutters – first seen on the 8-litre Bentley but standard on the Rolls-Royce 20/25 of the time – shed an interesting light on the benchmarks to which it and the car it was to power were being designed.

Meanwhile, a team had been established in the Experimental Department at Cricklewood to develop the new 4-litre Bentley. One of their first tasks must have been to cut down an 8-litre chassis to provide a frame of the right size for the new car. The shorter of the two 8-litre wheelbase options was 12 feet (144 inches), and the decision was taken to offer the new 4-litre with alternative wheelbases of 11 feet 2 inches (134 inches) and 11 feet 8 inches (140 inches). These dimensions would inevitably make the car larger than the rival Rolls-Royce, which came with wheelbases of 10 feet 9 inches (129 inches) or 11 feet (132 inches).

Shortening the chassis nevertheless left it with the massively deep double-dropped side-members originally drawn up for the 8-litre, and six of the seven sturdy tubular cross-members (the cross-member at the rear springs was omitted on production chassis, although seems to have been present on an early chassis photographed in May 1931). It was destined to be very strong indeed, and that strength must have been the reason why the strut gear used on the 8-litre was omitted, but unfortunately it was also going to be heavy. The rolling chassis of a long-chassis 4-litre Bentley weighed 32½cwt (3640lb), which was just half a hundredweight (56lb) less than that of the larger 6½-litre chassis.

By way of contrast, the old 4½-litre chassis weighed-in at 27cwt (3024lb). The difference was considerable.

The choice of axle ratios must have been difficult. A low axle ratio would give the expected level of acceleration, but would necessarily limit the top speed; a tall ratio would give the top speed but limit the acceleration. If there was no room for manoeuvre with the gearbox ratios – and we must assume that there was not, because the production 4-litre used the same gearbox and ratios as the 8-litre – then the only solution was a compromise. That compromise was to give the customer a choice of three axle ratios – 4.58:1, 4.75:1 and 5.18:1 – and for the sales force to make appropriate recommendations based on the intended usage of the car. The final drive was a 6½-litre type in the banjo of an 8-litre. In the end, most 4-litres were capable of around 80mph, with a best of perhaps 83mph, but they took quite a long time to reach such speeds. Later on, the gearbox casing was made from Elektron, although the internals were unchanged; these later gearboxes were known as G-type or "modified F-type" 'boxes.

Other chassis features reflected the car's conception as a rival for the Rolls-Royce 20/25. That was an owner-driver car, as distinct from the grander Phantom for which the inevitably wealthier purchasers often employed a chauffeur, or at least a mechanic. So the new 4-litre Bentley was conceived with the same thought in mind.

Regular greasing was a chore which the typical customer was not going to enjoy, and so the chassis was given the Tecalemit centralised lubrication system already seen in the 8-litre. This consisted of an oil reservoir on the engine side of the scuttle, with a hand-operated plunger under the dash and small-bore tubes running to a variety of places on the chassis which needed regular lubrication. One push on the plunger at appropriate intervals was all that would be demanded of the owner. And in case of problems with the ignition system, no owner wanted to be fiddling with electrical components by the side of the road. The most likely cause of trouble was the coil, and so this was simply duplicated. In case of failure, all the owner had to do was to open the bonnet and transfer the leads from the main coil to a back-up coil located next to it on the scuttle.

Then there was the question of brake adjustment. The 4-litre was to dispense with the servo which helped to inflate the cost of the 8-litre chassis. Instead it would simply have self-servo front brakes. The brakes were of course still rod-operated at the front, although the rods ran outside the chassis frame as they had on the 3-litre and 4½-litre chassis, and there were cables for the rear pair. This arrangement meant that they would need to be adjusted periodically to take up wear. So, as on earlier Bentleys (where it had been primarily an aid to racing performance), a convenient central adjuster was provided. One tweak was all that would be required to restore good braking.

Back, though, to WO himself. Ignored and by-

Again, the massiveness associated with earlier Bentley engines was simply not present when the 4-litre was viewed from the exhaust side. Below the exhaust manifold is a tappet cover plate that could be removed for access. Note the one-piece exhaust manifold: all earlier Bentley "sixes" had two manifolds.

The 4-litre engine incorporated some Ricardo patents, and a plate attached to the top cover advertised the fact.

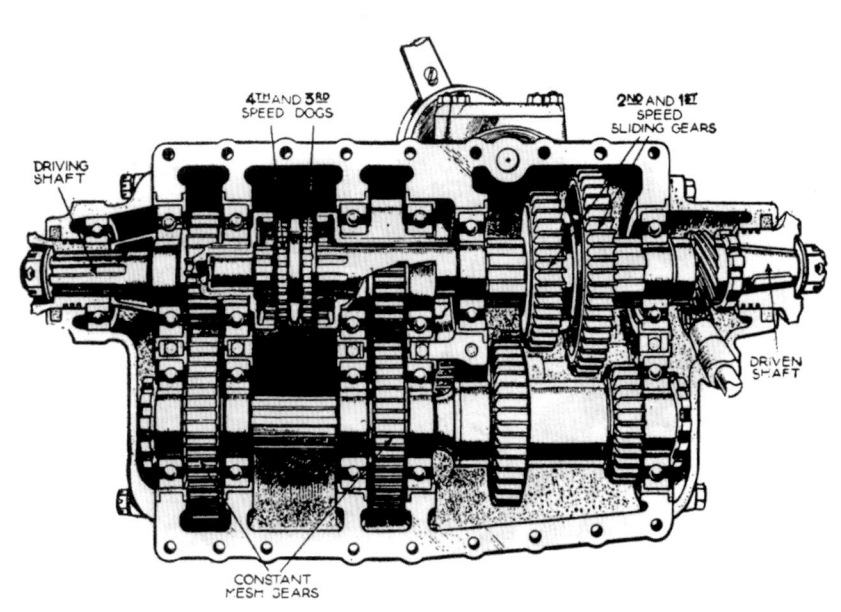

In the beginning, the 4-litre used the same gearbox as the 8-litre. This had been engineered for silence and refinement, and boasted bearings between each set of gearwheels.

passed, with his authority irretrievably undermined, his discomfort inevitably communicated itself to the team working on the 4-litre at Cricklewood. Almost every Bentley employee was intensely loyal to WO, and many of them clearly felt the slight over the design of the new car as keenly as he did. "None of us was really interested in the job," Wally Saunders told Elizabeth Nagle when discussing development of the 4-litre many years later. "It was simply bread-and-butter to us, and we didn't know what was going to happen. We didn't think of it as a Bentley – a shocking thing, it was."

Saunders had spent most of his time at Bentley as a racing mechanic, so he was probably feeling the loss of racing activity very keenly, too. He went on: "We all said at the time that it smelt – that 4-litre. It seemed very funny to us that certain of the high-ups insisted on that shocking thing over WO's head. There was one man in particular who'd come in from another firm; he had a lot to do with the 4-litre. It sort of stank to us – almost as if he was there to try to break the Company."

The target of that rather harsh criticism was probably Colonel Barrington, who had been brought in as Chief Designer after FT Burgess had died in 1929. Despite his elevated position in the company hierarchy, he was still a "new boy" when the 4-litre was being developed, and the longer-standing members of the workforce would inevitably have compared him unfavourably to Burgess, whom they had prob-

ably all regarded as a fundamental pillar of Bentley Motors. Barrington was in fact an experienced engineer who had worked at both Rolls-Royce and Napier, and it was he who guided the 8-litre into production. Nevertheless, in view of the involvement of both Rolls-Royce and Napier at the eventual demise of Bentley Motors, it is not hard to see how the poor man became especially associated in some people's minds with the collapse of the company.

With a dispirited WO in charge, a development team that lacked enthusiasm, and lurking fears of enemy infiltration, it is at least arguable that things which could have been done to improve the 4-litre were simply not done during the development stage. Perhaps suggestions were indeed put forward and then knocked back by management on cost grounds; we may never know. One way or another, though, the atmosphere at Cricklewood was not one from which a top-class new car was going to emerge.

"The engine wouldn't go into the 8-litre chassis to start off with; we had to cut a whole length right down the side of the frame to get in it." Such was Wally Saunders' recollection of the 4-litre's development period; the section cut out enabled the engine to be mounted on rubber-bushed sub-frames, which promoted refinement. "Stan Ivermee was in charge of the actual testing of it, and they played about with it for a long time – the head, valves, and God knows what. I know I took one of the first down to Gurney and Nutting to have a body fitted. It was a slow, heavy, cumbersome thing to drive – horrible." That car was probably VF 4001, numerically the first 4-litre chassis, which was indeed fitted with a Gurney Nutting saloon body and was first registered in June 1931.

"The heavy chassis killed it," Wally Hassan confirmed to Elizabeth Nagle. "We used to drive that prototype up and down Brockley Hill to compare it with the 4½, and, of course, the 4½ just walked away from it." Again talking to Elizabeth Nagle, Frank Clement added, "It was hopeless on power-weight ratio... it'd got no guts of any kind; it couldn't have with that weight. You had to kick it to make it go; and it had an awful habit of wheel wobble. It was a tramp, actually, and that was pretty dangerous. I know if you'd got past 70mph you'd got past all hope, nearly, and you had to have some guts to do it in that thing – dreadful car." And some years before these gentlemen had recorded their views, WO himself had written that the 4-litre was "a cumbersome makeshift, with an undoubted long-life expectation, but nothing else that anyone wanted."

It was a good thing that these views of the new Bentley did not spread beyond Cricklewood. Rolls-Royce, who had nevertheless managed to discover that a new Bentley was on the way as a rival to their 20/25, were certainly worried. The 8-litre was a direct threat to their Phantom, and some were saying it was actually a better car. If the new small Bentley lived up to those standards, they had a problem on their hands. It was Nick Walker who drew attention to a memo in the Rolls-Royce archives from the company's Managing Director, Arthur Sidgreaves, to Sir Henry Royce. "We knew that it was being brought out as a definite competitor of the 20/25, (and) we naturally feared that it might prove rather a severe competitor. Since we have seen the car, however, we all feel considerably relieved."

The 4-litre on sale

The new Bentley 4-litre was announced in May 1931, with a chassis-only price of £1225. Both 11ft 2in and 11ft 8in wheelbase versions cost the same. This compared with £1850 for the 8-litre chassis, and on the face of it the car was very much cheaper. However, it is doubtful if customers would have saved very much in the cost of the body, which was of course invariably hand-built by a specialist coachbuilder.

The leading British motoring magazines of the day both carried reports of the 4-litre's technical features. *The Autocar* gave it four pages in its issue dated 15 May, and *The Motor* gave it three pages in its issue of 19 May. Both were impeccably polite in the fashion of the times, *The Motor* noting respectfully that "few cars of this calibre are being built nowadays" while *The Autocar* focussed on what it saw as the car's novel features. These were the combustion chamber and valve layout, the separate gearbox with its large number of bearings and "silent" constant-mesh third gear, the strong double-dipped frame, the accessible single-point brake adjuster, and the use of Elektron to save weight.

Sadly, neither magazine ever published a road-test of the car when it was new. *The Autocar* did borrow an example for a test run (as we know from a later article published in its issue of 10 February 1945). However, the test was abandoned when the gearbox began to make nasty noises. Before a test of another car could be arranged, Bentley Motors had gone into receivership and was no longer in a position to make road-test cars available.

No more than half-a-dozen 4-litre cars had been delivered before the receiver was called in during July 1931. While negotiations for the company's future proceeded, the works continued to assemble 4-litres. The first sanction of 25 chassis had probably been completed by the time of the receivership, and a second sanction of 25 was approved, but they were to be the last. Many remained unsold for some time and a batch of chassis was snapped up by London dealer Jack Barclay, who had them bodied to suit various customers. The last example was not registered for the road until June 1933.

The 4-litre and its customers

The 4-litre certainly seems not to have had much appeal to the sporting motorists who had bought Bentleys during the heyday of the marque. In fact, the May 1931 sales brochure for the car clearly targeted the Rolls-Royce 20/25 customer – the owner-driver who wanted a quality car above all else. Bentley Motors, or their copywriter, described it as "the medium-size six-cylinder car of classic quality with economy and Bentley performance. Designed for those who desire distinction and suitable for all types of bodywork." The earlier small Bentley, the 4½-litre, had by contrast been described in sales catalogues as "The British Thoroughbred Sports Car".

It was, of course, from the same stable as those sporting cars of earlier times: "the Four-Litre has received a valuable legacy from its racing ancestry. Yet it would be hard to find a vehicle with less suggestion of this influence."

The real clue to the way the car was perceived, however, lies in the bodywork that customers chose to have fitted to their 4-litres. Right from the start, Bentley sales brochures steered them away from the open sporting styles and towards elegant closed bodies. Chapter 9 contains a more detailed examination of the bodies that were constructed for the 4-litre chassis, but it must be said that the sales brochure had summed up the car's appeal pretty well.

Of the six different types promised in that May

1931 sales catalogue, only the two-door Open Tourer by Vanden Plas had any suggestion of a sporting demeanour. HJ Mulliner had been selected to provide a close-coupled saloon (which had four seats but blind rear quarters) and a panelled Weymann saloon. Thrupp and Maberly would provide a Sports Sedanca, a Limousine de Ville (both with open driver's compartment), and an enclosed-drive Limousine (where the driver was protected from the elements under the same roof as the passengers).

The issue of weight always comes up in connection with the 4-litre chassis, and to an already heavy chassis were most commonly added heavy (and mainly closed) bodies. That was no real surprise, as buyers of cars in this class were in any case not especially keen on open bodywork. When open bodywork was fitted, it tended to be one of the more formal styles that were beginning to emerge, such as the drophead coupé; four-seaters and tourers were built in only penny numbers.

Those heavy closed bodies can have done nothing for the performance of a 4-litre Bentley. The typical closed car, according to *The Technical Facts of the Vintage Bentley*, weighed a massive 44cwt (4928lb). Comparing that with the typical weight of an open 4½-litre, which the same source gives as 33cwt (3696lb) makes clear why the car was never going to have the sort of performance that sporting enthusiasts had enjoyed so much in earlier cars from the Bentley stable.

The views of those who worked at Cricklewood have already been quoted, but it is worth turning for an opinion to one other, anonymous, member of the Bentley staff. This man wrote to *The Autocar* in early 1945, recalling what the 4-litre was like to drive and wondering whether anybody now remembered the car. In its issue of 10 February, *The Autocar* printed his views, which were noticeably more sober than those his former colleagues passed on to Elizabeth Nagle nearly 20 years later: "From the enthusiast's point of view it certainly had a poor performance low down in the speed range....In traffic and on narrow twisting roads this model felt under-powered, and it had poor acceleration for a Bentley. The brakes, on the other hand, were excellent and the steering was not heavy compared with that of contemporary cars of similar size. Once out on the open road, however, and over 40mph, some liveliness was discernible in the engine and the car could be cruised at a speed very near its maximum, which was about 80mph, this, of course, being a disappointing figure compared with the performance of other Bentley types."

For confirmation of that last comment, the 3-litre in some forms, the 4½-litre and the 6½-litre had all been capable of 90mph, while the 8-litre could of course just exceed 100mph.

The 4-litre on the road

In the absence of any independent assessment of the 4-litre when it was new, it is worth turning to one made much more recently that was not only finely judged but also displayed a sensible understanding of the 4-litre and its aims. It was written by Tom Threlfall – best known for racing various Lotus and Cooper products in the late 1950s and early 1960s – and was published in *Classic and Sportscar* magazine for November 1989. He was fortunate to be able to compare a short-chassis Thrupp and Maberly saloon (VA 4088) and a Vanden Plas tourer (VA 4098), both of them delivered to their first owners in March 1932 but both with chassis built in 1931. Both had almost certainly been among the chassis bought by London dealer Jack Barclay at the end of that year.

CHASSIS NUMBERS AND BUILD DATES OF THE 4-LITRE CARS

The chassis number of a 4-litre Bentley was always stamped into a ledge on the left-hand side of the bulkhead.

There were just two build sanctions for the 4-litre chassis and, as was already Bentley practice, there were 25 cars in each sanction. Each sanction was identified by a pair of initial capitals, and these were followed by a four-figure serial number.

The construction of bodywork typically took between two and three months, although some bodies took much longer, and there would have been other delays when Cricklewood sent a completed car back to the bodybuilder for modifications before it would issue the Five-Year Guarantee.

Build dates here have been calculated from delivery dates shown in Bentley Motors records. The actual build date of most chassis was two or three months earlier than their delivery dates, but there were cars which took longer than the usual time to complete.

Chassis numbers	Delivery dates
VF 4001 to VF 4025	May 1931 to summer 1931
VA 4076 to VA 4100	Summer 1931 to end 1931

Of the saloon, which had a 4.58:1 axle ratio, Threlfall wrote:

"The engine responds at the first touch of the starter (a pre-engaged one, with no mashing Bendix) and settles quickly into a pleasant six-cylinder burble more suggestive of Meadows than of Bentley or Rolls-Royce. There is none of the usual Bentley valve-gear clatter.

"The transmission is unmistakably and heavily Bentley, however, needing a three-second push on the clutch-stop before first gear can be engaged.... The gearbox has a wide gap twixt first and second speeds, requiring further use of the clutch stop when accelerating from rest up a hill.

"The steering is heavy at taxi-ing speeds, but easy once the car is under way. The acceleration is gradual rather than rapid, with the engine apparently working quite hard. The cruising speed on the flat seems to be a happy 50-60mph, and the amount of power then remaining available for overtaking makes the manufacturer's claim that the car is 'capable of exceeding 80mph with closed bodywork' look something less than a racing certainty.

"The car rode comfortably over any irregularities left in the road by the Surrey County Council, as did its crew – in seats of armchair quality."

The tourer, which seemed to have a taller axle ratio fitted, was suffering from an occasional misfire, but its

"ride was irreproachable, and the steering light enough once one was under way.... With the help of the rev counter, it is noticeable that the power stopped coming through very readily at engine speeds over 2500rpm."

However,

"Although I have never piloted an aircraft carrier down the Panama Canal, having driven the 4-litre through the narrower lanes of East Nottinghamshire I know how it would feel; for tight parking a strong bow-thruster would be very helpful, too."

Ultimately, Threlfall concluded that the 4-litre *"is good, solid, vintage-style transport right through – but it is not really a sportscar. That is the shortcoming for which history (and, it must be said, much of the more extrovert moustachioed Bentley Mafia) has blamed the car. That is about as logical as blaming your Labrador for not being a Greyhound. Since the 4-litre has never tried to be a sportscar, it is possible that history may have been barking up the wrong tree."*

SPECIFICATIONS FOR BENTLEY 4-LITRE MODELS

Years of manufacture
1931

Build quantity
50

Engine
3915cc (85mm x 115mm)
IOE six-cylinder with two valves per cylinder

Two SU HV5 carburettors

5.5:1 compression ratio
120bhp at 4000rpm

Transmission
Four-speed "crash" gearbox.
F-type gearbox
(Note: most cars had the "modified" F-type gearbox with Elektron casing)
3.243:1, 1.792:1, 1.345:1, 1.00:1; reverse 2.926:1
Final drive ratio: 4.58:1, 4.75:1 or 5.18:1

Suspension
Semi-elliptic leaf springs on front and rear axles; Bentley & Draper friction dampers on the front axle, and Bentley & Draper hydraulic dampers on the rear axle

Steering
Worm and wheel steering

Brakes
Four-wheel drum brakes with leading-and-trailing shoes. Rod operation for the front brakes and cable operation for the rear brakes; handbrake acting on rear shoes.

Chassis dimensions
Wheelbase:	11ft 2in or 11ft 8in
Overall length:	15ft 10⅜in (short chassis)
	16ft 4⅜in (long chassis)
Overall width:	5ft 8½in
Track:	56in front and rear
Weight:	32cwt (short chassis)
	32½cwt (long chassis)

Performance
Max. speed:	80-83mph
0-60mph:	No figures available
Fuel consumption (typical):	14-15mpg (2.64 miles per litre)

Drophead coupé bodies were becoming more popular in the early 1930s, and the very last 4-litre Bentley was fitted with this one by Freestone & Webb, which was typical of the type. The car is on chassis VA4100, and was not delivered until 1933, the supplying agent being Jack Barclay in London. The current owner is George Tanner

From the front, there was no mistaking the 4-litre as a member of the stable which had produced the earlier six-cylinder cars, but from the rear the parentage was less obvious, especially with this modern style of bodywork.

BENTLEY SIX-CYLINDER MODELS IN DETAIL

The rear seat gives plenty of room for two passengers. The soft top has a high-quality woollen headlining.

The door trim features a rope pull and a very generous map pocket.

By this stage, Bentley Motors was increasingly wedded to Bosch electrical equipment, for the simple reason that it was the best then available.

152

THE 4-LITRE

There is a delightful patina of age to those seats. At some stage, the fuel gauge has clearly proved unreliable, as a modern substitute has been added just below the steering column.

Another attractive arrangement for the instrument dials – but in this case the rev counter is a modern addition.

Handbrake and gear lever were outboard of the driver, as they always had been on the WO Bentleys.

153

... and this is what all the fuss has always been about. The engine departed from the hallowed principles that WO had laid down in 1919, and that was enough to condemn it in the eyes of many traditionalists both inside and outside the company.

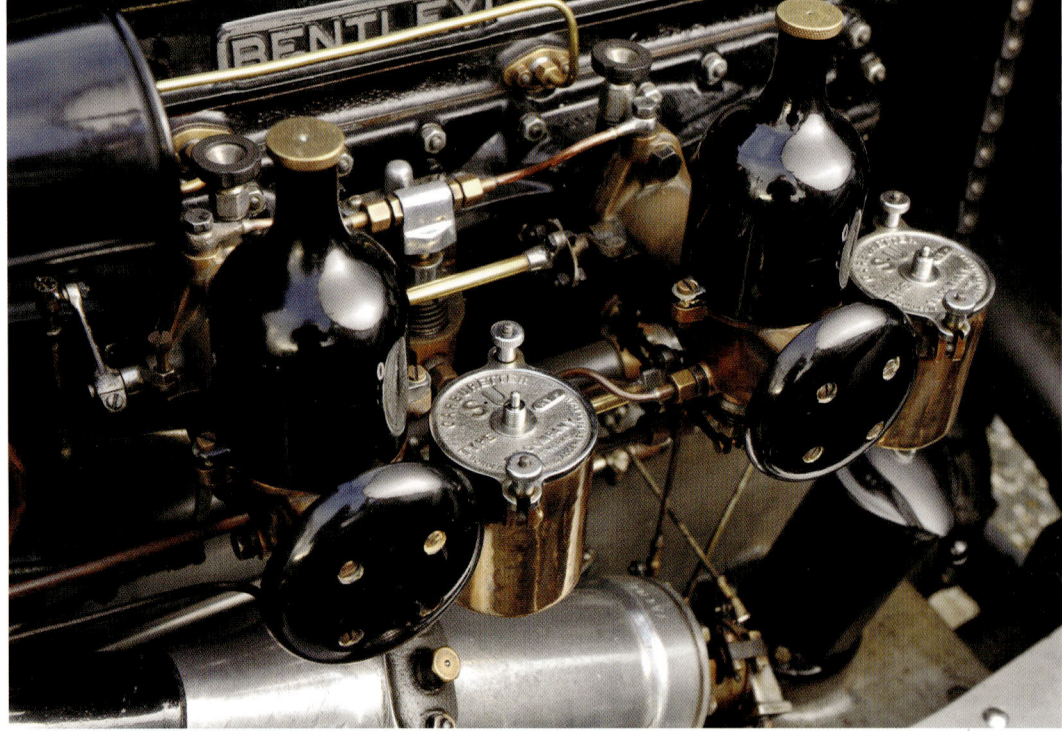

The 4-litre remained loyal to SU carburettors.

THE 4-LITRE

The four-bladed fan on the 4-litre engine had the same type of belt drive as was used on the 8-litre, although the fan itself was mounted higher up.

It was certainly more compact than earlier Bentley engines – note how much room there is between the rocker cover and the bonnet – but had as much power as the older and larger 4½-litre.

Taking no chances: the 4-litre equipment included a spare ignition coil mounted on the bulkhead. The black box is the oil tank for the Tecalemit one-shot lubrication system.

155

BENTLEY SIX-CYLINDER MODELS IN DETAIL

The numerical element of the chassis number – 4100 – was stamped into the engine side of the bulkhead top, just behind the Autovac. The position of the horn differs from that on earlier six-cylinder cars,.

The slotted flange on the side of the steering box allowed the rake of the steering column to be adjusted to suit the coachwork fitted to the chassis.

THE 4-LITRE

This was a three-position drophead body, and the top could be fully erected, fully opened, or left in the half-erected "de ville" position.

157

Chapter Nine

Coachwork on the 4-Litre Chassis

No 4-litre ever graced a Bentley Motors stand at Olympia, because the model was introduced between shows. Too late for the 1930 show, it did not appear at Olympia in 1931 because by the time of that event Bentley Motors was in liquidation. So it is not possible to deduce from "show" cars what Cricklewood thought was most appropriate for the chassis.

For that, we have to turn to the 4-litre sales brochure, no 36 of May 1931. Here, Bentley's copywriter said very little about the coachwork

COACHWORK ON THE 4-LITRE CHASSIS

Photographs of 4-litres in original condition are as rare as hen's teeth: there were relatively few cars anyway, and enthusiasts generally seemed not to care about them. Fortunately, a handful of cars still survives with original bodywork intact, and VF 4018 is among them. Variously described as a coupé and a saloon, it had a two-door body by HJ Mulliner incorporating certain design features to its original owner's specification. Among them must have been the curious half-window below the dummy landau-iron, similar to that seen on the Freestone & Webb body on Speed Six BA 2591 (see Chapter 4).

for which the car was intended, except that "the frame... lends itself... to the mounting of commodious bodywork having the character of an exceptionally suave and attractive line." Was the company hedging its bets? Or was it trying to say that the 4-litre chassis was not cast in the same high-performance mould as earlier Bentleys and was ideal for large saloon bodies?

The theory

Nevertheless, that sales brochure did contain illustrations of four different types of body on the 4-litre chassis. These were all drawings – probably no genuine 4-litres had been completed by the time the brochure was drawn up – but they showed a quite wide variety of options.

The only open car was an "Open Tourer by Vanden Plas", a very sober-looking two-door model with louvred side valances, disc wheel covers, a trunk built into the back of the body and a fabric top that folded flat behind the rear seats. Only two 4-litre tourers were in fact built by Vanden Plas, and the surviving example has an altogether more conventional style of body than the one illustrated in the brochure. So perhaps none of the "approved" style were ever actually made.

This photograph was taken in 1949, and is the only known one to show the Vanden Plas drophead coupé body on VF 4017

The second car illustrated was a "Close-Coupled Saloon by HJ Mulliner". It was presumably on the short chassis, and featured two doors, the latest style of dummy landau irons on the rear panels, a two-tone paint scheme, and what looked like a quite spacious boot built into the back of the body. As on the tourer, the wire spokes of the wheels were concealed behind disc covers. It is impossible on surviving evidence to say whether any of the 4-litres bodied by HJ Mulliner did have this design, but VF 4018 did have a body that looked very similar indeed, although an additional triangular window had been fitted to the rear quarters, below the dummy landau iron.

The third and fourth designs in the brochure were both formal types by Thrupp & Maberly, and both sported wheel discs. One was a "Sports Sedanca", and the other a "Limousine de Ville". Neither term was exactly standard in the coachbuilding trade at the time, and both reflect the confusion that existed even than about the meaning of certain terms. The key differences between them were that the Sports Sedanca had blind rear quarters and a large trunk built into the back of the body, while the Limousine de Ville had no external trunk, a much longer passenger compartment (presumably with room for occasional seats as well as the usual rear bench), and side windows in the rear quarters behind the doors.

Both designs represented wishful thinking. In practice, Thrupp & Maberly bodied no 4-litre chassis with any kind of "de Ville" coachwork.

One reason might have been that heavy bodywork of this kind on the long-wheelbase chassis was simply too much for the 4-litre to power at respectable speeds. Although such bodies had occasionally been fitted to the four-cylinder Bentleys, which all had less power than the 4-litre, times had moved on and customers expected better by 1931 – especially from a marque with the sporting heritage of Bentley.

That May 1931 sales brochure had probably been prepared in rather a hurry, and by mid-May other body styles were on the agenda. The Autocar magazine was clearly briefed about planned bodywork, and its issue of 15 May 1931 added three other body types: a four-door four-seat tourer, a four-door four-light saloon, and a four-door sportsman's saloon with sliding windows. The two enclosed bodies were to have Weymann panels, and although there was no indication of who was intended to supply these additional three bodies, it is fairly clear that the sportsman's saloon with its sliding windows was by HJ Mulliner, who had by this time probably completed the first example on chassis VF 4004 (see sidebar).

The practice

A few Bentley customers clearly did find it hard to get away from the marque's sporting heritage when ordering coachwork for their 4-litres, but the majority bought the chassis to have it fitted with sober and relatively unadventurous bodies. That was no great surprise: most customers for the Rolls-Royce 20/25, for which the 4-litre Bentley was intended to be a direct rival, also stuck to such bodywork.

Bentley's guarantee records show that very large numbers of 4-litres were not delivered until as late as 1932 or 1933. As a result, some

TOTALS OF INDIVIDUAL BODY STYLES ON THE 4-LITRE CHASSIS

Saloon	33
Coupé	2
Sedanca and Sedanca de Ville	2
Drophead coupé	4
Tourer	2
Four-seater	4
Coupé Cabriolet	1
Coupé de Ville	2
TOTAL	50

COACHWORK ON THE 4-LITRE CHASSIS

VF 4004, A LIGHTWEIGHT SPORTS SALOON

HJ Mulliner were WO's favoured builders of saloon bodies, and the company built the majority of the saloons constructed on the 4-litre chassis. However, not all were as attractive as the body fitted to chassis VF 4004, which was one of the first chassis and was delivered in May 1931.

This car was on the short, 11ft 2in, wheelbase and was bodied as a special lightweight sports saloon, with a most attractive two-tone colour scheme of black upper quarters and wings over blue main panels. Among other things, the short chassis minimised weight, and further weight was saved by the use of sliding windows in the doors instead of winding types. The light overall weight presumably aided performance, which made the car an obvious choice for the Bentley showroom demonstrator.

The car was also used by Woolf Barnato, who retained it until April 1932. By the 1940s, VF 4004 had deteriorated and was destined for the scrapyard, but fortunately was rescued by an enthusiast. Having been carefully brought back to top condition, the car still survives today.

HJ Mulliner built the saloon body on this 4-litre for Woolf Barnato. VF 4004 also spent some time as a Bentley Motors demonstrator.

of these cars carried bodies reflecting the changing trends of the early 1930s. One final group of chassis was acquired after the liquidation by the London dealer Jack Barclay, and several of these were bodied in what were then very modern styles.

The vast majority of 4-litre chassis – 33 out of the 50 built – were bodied as saloons. There were no limousines, probably because the 4-litre did not have the power to move such heavy bodywork at respectable speeds, but perhaps also because the chassis was just not long enough.

The next most popular body types were drophead coupés and four-seaters, of which there were four each. Tourer bodies accounted for just two chassis, coupés for another two, and there were two sedancas, one of them actually described as a sedanca de ville. There was then one coupé-cabriolet body. Details of the bodies fitted to two chassis are not known.

The relatively small number of open bodies can be explained in two ways. First, by the start of the 1930s closed bodywork that offered proper weather protection had taken the lead in popularity. Second, the 4-litre chassis did not offer a traditionally Bentley type of sporting performance and therefore probably attracted fewer buyers who would have been likely to choose open bodywork.

Also quite noticeable is that the majority of known 4-litre bodies were by the first-division

Most 4-litres were bodied as saloons, but there were several different styles because fashions were changing in the period from 1930-32 when the majority were built. This one on VA 4088 was delivered in March 1932, and was by Thrupp & Maberly. The car has remained in one family ownership since new.

carried a body by HJ Mulliner, and that on VA 4091 was by Carlton.

Coupé-cabriolets

The coupé-cabriolet style was really a predecessor of the drophead coupé. Its key characteristics were two doors, two seats (or four close-coupled seats), and a folding top. The sole example on the 4-litre chassis was on VF 4020, delivered in September 1931 and constructed by Freestone & Webb. An early photograph suggests that the car was in fact a drophead coupé, broadly similar to the Freestone & Webb body of that type on VA 4100 (see below); the choice of the term coupé-cabriolet perhaps deliberately looked to the past rather than to the future.

Drophead coupés

Vanden Plas had made a speciality of the drophead coupé, and it was no surprise that they built three of the four bodies of this type on 4-litre Bentley chassis. These were VF 4017 (delivered in September 1931), VA 4079 (March 1932) and VA 4083 (October 1931). The fourth body was by Freestone & Webb on the very last chassis, VA 4100. Delivered in June 1933, this car was created from one of the chassis that passed to London dealer Jack Barclay when Bentley Motors was wound up.

coachbuilders – HJ Mulliner, Freestone & Webb, Thrupp & Maberly, and Vanden Plas. Although other coachbuilders did build a handful, there were no 4-litres bodied by lesser-known provincial firms. All were by established, well-known coachbuilders who belonged to what might be called the second division. On the other hand, top-quality companies such as Barker, Hooper and Park Ward were notable by their absence from the lists. Exactly why this should have been so is hard to pin down; perhaps the reason was simply a combination of chance and the relatively small numbers of 4-litre chassis.

Coupés

The two coupé-bodied 4-litres were both delivered in April 1932. Chassis number VA 4082

Saloons

The lion's share of saloon bodies on the 4-litre chassis was taken by HJ Mulliner, who built ten of them. Freestone & Webb were only just behind, with a total of nine. Thrupp & Maberly

Again dating from 1932, this saloon body was by Gurney Nutting on chassis VF 4097. The forward sweep of the front door is an interesting feature.

COACHWORK ON THE 4-LITRE CHASSIS

As so often with vintage Bentleys, things are not quite what they seem here. This is actually a replica Gurney Nutting saloon body on VF 4011, incorporating elements of the original body from VA 4076. The body was reconstructed faithfully on the basis of photographs.

Vanden Plas built the touring body on VF 4021, seen here in open guise with rear windscreen erected, and also with hood and sidescreens erected.

built six and Gurney Nutting three, but the remaining five were constructed, one each, by Charlesworth, Lancefield, Mayfair, Maythorn and James Young.

Several of these bodies had a luggage boot built into the rear of the body, which inevitably moved the back of the passenger compartment forward on the chassis and so reduced rear legroom. The reduced space at the rear also meant that there was no room for an extra side window, and so these bodies had blind rear quarters.

The boot was handy for the sportsman (providing somewhere to stow golf bags, for example), and so a number were built as "sports saloons" with four doors and a lower roofline

163

Old chassis never die; they just get rebodied. This is 4-litre VF 4006, which originally had a Harrison four-seater body but was rebuilt in 1938-39 with this coupé de ville body by Bowler, a specialist Bentley dealer. It was also fitted with a Speed Six engine, as was quite common at the time. Since these pictures were taken (around 1960, at the dealer Jack O'Lantern's in Hampshire) it has had two more bodies. One was an open four-seater replica, and the latest is a convertible inspired by the Gurney Nutting coupé built for Woolf Barnato on a Speed Six chassis. The car now has an 8-litre engine.

than an orthodox saloon which helped to make them look sleeker and more sporting. Some were also built with just two doors, when they usually took the name of "close-coupled saloon".

Sedancas and sedancas de ville

It was perhaps a little surprising to find this somewhat outmoded style of body still being ordered in the early 1930s, but two were constructed on 4-litre chassis.

HJ Mulliner built one of them, on VF 4016. It was delivered in February 1932 and was described as a sedanca de ville. The other car was on chassis VA 4099, delivered in December 1932, and this time the body was by Freestone & Webb.

Tourers

Old favourites Vanden Plas were responsible for both the tourer bodies on 4-litre chassis. The earlier one was on VF 4021, delivered in November 1931, and the later one on VA 4089, delivered in March 1932. This second car had a body that was very much in the mould of the open tourers popular on Bentley chassis in the 1920s.

Chapter Ten

Legend: The Afterlife of the Six-Cylinder Bentleys

One of the most striking facts that emerges from any study of the Cricklewood Bentleys is how inaccurate is most people's perception of the cars today. Attending a vintage Bentley gathering at the start of the 21st century, a visitor could be forgiven for thinking that an open touring car, finished in green and kitted out to take on the Le Mans 24-hour race, was what Bentley stood for in the 1920s and up to the demise of the old company in 1931.

As this book and its companion volume on the four-cylinder cars from Cricklewood make clear, nothing could be further from the truth. Real Bentley enthusiasts have been aware of how the truth has been eroded over the years, and have done their best to record the way things were in a number of standard books on the subject. First, perhaps, was Johnnie Green's *Bentley – Fifty Years of the Marque*, originally published in 1969 and subsequently updated. Next came the Bentley Drivers' Club's own Stanley Sedgwick, who wrote *All the Pre-War Bentleys - As New*, with Hugh Young, and published it in 1976. Michael Hay did an even more comprehensive job ten years later with his *Bentley: the Vintage Years 1919-1931*. Today, fortunately, he tradition is continued on the internet, with Robert McLellan's superb web site www.vintagebentleys.org, which has the advantage of being updated regularly as new information comes to light.

So how exactly has the truth about the Cricklewood Bentleys become so distorted over the years? Perhaps the best way of explaining that is to begin with an analogy. Imagine a time, 30 years from now, when the majority of surviving Range Rovers were examples which had been modified by enthusiastic owners for hardcore off-roading activities, and only tiny numbers survived in original condition. Onlookers would get a very distorted picture of what a Range Rover was all about in its heyday. It would be a nearly exact parallel with what has happened to the Cricklewood Bentleys.

Over the years, a number of factors have influenced perceptions of the cars. First, many cars lost their original bodies during the 1930s. Coachbuilt bodies, especially those with Weymann construction, did not last anywhere near as well as the chassis on which they were mounted. As the chassis flexed, so they gradually undermined the integrity of the bodies, and owners of expensive chassis such as the six-cylinder Bentleys saw it as quite normal to have their cars rebodied after a few years.

The notion of updating older cars was also given something like factory approval through the activities in the mid-1930s of HM Bentley & Partners. HM Bentley was WO's older brother, and had been a co-Director of Bentley Motors until the company had been sold to Woolf Barnato in 1926. In the 1930s, he set up a business refurbishing older chassis with open sporting bodywork, mostly racy-looking and

BENTLEY SIX-CYLINDER MODELS IN DETAIL

Rather lovely in its own way, this is Speed Six LR 2780 with its second body. The original Gurney Nutting saloon body was replaced in 1934 when it was four years old by this Mayfair coupé. Sadly, the car has now been rebodied yet again, this time as a tourer.

KD 2106 started life in 1927 as a Hooper-bodied coupé, but was rebodied with this open four-door style by Corsica in the late 1930s. Such rebodies were quite common – and necessary, because the original bodies often literally fell apart.

fitted with no more than two seats. Though this was not a factory-sponsored operation, to the Bentley faithful it helped to suggest that the marque was still alive and that its old traditions had not been allowed to die.

Not every car was so well treated, of course. Those which had been sold on to new owners gradually worked their way down the food chain until they had fallen into the hands of impecunious owners who were unable to maintain them to anything more than very basic standards. Bodies rotted or collapsed, and by their very nature were far too expensive to rebuild or replace with similar types. The chassis were stored or discarded, or passed on for little money to enthusiasts.

Many of those enthusiasts were attracted to Bentley chassis because of the marque's legendary exploits at Le Mans and elsewhere and, as explained later in this chapter, the

Bentley legend was still very much alive at Brooklands during the 1930s. It is not hard to understand an enthusiastic young man buying a powerful Bentley that had fallen on hard times, removing its decayed body and fitting it with the most minimal body he could construct or cannibalise from elsewhere. Such a body would be cheap, it would be light in weight and so promote better performance, and it would bear some resemblance to the great Le Mans cars or to their Brooklands successors. The chassis themselves were not sacrosanct, of course. Michael Hay points out that there was a thriving trade in the 1930s, fitting 6½-litre engines into 4-litre chassis.

Not much had changed by the end of the 1940s. Brooklands was no more, of course, having closed for racing in 1939 when the site was turned over to military aircraft production. That made it a target for enemy bombers, and the track was also disrupted by a new access road to one of the aircraft production factories. So although motor racing resumed at other sites in the late 1940s, the conditions were rather different. New cars entered the scene, and the old Bentleys were no longer as popular. Unwanted chassis could be picked up for a few pounds, and it was realistically feasible for an enthusiast to buy two or three and to create one good car out of them. The results of that are still with us today; even the best authenticated cars are often still running only because of judicious cannibalism at some time in their past.

By 1965, enthusiasts had become past masters at borrowing pieces from one model to keep another one running, and an extract from the third edition of *The Technical Facts of the Vintage Bentley*, published by the Bentley Drivers' Club, gives a strong flavour of the sort of thing that was going on to keep the cars on the road:

"Complete nose pieces of the 4½ (S), 6½ and 4 Litres can be made to fit the rear axles of the 3 and 4½ Litres by modifications to the casing and using the domed back plates from the nose pieces of the former to take the larger crown wheel. The propellor shaft will have to be shortened as necessary."

Finally, we come to what might be called the modern era, beginning some time around the early 1970s. Old Bentleys were beginning to command higher prices, and of course the legends created by the Le Mans team cars and by the Brooklands "specials" lingered on. Dilapidated coachbuilt bodies were just as expensive to restore as ever, and perhaps even more so; besides, their weight slowed a car down, and a 1920s sedanca body with its driving compartment out in the open was hardly the most practical hobby car to have. So, where new bodies were needed, enthusiasts demanded open touring bodies – and for the sake of retaining some authenticity and credibility, they wanted them to look like the classic open touring bodies on the Le Mans cars. It would now take a brave and very wealthy owner to

This genuine basket case illustrates the dilemma facing Bentley enthusiasts before the cars became valuable. 6½-litre BX 2411 originally had a landaulette body constructed by Harrison for Offord; it was found in this condition in Uganda in 1969. Initially given the Park Ward coupé body from another 6½-litre chassis, it is now a replica tourer.

scrap one of these bodies, perhaps reinstating the foot or so cut out of the original chassis when it was rebodied, and reconstruct one of the grand formal bodies of the 1920s.

Specials: creating the legend

Once Bentley Motors had gone into receivership and had come out on the other side as the makers of the "Silent Sports Car", there were many who believed that the game was over. However, there was also a hard core of enthusiasts who were determined to keep the Bentley name alive in motor sport. Their efforts resulted in a small number of what Michael Frostick (in *Bentley, Cricklewood to Crewe*) so aptly called "Bentleys that kept the Cricklewood flag flying, long after the flag post had been removed". Among these were some six-cylinder cars – although it must be said that not all of them started life with six-cylinder engines.

The focus of club-level motor sport activity in Britain in the 1930s was still the Brooklands track, and it was largely on this track that the Bentley legend was kept alive. It was also largely thanks to the regulations applied at Brooklands that the idea of keeping a vintage Bentley in its original condition quickly disappeared from view. Motor racing enthusiasts want to win, and if winning meant modifying the cars that WO had created, then they would do exactly that. As a result, a distinctive culture arose around the vintage Bentley, which not only permitted but actually encouraged changes to the chassis, the body, the engine and anything else that was simply not up to the job of winning at Brooklands.

There were many four-cylinder cars that upheld the Bentley honour at Brooklands in the 1930s. Notable among them was Tim Birkin's "Brooklands Battleship", which was a single-seater evolution of his first supercharged chassis. From 1936, there was the Pacey Hassan Special, which featured a 4½-litre Bentley engine but not a lot else that had originated at Cricklewood. And there were, of course, several legendary six-cylinder cars. Their stories have been covered in far more detail elsewhere, but it is worth looking briefly at some of them here in order to understand something of how the Bentley legend was kept alive in the years just before the Second World War, and also something of how it was altered from its purest form.

The Barnato Hassan Special

Probably the earliest of these six-cylinder cars was the Barnato Hassan Special, which was constructed in 1933-34. The two names associated with it had their own special appeal to Bentley enthusiasts, because Woolf Barnato had been the Chairman of Bentley Motors and its most successful Le Mans driver, while Wally Hassan had been the Cricklewood company's top mechanic. The two had become close friends during the late 1920s, and after the old company closed down, Barnato offered Hassan a job looking after his stable of racing cars. In practice, Barnato preferred to let others drive his cars, and after Clive Dunfee's fatal accident in one of those cars at Brooklands in 1932, he gave up driving in races altogether.

It was Wally Hassan who had rebuilt the car in which Clive Dunfee was killed, fitting an 8-litre engine into Speed Six "Old Number One" which at that time was still owned by Barnato. Meanwhile, the original 6½-litre engine had been put on one side, and in 1933 Barnato asked Hassan to use it in a single-seater "special" that would use a number of other Bentley parts.

The car that Hassan built incorporated a number of Bentley parts that he was able to obtain from the old Bentley Service Station, which was still open at Kingsbury. It was also built on a specially-designed chassis frame, which was very nearly as narrow as that of the typical single-seater racing car of the period but had Bentley steering components in more or less their usual positions. As a result, the driver was actually offset to the right of the car. The car was deliberately low-slung – much more so than any car that had come from Cricklewood – and its body was as narrow as it could be made while enclosing all the mechanical components. Hassan fitted the rear springs on outriggers to improve the car's cornering power, and grafted Lockheed brakes into the Bentley backplates to make sure that it stopped.

Completed in 1934, the car took to the tracks. Despite the large number of Bentley mechanical components in it, the Bentley name was not overtly associated with the car. Indeed, Rolls-Royce would probably have objected strongly if it had been, as the Bentley name now belonged to them. Nonetheless, to enthusiasts, the Barnato Hassan Special was a kind of embodiment of the old Bentley spirit, and as far as many of them were concerned, it might just as

The Barnato-Hassan Special was pictured here at a VSCC meeting in April 1988.

well have been badged as a Bentley.

Throughout its Brooklands career in the 1930s, the Barnato Hassan Special was almost always driven by Oliver Bertram, a barrister friend of Barnato's. However, its original 6½-litre engine did not last long. It broke a connecting rod during the 1934 500 Miles race at Brooklands, and so Barnato had that engine removed and replaced by an 8-litre Bentley engine. In this guise, Bertram used it on 5 August 1935 to take the Brooklands outer circuit record with a time of 69.85 seconds and an average speed of 142.60mph. That this speed was far in excess of what even the Le Mans Bentleys had been able to achieve (about 125mph seems to have been the maximum for a Speed Six) shows just how special this "special" really was.

With that run in August, Bertram had actually secured two records, one being for Class B cars and the other being the overall Brooklands record. The Class B record stood until Brooklands closed down at the start of the Second World War, but the overall record lasted for just over two months. On 7 October, John Cobb claimed it at 143.44mph in his Napier Railton Special.

Still competitive, the Barnato Hassan Special was rebuilt in 1936, with the steering now centralised and a new body that was painted pearl grey instead of the racing green of the original. It again took to the track, although its best was a lap of the outer circuit at 143.11mph during 1938. For that, it had been carefully lightened, even to the extent of dispensing with brakes on the front wheels. However, the Brooklands handicap system effectively made the car uncompetitive and Barnato understand-

This is the Marker-Jackson Special, pictured when it was undergoing some work at the premises of well-known Bentley specialist Stanley Mann in 1989.

ably lost interest in it. By then in new ownership, the car made a few appearances at race events in the late 1940s, but was no longer really competitive and by the 1950s was seen as a vintage racer worthy of preservation and more occasional use.

The Marker Jackson Special

Like the Barnato Hassan Special, the Marker Jackson Special was based on parts of a former works team car. In this case, the car was "Old Mother Gun", the prototype 4½-litre which had made its Le Mans debut in 1927 and had been caught up in that year's infamous White House Corner crash.

The car, on chassis number ST 3001, had been sold to Richard Marker in 1932, and in 1934 he replaced its original engine with a Speed Six type for use at Brooklands. For the next two years, it was campaigned successfully at the track by Marker and by Margaret Allan. Sold on in 1936, it passed into the hands of Robin Jackson, who overhauled the chassis, fitted a single-seater body and did some work on the engine which included fitting new pistons and conrods. Emerging in this guise for the 1937 season, it achieved a best lap average of 134.97mph with Kitt Baker-Carr at the wheel.

Again like the Barnato Hassan car, it made some post-war appearances in the late 1940s but was then retired from active campaigning.

However, the car's career was revived anew after a 1989 restoration by vintage Bentley specialist Stanley Mann. With a three-carburettor 6½-litre engine developing around 290bhp at 5000rpm, and a top speed of just under 150mph, the car is now regularly seen at vintage racing events in Europe. On 26 April 1992, it took the UK Class B standing-start 1000 miles record at a speed of 104.49mph. The record runs, driven on the high-speed circuit at the Millbrook test track, were shared by Stanley Mann, HRH Prince Michael of Kent, Vaughan Davis and Phil Greenwood.

The Forrest Lycett 8-litre

Another notable car of the post-receivership period is the 8-litre owned and modified by Forrest Lycett. This car in fact carried the great enthusiast tradition of making old Bentleys go ever faster right through into the 1970s, which was some 40 years after it was originally built.

Forrest Lycett was a renowned Bentley enthusiast and one of the founders of the Bentley Drivers' Club in 1936. He owned a succession of Bentleys and modified many of them. He

Lowered and designed for speed, this is the Forrest Lycett 8-litre special.

bought his 8-litre, on chassis number YX 5121, at the end of 1931 and had it bodied as a rakish and sporting open four-seater by Corsica. This, however, was not good enough for him. He went to LC "Mac" McKenzie, a vintage Bentley specialist of the time who was responsible for improving the performance of a number of examples, and asked him to improve it.

McKenzie rebuilt the car on a shorter wheelbase, using side-members from a 4-litre chassis to reduce the wheelbase from the original 12ft to 11ft. The whole car was lowered to reduce aerodynamic drag, and weight was reduced by fitting a specially-designed body made of lightweight duralumin. The engine was progressively modified to reach a peak output of 340bhp, which represented an improvement of 140bhp over the 8-litre's standard 200bhp.

During the 1930s, this 8-litre was considered to be one of the fastest road cars in the world. Lycett regularly campaigned it at Brooklands and elsewhere, setting the International Class B standing-start kilometre record there in 1937 and going on to take the British standing-start mile record at the same track in 1939. On this second occasion, he famously drove to Brooklands from London, took the record and then drove back to finish the day at his desk in the City.

After the war, Lycett continued using the car for all manner of speed trials. In 1959, he took the car to Belgium for an assault on the flying mile record on the Jabbeke motorway. He achieved that record with a speed of 140.845mph, claiming several additional Belgian national records from Maurice Trintignant, who had set them with a Facel Vega. Four of these class records stood for eight years before being broken.

BENTLEY SIX-CYLINDER MODELS IN DETAIL

This 3/8-litre special was constructed in the first decade of the 21st century by Stanley Mann Racing on the basis of a 1927 3-litre Speed chassis. The engine is a Speed Six bored out to 8 litres, fitted with triple carburettors and delivering some 330bhp. Not surprisingly, it was considered prudent to uprate the brakes to full hydraulic actuation.

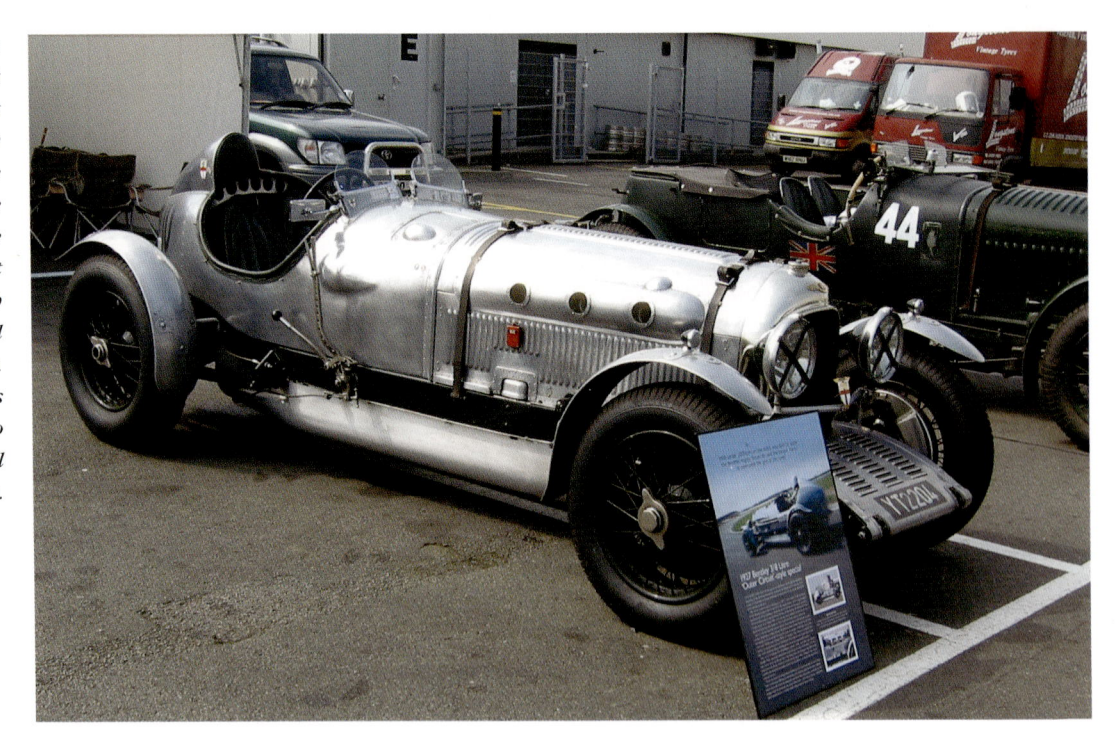

... and still they come

The great Brooklands tradition of high-performance cars racing for public entertainment still affects the vintage Bentley scene today. The six-cylinder cars, often modified to give performance far beyond anything WO or his colleagues could have dreamed, are favourites at the Bentley Drivers' Club's track days, of which the best known is at Silverstone every summer. That they continue to provide fun for their owners and entertainment for those who go to watch is certainly an enduring tribute to

Creating "specials" sometimes calls for ingenuity. Space had to be found alongside the 8-litre engine for the supercharger and twin carburettors on this one. Would WO have approved?

the machines that WO Bentley created.

There have even been some modern re-creations of the spirit of Brooklands, based on elements of the six-cylinder Bentleys. Today's well-known Napier Bentley started life in 1968 as a "special" built by David Llewellyn on a Sunbeam chassis to re-create the giant aero-engined "specials" that were so much a part of the Brooklands scene in the 1930s. The engine was a 24-litre Napier Sea Lion W12 from an RAF rescue launch, developing around 550bhp and 1400 lb ft of torque.

After a serious accident, the car needed a new chassis, and one was created out of a pair of 4-litre Bentley frames (which is a sad reflection on the lack of affection among enthusiasts for the 4-litre in the late 1970s and early 1980s when the rebuild took place). Now known as the Napier Bentley, the car is generally considered to be a real handful to drive, but it certainly fulfils its role of entertaining the crowds. Standing-starts are almost invariably accompanied by clouds of smoke from the tyres, while the multiple exhaust stubs spit flame and the accompanying noise adds to the experience. A Bentley it is not, in the strictest sense of the term, but it does pander magnificently to the expectations of those who watch it in action.

An even more recent creation is the Packard-Bentley, familiarly known as "Mavis". This is a single-seater, built between 2003 and 2010 on an 8-litre chassis by VSCC member Chris Williams. It has a Bentley gearbox and axles, too, but the engine is a 42-litre Packard V12 from a Second World War motor torpedo boat, and puts out around 1600bhp. Once again, noise, flames and smoke all contribute to the crowd-pleasing appeal of this monster which can be seen at vintage racing events during the summer months.

This is the Bentley-Napier, pictured on an early outing at Silverstone in 1979. With cars like this the spirit of vintage racing remains alive and well.

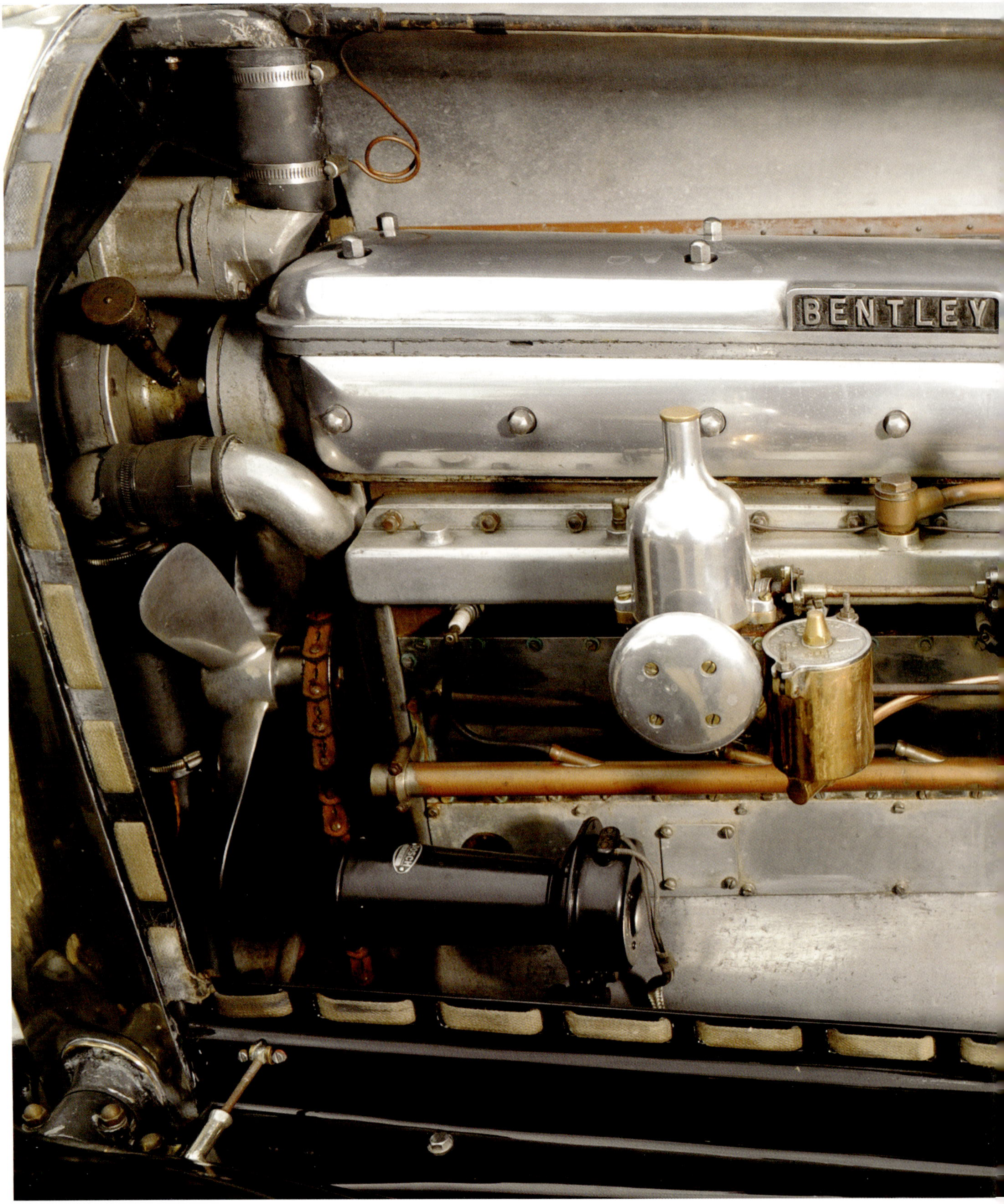
BENTLEY

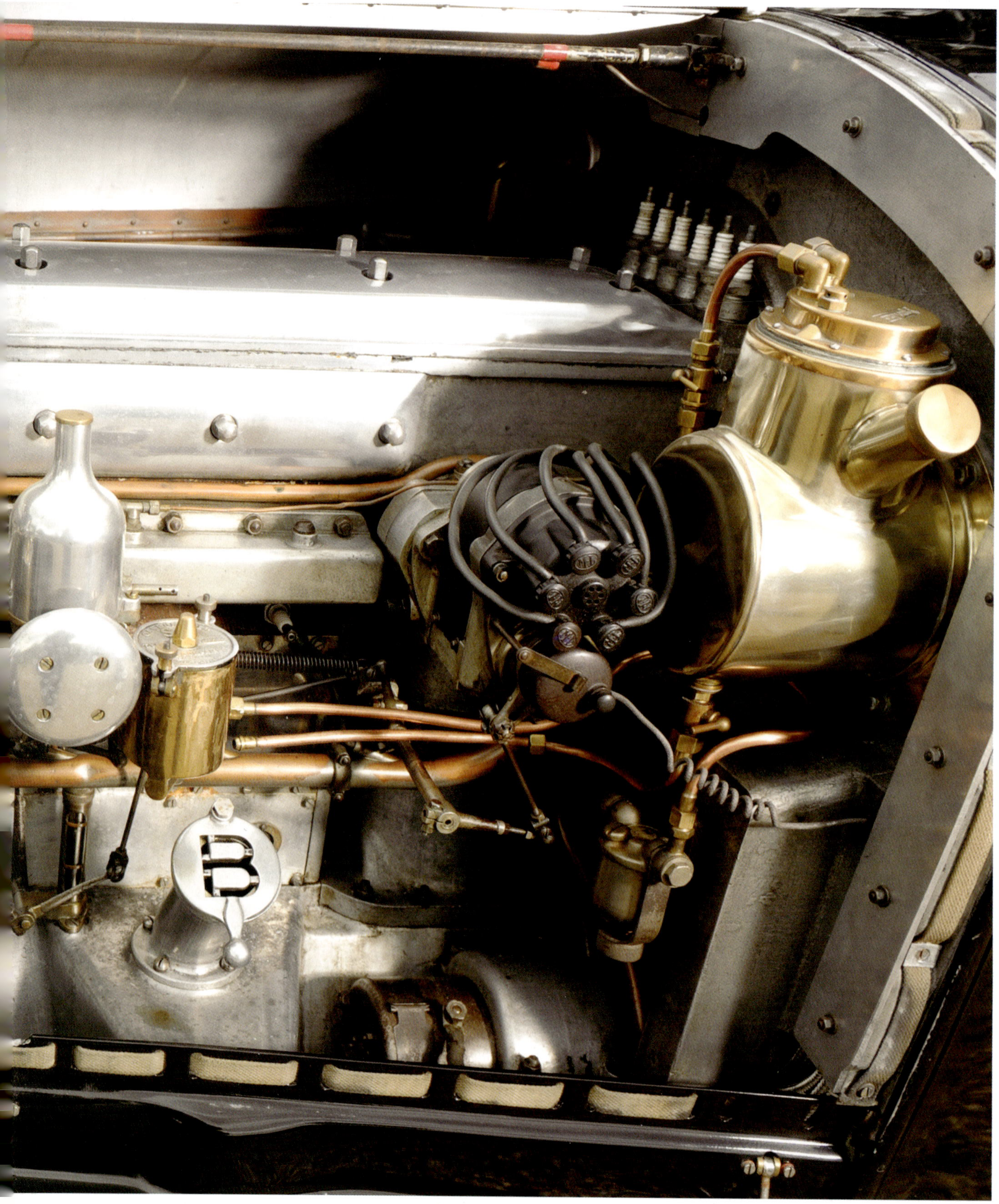